THE END IN AFRICA

BY THE SAME AUTHOR

MEDITERRANEAN FRONT
DON'T BLAME THE GENERALS

THE
END IN AFRICA

BY

ALAN MOOREHEAD

Harper & Brothers, Publishers
New York and London

This book is complete and unabridged
in contents, and is manufactured in strict
conformity with Government regulations
for saving paper.

To

DAVID HOLMSTED

a soldier who died in Africa

Preface

This is the story of the fall of Tunis and the third and final year of campaigning in Africa from the summer of 1942 to the summer of 1943.

I find it a difficult story to tell coherently. Up to 1942 the Mediterranean war was a fairly compact thing, an arena by itself, and it was possible for an observer to see something of nearly every action. But then the Eighth Army joined the Battle of Alamein, General Eisenhower's forces landed in North Africa and the fighting spilled right along the floor of Europe. It became quite out of the question for one man to follow the troops as they marched on the Axis from several different directions at once.

Trying to get this huge spectacle into focus, to reach some sort of perspective, I spent the first four months of the year making a journey round the world, starting from Egypt in the summer, calling at New York in the fall and London in the winter and ending a little breathlessly in Tunisia in the spring. It was hardly a success. I "heard great argument . . . but came out by the same door as in I went," and with a feeling of relief got back to the simpler values of the battlefield.

However, at least I learned that you cannot write about the war as a straight military struggle any longer. And so I have tried to tell the story of the end of the African campaign in what seems to me to be the only possible way: as an imbroglio of politics and warfare.

In North Africa there was no clear-cut military issue as there was in the desert or indeed through most of the Middle East campaigns. The army in Tunisia and Algeria fought amongst civilians and its movements were directed just as much from the State Department in Washington and the Foreign Office in London as from General Eisenhower's headquarters.

Then, too, we were not fighting for our lives or the protection of our homes but for the victory and the political reorganization of Europe. For the first time we engaged in outright offence—not defence—and the politicians emerged from their long hibernation which began at the fall of France in 1940.

Heaven knows what you will make of the first three chapters. I leave them in as a sort of personal synopsis for this complicated serial story which began so long ago in the dust of the Western Desert. If this book leaves you with the impression that we succeeded militarily in Africa and failed politically then I can only say that it seemed so to quite a number of us who were there at the time, and it seems even more so now. But that part of the story, the political part, still goes on. I must put down here my thanks to Sidney and Zoë Bernstein who gave me the hospitality of their farm in which to write this book, and to my wife who helped from the beginning.

ALAN MOOREHEAD

Kent
August 1943

CONTENTS

PART ONE. THE BACKGROUND

I.	Durban	3
II.	New York	20
III.	London	31
IV.	Londonderry	42
V.	Gibraltar	59

PART TWO. THE FOREGROUND

VI.	Algiers	67
VII.	Thibar	80
VIII.	Djedeida	97
IX.	Medjez el Bab	108
X.	Tripoli	126
XI.	Casablanca	143
XII.	Kasserine	153

PART THREE. THE ASSAULT

XIII.	El Guettar	163
XIV.	Kairouan	176

XV. Sousse   195

XVI. Longstop   207

XVII. Mateur   219

XVIII. Tunis   230

XIX. Bizerta   248

XX. Cape Bon   259

PART ONE

The Background

Chapter I: Durban

THIS was one of the last luxury liners in the world. There would never again be a ship like *Zola*. The company built her in the last year before the war when there was still the hope of peace and the habit of extravagance; and men still believed in a world of luxury and profits because they could not get themselves to face the dreadful prospect of war.

As the last declining months of peace ran out they streamlined *Zola's* hull and built a row of luxury shops along the promenade deck. They lined her state-rooms with padded silk and placed a floodlit statue at the end of the great dining saloon where you might sit over your *huîtres marinées* and *Liebfraumilch* and watch the sea go past at forty miles an hour through huge plate-glass windows. And in the hot afternoon you could go through the air-conditioned corridors to play tennis on the upper decks or swim in a marble pool where the artificial waves were kept at just the right temperature.

On *Zola* you could have a mint julep or an electric massage, a love affair or a game of baccarat, a major operation or a Brahms recital. There was hardly an artificial pleasure on earth that you could not have had on *Zola*. She was many thousand tons to carry only a few hundred passengers with a huge crew to look after them. Of these passengers just one hundred and fifty were first class and to them was given two-thirds of the ship—they would pay for the tennis courts and the Burgundy so let them have everything they wanted. *Zola*, you see, was built to carry millionaires from America to Europe and she was designed to make that journey across the Atlantic in just a few days.

The beef baron could step aboard with his overjewelled wife and she need never look at the sea or hardly feel its existence

3

until she began arguing with the customs in France. Then Paris; and with Paris the dress shows, the Champs Elysées, the racing at Auteuil, the Bal Tabarin.

Zola, a miracle of white paint and chromium and soundless, vibrationless engines, was ready to put to sea just about the time Hitler was ready. She was one of the last luxury liners in the world.

This was the ship that arrived off Suez at the end of the third year of war. The unbearable heat of the Red Sea in August sweated out of her drab grey plates. Not hundreds of passengers but thousands tumbled down her gangways on to the lighters and they were young American troops wearing steel helmets and carrying packs. The ship they left behind was as gloomy as a gaol, as comfortless and unlovely as only an army barracks can be. The padded silk of course was gone from the walls but that was only the beginning. In the ballroom crude wooden bunks were piled tier on tier leaving only two feet six inches between each sleeping man and his fellow passenger above. The swimming pool was full of potatoes, the shops were cabins, six, ten and twelve men to a cabin. The statue was boarded over and in the first-class dining saloon where neither oysters nor German wine were ever served you could see nothing outside for every window was boarded over with jet-black three-ply wood. The open decks and the tennis court where the men had slept in thousands through the Red Sea were filthy with dust and discarded papers and orange peel. *Zola* was long overdue for fumigation and she was lousy—lousy with vermin.

Because His Majesty's Troopship *Zola* appeared so drab and dirty with her one lofty funnel you would never have guessed as you looked at her from the docks of Suez that she and her fellows were a major factor in the world. Dirty, lousy, hot and overworked, she had arrived on this sweltering August day to land Americans in Egypt and take on board hundreds of Germans who had been captured in the Western Desert.

These Germans marched through the squalid dockside streets

of Suez with great sureness and confidence. They were short and lean little men and many of them carried under their arms a roll of bedding or an unpainted box containing perhaps an extra shirt and a few personal things they had managed to salvage in the battle. They were still dusty with desert sand and their thin green-grey gabardine uniforms and cloth caps were soiled and worn. They whistled as they marched. As they crammed into the lighters that took them out to the troopship they sang "We March Against England Today." Twenty or thirty officers, including a U-boat lieutenant, were in a little group by themselves. They smoked and contemptuously did what they were told. German privates followed behind carrying the officers' luggage. There was no atmosphere of defeat here, no depression, no apprehension. They were Aryan Germans walking through a rabble of Arabs and Jews and black men and they wore their medals on their tunics to show that they had fought with Rommel and the Afrika Korps. Lately they had won a great victory in the desert and even now Marshal Rommel stood at the gates of Alexandria. It appeared almost certain that within a few weeks he would be in Cairo and Alexandria. No, they had nothing to be ashamed of, these Germans, and now they were leaving their comrades to carry on the conquests they had so magnificently begun.

I stood at the rail of *Zola* watching the Germans come aboard from the lighters, and the third mate spat into the oily sea.

"More trouble," he said. "I expect we'll be having more trouble with these bastards."

He had indeed good reason to dislike German prisoners. A remarkable thing had happened aboard this ship on her last trip. In the same way she had arrived at Suez and taken on board a batch of Germans including General Ravenstein, who had ranked second to Rommel until he was captured outside Tobruk. The German troops had been drafted into quarters between decks at the forward end of the ship and their officers segregated on the boat deck aft. The officer in charge of the British escort had failed to take proper security measures. There were the Germans under lock and key, he argued, what could they do at sea? That British officer did not know General Ravenstein.

The third day out from Suez a guard who spoke German heard one of the prisoners say quietly, "It won't be long now." The guard promptly reported to the orderly room what he had heard. He had the impression the prisoners were plotting something, he said.

The soldier was waved aside with a reprimand by the British officer. He was told not to bring fanciful stories to his superiors and to get on with his job. A Czech doctor who was a member of *Zola*'s crew heard the incident in the orderly room and he was by no means convinced that everything was well. His Czech instincts told him there was likely to be danger wherever you have Germans. He had seen the slovenly arrangements made for the guarding of the prisoners. The doctor went to the captain with the story.

Wars make no difference to the status of captains. The captain is undisputed master of his ship whether he carries a president or a field marshal or merely an army officer in command of German prisoners. This captain, being a shrewd and dynamic little Scot, sacked the British army officer on the spot and ordered an immediate search of the ship. Within the hour— the eleventh hour—an extraordinary plot was uncovered.

British tommies going through the prisoners' quarters found broken chair-legs secreted in the stanchions. A score of pepper pots, each one capable of temporarily blinding a man, were dug out of the Germans' bedding. Some had razor blades bedded in potatoes. Others had filed table knives to a point or somehow managed to hide rifle bayonets down their trouser legs. There were roughly drawn sketch maps showing a plan of the ship's interior. Other charts showed the position of the ship off Africa. The Germans had divided themselves into assault parties, each party under the command of an NCO.

All this had been organized by Ravenstein from the upper

deck. Under Ravenstein's instructions a German doctor in the officers' quarters had asked permission to attend the German sick and this had been granted. In this way liaison was made between the officers and the troops below decks. To his first patients the doctor said, "Go back and tell as many of your comrades as you can to report to me with colds and stomach trouble." To each of these faked patients the doctor passed on orders: "You will assault this companionway . . . you will stand here and cause a diversion . . . you will lead the break-through to the upper decks."

Meanwhile a U-boat officer among the prisoners noted from the speed of the ship and the position of the sun that she was proceeding down the Red Sea and would be off Cape Guardafui on the third night out. He drew up charts accordingly and the early hours of the fourth morning were selected as the time the mutiny should begin. Ravenstein's plan was very simple. Shortly after midnight a small party of the troops should cause a disturbance along the passages leading to the interior of the ship. The main body of the Germans would then rush and overwhelm the two British soldiers who guarded the two doors leading on to the open decks in the bows. Once outside it would be no difficult matter for the Germans to swarm up over three decks to the bridge and deal with the British officers on duty there. Arms would be found in the bridge.

Then the German NCO's were ordered to run across the tennis court on the boat deck and release Ravenstein and his fellow officers. While the remainder of the British escort and the crew were being subdued the U-boat officer would take control of the vessel and steer her into port in the Vichy-controlled island of Madagascar which lay a few days' steaming to the south. This was the mutiny which was discovered and put down just two hours before it was to take place on *Zola*'s previous voyage. This was what made the third mate spit over the side and say bitterly, "I expect there will be more trouble."

But there was no trouble. In the pitiless Red Sea summer glare the prisoners were stowed away. A couple of hundred South African soldiers and woman volunteers who were going on leave came aboard. My wife, myself and our baby found a fairly comfortable cabin on the upper decks. We shouldered our canvas life jackets which we were to have by us day and night for the next six weeks. We gathered in the lounge to hear a lecture on the dangers of smoking on deck at night, of leaving lighted portholes open, of being off our guard with the prisoners, of not having a convenient water bottle in case we were shipwrecked and on all the other menaces which follow the sailor through the wartime sea.

But it was the heat that governed all our actions, the damp, exhausting Red Sea heat that throws up red spots in front of your eyes in the daytime and leaves you tossing all night in the sweaty damp sheets of your bunk.

Sixty Germans between decks collapsed with heat stroke and as their unconscious bodies were dragged out to the open decks they left behind them on the planks a thin trickle of sweat until they could sweat no more.

After that the Czech doctor had to allow the prisoners on deck at night, a highly dangerous move in normal times but at this moment reasonably secure since the men simply lay about gasping and sucking at the dead air like fish that have just been brought ashore from the sea.

In the Indian Ocean the weather freshened. Across the equator it was almost cold. Each day while the great ship rolled steeply on her beam ends the people of this little moving island grew together and in their isolation the Germans and the South Africans and the crew came to know one another. Each morning it seemed one left behind a little more of the past and the habits of the land fell away. One did not even look forward very far into the future. It was sufficient to fulfil the same daily routine and let one's mind rest in a sort of suspension from the world. The ship would take one back quickly enough. You could feel it all night and all day tugging forward through this immensity of space and since there was nothing one could do to hasten it or retard it or alter its direction the natural instinct was to lie back passively and let the sea and the clouds go by.

We saw no other ship, no sign of land. As we crept down into the southern ocean a young albatross swung back and forth over our wake as though it were suspended from a pendulum. Sometimes I would hold my son John up to watch the flying fish spring in shoals from the crest of a wave. There was no other sign of life, and nothing anywhere to suggest that to-morrow would be any different from to-day or yesterday. We did not think of being torpedoed, we did not imagine we would be bombed. We seemed to be remote not only from the war but from the peacetime world as well. Neither money nor position nor ambition nor talent could affect one's condition either way in this narrow space; and every day that went by our world grew narrower and more remote.

I imagine that a prisoner in a cell will come to feel like this and with that idea in mind I began to watch the prisoners on board this ship. Almost imperceptibly they were changing. There was nothing much at first you could point to with certainty, but the general atmosphere of hostility was gone. Instead of bothering to look contemptuous, the officers used their hours on deck to run and walk about. Once I found them playing hide and seek with John and they seemed to be enjoying it just as much as he was.

The truth was that many on that ship were very tired. A great number had been for a year or even two years in the desert. It had been fighting without decision and without relief. It began to appear that it would go on for ever and that when the armistice came it would still find the Eighth Army and the Afrika Korps swaying back and forth over that dreary worn-out waste. In the minds of the prisoners and their gaolers there was no romance and little excitement left in the desert. Mersa Matruh, Alamein, Sollum, Capuzzo, Bardia, Tobruk, Derna, Barca and Benghazi—we knew these places for what they were,

broken, wretched, shell-holed villages surrounded by deep clinging dust and a stale atmosphere compounded of heat, flies, petrol
fumes and boredom.

Just for a moment in the past month there had been wild hope
in the Afrika Korps that they would break through to the green
Nile and there had been a proportionate despair on the British
side. The fall of Tobruk had been a disaster for the British and
a major triumph for the Germans. But now all that was finished,
as all the other great desert moves were finished. We had thrown
back the exhausted Germans from Alamein at the last moment.
Living in the Alamein line that August I had felt again the lift
and excitement of the first days of the desert war. The Germans
came on again and again and we always held them, and thrust
forward on our own account. But gradually that movement
levelled down into a tedious war of position. It had been an
overwhelming relief to leave it, to come down to the sea and get
away in this ship.

More and more one felt, "All that is over and finished with.
We can start a new life now—somewhere there are trees and
mountains and rivers." You could see that look forming in the
faces of the Germans. They began to relax. They began to
throw off the stiff military system that had hemmed in their
lives since the day Hitler had marched into Poland. They began
to think and they began the process of becoming normal human
beings again.

This change had not yet gone far when we reached Durban.
It was winter at Durban and a cold soft rain blew across the
Bluff, the green headland that blankets the port. As we tied up
alongside, a company of troops in battle dress began to form
up on the docks. These were the Poles who by some freak of
the war had been landed in South Africa on their way from
Russia to England. Now they were coming aboard to take over
the escort duty from the South Africans who were going ashore
on their leave.

Somewhere in the change-over the trouble occurred. There

was a hubbub in the middle of the night and much running along the decks and shouting. A porthole on E deck had been prised open and seventeen of the prisoners had slipped over the side into the sea. The hue and cry went on all night and all the next day. Under the ship's floodlights some of the Germans had been picked up with boat hooks from the water. Others had drowned near the harbour bar or been taken by sharks. Others had gone ashore on to the green headland which at that time was said to be swarming with black mamba snakes. In the end all were accounted for except six and we sailed without them.

We turned now towards the west around the Cape of Good Hope and into that interminable expanse of the South Atlantic. All the land in the world could be lost in this one ocean where nothing lies in a straight line between the North and the South poles. We drove on day after day, and for many hundreds of miles there was no land in any direction. An island was a tiny unseen speck to the west.

No U-boat had lately been heard of in these latitudes but still we zig-zagged back and forth and sent out a jagged wake behind. And still each morning at ten the ship's syren blew and we went through our lifeboat drill.

Each night the Poles would form up in line on the port deck and with their faces turned towards the sunset would sing their ancient national hymn. It was a lament that might have touched your heart anywhere. But here in this wilderness, sung by these homeless men, mere boys some of them, and without accompaniment except the sound of the waves against the ship, it had a quality of nostalgia and pathos that left you embarrassed and afraid. Each man had lost his family years ago in Poland and now, dressed in foreign uniforms on a foreign ship, they were divided from their homes not only by the Germans, but by many thousands of miles of sea and land, and their cause looked more hopeless than ever.

The Poles were tough but very correct with the Germans.

Put a young lad on sentry duty and he would never budge until he was relieved. The Germans were not allowed to smoke between decks and one day a Bavarian NCO began taunting a Polish sentry by putting a cigarette in his mouth and pretending to light it. The Pole told him to stop. The German persisted and finally struck a match. In a second the Pole had his gun in the German's back and was marching him up to the orderly room. There was no more fooling with the Poles after that.

With the handful of British guards on board it was different. The British despite everything were very easy-going, and the Germans seemed to feel more at ease with them. One of the prisoners who had been recaptured at Durban was isolated in a cell as punishment and he was known as a tough character. There was some surprise therefore one day when he reported to the orderly room that the British sergeant in charge of him had gone off, leaving a rifle and forty rounds of ammunition in the cell.

The Poles never relaxed on duty for an instant. Off duty they never walked about the ship. They simply lay on the deck and slept and ate or played cards quietly and sometimes they would gather round a man who had a concertina. None of them spoke anything but Polish. They were a strange and secluded group aboard the ship and although we all had great goodwill for them there was no real point of contact. It was just in the evening when their hymn was sung that one suddenly had a vision of the unconquerable pride that kept these men together. Some of the older men had tears in their eyes as they sang and if you will concede that these were the tears of men who had nothing to lose except their spirit you will understand their religious desire to kill Germans. I have seen Poles killing Germans and they do it with the same passionless coldness with which a surgeon cuts out an ulcer. There is some motive which is beyond hate or revenge. It is a direct physical reaction, something that has made the Germans more brutal in Poland than anywhere else. In the end it is probably the primitive desire for survival.

Soon we were in the Gulf Stream. It was warmer and clumps of gulf weed, like great bunches of bright yellow grapes, floated constantly by. Points of white phosphorus flashed away from the ship's sides like sparks from an anvil. And so we went into port to oil. Hills and islands sparkled in vivid sunshine on this morning, a breath-taking pleasure after so many weeks in mid-ocean. From the heights to the pavements in the town below, the port glowed with light and fresh colour. We were not allowed ashore. While motor launches plied round and round the ship on the watch for Germans trying to escape overboard we sat there all day gazing at the lovely scene.

And now at last I began to break off the remaining links that held me to the Mediterranean and the war in the Middle East. This was the new world. For nearly three years I had lived in uniform and that alone is enough to bind you into army habits so that you do not think very much outside the army and even the method of your thinking becomes conditioned by the routine. For most people the army is a physically better life than the life of civilian peace, but you lose your mental independence. All of us who had been in the Middle East since the beginning had increasingly felt that our lives were becoming narrower and narrower. We saw the war only from the point of view of Egypt and the desert. We felt we were missing the main thing. For years I had been writing dispatches, articles and books for people I had never seen and whose reactions were almost unknown to me. England was a blur on my memory. I had missed the blitz. America I had never seen. For a long time we had been getting tantalizing scraps of information about the great changes that were going on in England and America. It was said there was a great left-wing movement in Britain; that the whole country had swung over to a pro-Russian line. The steel mills and assembly lines of America were simply fables in our minds, things of which we heard with wonder because they were utterly new and we had no points of comparison and assessment. We had seen the American guns fire often enough, but who made them and how many and when would the new machines they spoke about be delivered?

Above all this, how was the war going to be fought? Were we going to flounder on forever in the desert, getting nowhere? They spoke of a second front from England but where was it? Where were the Americans going to throw their full weight—in the Pacific or Europe? There were whispers from time to time that Africa and the Mediterranean were going to be made a major front but you could never believe this entirely any more than you could believe the stories of a new landing in Norway.

It was exasperating never to know for certain. For years it seemed we had blundered on in the darkness and inevitably a phobia sprang up in our minds that there was no direction anywhere, no plan for the war and no hard prospects for the peace.

And so this was for me a voyage of personal discovery, a voyage round the world to find out what was happening and where the orders were coming from and who was giving them.

I believed in the African war; I knew or thought I knew that if we had enough arms we could clear the Mediterranean and get at Europe through France, Italy and the Balkans at far less cost than by making a frontal assault from England.

There were a thousand things I wanted to know and experience and somehow I felt that I was going to get the answers in America and Britain. For the first time now I felt that the story was about to unfold and I began to look forward to the next few months with the excitement of a child watching the curtain go up on his first pantomime.

That night *Zola* rode out into the Atlantic again and turned north. We had heard many stories of U-boats ranging these seas, but after so many weeks it was impossible to believe that this safe, fast ship would be attacked. They say the crew of a bomber after a number of trips become convinced that their machine is lucky and will never be shot down. Something of the same thought enters the nature of the sailor at sea and he seals up his mind against the prospect of shipwreck.

At all events we saw nothing as we came through this dangerous bit, and in weather that got steadily fresher we passed along the coast of the United States and turned at last towards Halifax in Nova Scotia, our journey's end.

By now the prisoners had become entirely part of the ship's life. We would have missed them had we not seen them exercising on the deck in the morning. We got to know them individually by sight—the short, flaxen-haired gunnery officer with the knee-boots, the serious dark-haired group who always played some game with their strange and gay German cards, the Luftwaffe pilot who kept a little apart, the younger ones who could scarcely have been twenty and who used to practise jumps over one of the hawsers. As soon as they filed out from the dim interior of the ship on to the bright deck they smiled and looked at the sea. Then since they were not allowed to carry matches they thronged round the British guards to get lights for their cigarettes. The guards and the prisoners had grown through habit to know one another well enough to communicate by signs and broken words. Once the prisoners had complained that their rations were not good enough, but it was not a bitter or mutinous complaint—just the sort of complaint that a group of boarders will make to the landlady at a holiday pension.

God knows we all got tired of the food but it was still much better than the food in England. I went down to the prisoners' quarters one day and tasted the meat and vegetable stew and the rice and stewed fruit. There was white bread and occasionally fresh fruit from the refrigerators.

When we had got aboard at Suez only one man, an avowed anti-Nazi, would give his parole that he would not attempt to escape. He was made into a dish-washer and kept apart from his fellow prisoners lest they should molest him. But now the Germans were all willing enough to help with the work. They were divided into a score or so of "messes" of about twenty or thirty men each. Each mess appointed its leader, who was responsible for keeping order and getting the men's quarters cleaned out each morning. Two men from each mess collected the food at mealtimes from the galleys and Germans volunteered to work in the galleys as well.

For the most part they kept their quarters spotlessly clean and most of the men shaved regularly. Their talk now had drifted away from the desert and the war. Mostly they liked to discuss how it would be in camp in Canada, whether they would be able to send and receive mail, what clothes they would be issued and what the food would be like ashore. They began to look forward to Canada with interest and even pleasure.

One day they sent up word to the orderly room that they had an excellent pianist among their number and they would like to provide a concert for the British officers. All this was a long way from the sort of atmosphere in which we had set out from Suez.

Off Newfoundland we plunged into the heavy fog that hangs off the coast in the late summer. This fog is dangerous, since it lies across one of the busiest sea-lanes in the Atlantic and it can descend out of a clear sky within half an hour. Long before we picked up the pilot from Halifax we were creeping very slowly through the grey, wet mist and all around us the sudden eerie blare of fog-horns kept sounding. We knew we had to pass the noise of these fog-horns that float at the approaches to the harbour and for a time we heard them steadily—moaning, drawn-out blasts that seemed somehow to accentuate the weight and mystery of the fog. But then other fog-horns, coming from many different directions and never remaining in one place, began to rise and fall over the calm water. These were other ships and they were close. Every available officer on *Zola* stood round the bridge peering vainly through the mist that some-times lifted for a quarter of a mile and then abruptly closed in again.

Without warning the fog dissipated entirely and the bright sun poured down on the sea like a spotlight coming from the wings of an immense theatre. Within a split second the captain was shouting orders. Ships were all around us. One freighter was right under our bows. Behind them the green cliffs of Halifax glowed strongly in yellow light. We were passing straight through the middle of a convoy setting out for England.

At six or seven knots a great liner answers with painful sluggishness to the helm. There was the freighter a few yards away, a tiny matchbox on the sea; here were *Zola*'s hundred-foot grey bows bearing down on it and there was nothing much any one could do. I, for one, just stood there holding my breath. Then the freighter vanished from my sight under the bows. We waited. Then the freighter slid out the other side. She trailed a fog-line behind her and this we sliced in half. For a full minute it was possible to look down on to the freighter's decks and see the scared and working face of the commander on his little wooden bridge. He had hoisted a rope ball to his masthead which is the signal that a ship is out of control. With that signal aloft the freighter's captain knew that we would be held responsible for any damage that occurred; but who cares for responsibility at the moment of disaster? Can the falling parachutist argue with the manufacturer who supplies him with a parachute that won't open? So as the tension broke on *Zola*'s bridge we laughed in a mixture of callousness and relief at the freighter's distress signals.

But still there were other ships all around us. I began to count them and got to six and suddenly the fog slid down again and where there had been ships, now only the angry groan of moving fog-horns sounded. In and out of gloom we edged towards the harbour mouth and back into the sunshine. An unemotional pilot took us in. That night while we tied up alongside the railway station there was tremendous commotion on board. The prisoners were to be taken off in the morning. They had to be counted, searched once more and drafted section by section on to a waiting Canadian train. The sick had to be carried ashore.

All the next morning I watched the Germans filing off. They stood in long lines spiralling down the main staircase leading to the gangway, each man with his pack on his back and his prisoner's card in his hand. The prisoners were in high spirits. One flaxen-haired boy winked broadly at my wife, the only woman on board since leaving Durban. You could hardly believe that these were the same men who had fought so bitterly in the desert. They were eager to get ashore and they kept laughing and making jokes among themselves as they waited.

A ship bringing the wrecked survivors from a ship which had been attacked outside Halifax a few days before slid into a berth beside us. Haggard-looking women and despondent men with blankets round their shoulders looked across to the prisoners on Zola with bitterness and hatred.

There was one last little incident. All the German troops got off first and this left no one to carry the German officers' luggage. (Under the Hague convention captured officers are entitled to have their bags carried.) With a tactlessness that passed all belief the British officer asked the Poles to carry the baggage. He might as well have asked the survivors from the convoy. The Poles refused point-blank.

Now this sort of argument and misunderstanding had been growing aboard Zola. There were many differences between the crew, the British escort and the Poles. While the prisoners had grown more quiescent, the men set to guard them had fallen out with one another. While the Germans in defeat and captivity had been drawn more closely together, we the victors were finding points of difference in our victory. It had been like that too at Versailles at the end of the other war. But no one on board was willing to create an incident at this moment and so the British tommies were ordered to take the German luggage ashore.

First came the German officers, after them the tommies lumping their suitcases; and the language of the tommies was a thing to marvel at. They were angry with the Germans, angry with the Poles and most of all angry to the point of mutiny with their own officers. It was a slight and silly incident, one of those little things that make men hate the army. A British corporal paused on the gangway and deliberately dropped one of the German suitcases over the side. No one spoke. No officer cared to raise his voice. The corporal, a man with his soul refreshed, continued with dignity up the gangway.

Chapter II: New York

THEY were putting the last touches to the North African plan when I arrived in America and a strange business it was. While half the newspapers of the country were shouting for a second front the thing was being organized in an atmosphere of secrecy that you would not have thought possible in a democracy. Already in October the troops had sailed from the United States, the tanks and guns had been allotted and the deal with the French generals had been signed, sealed and delivered.

But the country knew nothing of all this. Even in the train journey from Halifax to New York I felt the unrest and discontent at the way the war was going. As the rich pine forests and the lakes of Nova Scotia went past, the man in the next compartment was saying:

"Why don't they DO something? What's wrong with them? Why can't they start a second front?"

There had indeed been no good news for a year.

In the Pacific it had been one calamity after another; Pearl Harbour and Singapore, the sinking of the *Prince of Wales* and the cutting of the Burma Road. Nor had our occasional naval successes been able to stop the Japanese avalanche that swept on over Malaya and Java, Borneo and the Philippines, Burma and New Guinea. Even now things were going badly for the marines on Guadalcanal.

In India the Cripps negotiations had crashed and in the bitter political shambles that followed there was shooting in the streets of Bombay and Calcutta and sabotage all the way across the peninsula.

Tobruk had surrendered, the worst humiliation in the desert

war, and at any moment it seemed likely that Rommel might fling the British out of the Middle East altogether.

The U-boat war had touched its climax. One submarine penetrated far up the St. Lawrence. Another destroyed an Allied ship off Long Island and there was a long list of sinkings right down the eastern American seaboard.

Dieppe with the swift loss of more than half the British expedition seemed merely to prove that we could not invade Europe.

The Red armies were reeling back in the face of one massed German offensive after another. The Ukraine was overrun as far as the Caucasus and the Volga; and now the last buildings in Stalingrad were being demolished.

Nowhere on the whole globe was there any real progress or indeed any real sign that the rot would ever stop.

All this was reflected in the harshest possible lines about the time I reached New York, towards the end of September, 1942. Morale during bad times is nearly always lowest at the base and highest at the front. I knew that. But for me there had been no chance to make a gradual adjustment in my mind. I had come straight from the Western Desert, one of the remotest and most changeable of all the fronts. The intervening period at sea had been a vacuum. And now I stepped suddenly into the biggest of all the rear bases and the shock was much greater than it would otherwise have been.

Everywhere I went people seemed to be gripped by the same sense of irritation and frustration. It made no difference whether you talked to a cab-driver on Fifth Avenue or a business man just in from the Middle West. They were in the war but not of it. They were beginning to suffer the discomfort of war without seeing any definite result. The papers were full of war talk and the streets full of slogans, but where was the action? Where was the money going? Production was coming along fine but what happened to all the thousands of tanks and guns and jeeps? Why didn't somebody use them? Were the Russians the only people who could fight?

Every stop in the propaganda organ had been pulled out wide in praise of the American soldier. There was religious fervour in the phrase "our boys," and while you could criticize everything else on earth, even the most hard-boiled columnist or politician would never dare to question the skill and courage of the American soldier. But the ugly, unthinkable thing that nobody dared mention was beginning to creep into the back of people's minds. Did the nation really want to fight? Were not the Germans and the Japs really better soldiers? Look what was happening on Guadalcanal. . . .

And because this suspicion was unthinkable and I imagine the people in their hearts knew it to be untrue they vented their discontent with twice the force in other directions. The leadership was wrong, they argued. Washington was a hell's kitchen of double-dealing politicians and war profiteers. The cynicism about Washington was so intense it was bewildering. That was the place where rogues bribed one another to get government contracts, where foreigners intrigued, where men bought themselves out of active service, where fools and incompetents were falling over one another in every government department. American boys were paying with their lives for the mistakes made in the White House. The navy was at loggerheads with the army. There were rows with Russia, rows with Britain, rows with the Chinese. Big business was piling up more big business for after the war. The draft was crooked. The whole thing was crooked and there was no firm direction anywhere.

What was needed, one was told, was more honest-to-God Americanism in America and especially in Washington. Once let the Americans get started and they would see this thing through by themselves.

Because they had never seen war and had been brought up to hate it and fear it more than disease, more even than poverty, many of the people I met imagined it was far worse than it was.

In the absence of facts and in the presence of lurid, exciting propaganda people's minds were beginning to fill with horrific images—the raped girl in Tokio, the dying soldier in the mud, the tortured face of the sailor going down for the last time, the blazing homestead and the mother fleeing with her children from the monstrous Jap. These were the subjects of the posters and the daily cartoons and all the time the long horror of Stalingrad went on making these images seem all too real.

Nothing it seemed was being done to get on with the war—that was the thing. The boys were being sacrificed without reason, without direction and without care. Unless there was a second front soon the war might go on forever.

I do not suggest that these feelings were universal or even obvious. I simply say that within a few minutes of talking with the average citizen you began to sense his underlying discontent. It was the same discontent and uncertainty that had assailed every country in Europe on the eve of going into action, the same fear that attacks a patient on his way to the dentist. They say there is no moment for the soldier which is worse than that short period of nervous tension before he goes over the top. Once in action his mind clears and his courage leaps up. To a stranger America appeared to have reached that difficult moment just before going over the top.

Meanwhile in Washington the plans went steadily forward. Newspaper friends took me to one of Mr. Cordell Hull's conferences at the State Department. The Secretary stood patiently behind his chair and he had the air of a man who feels he is about to say No to a lot of questions which have been asked him many times before.

"Is there any change in our relations with Vichy?" some one asked.

"I have nothing more to add," said the Secretary and waited for the next question.

There were of course the most violent changes with Vichy going on behind the scenes. The matter had been most carefully discussed with Winston Churchill on his visit to Washington in the previous July at the time of the fall of Tobruk. As the Prime Minister has since revealed, that conference was the seed of the whole North African adventure—the conference that decided the Americans to put their main effort first into Europe and let the Japanese war wait; the conference that settled the blow should fall in the Mediterranean and that the Vichy generals (and not de Gaulle) should be asked to co-operate in the landing.

One can imagine the Prime Minister's arguments. Since the days of the Gallipoli landing in the last war he had been an ardent devotee of the Mediterranean policy—the policy of fighting the war on long lines of communication. Since 1918 he had argued at length and with reason that had the Gallipoli campaign been pressed home it would have considerably shortened the last war by throwing Turkey out of the struggle and opening up a supply line to Russia.

Clearly Churchill had argued these points again in Washington. Just as urgently as in 1915-1916 we needed a strong highroad into Russia through the Mediterranean. The Persian and Murmansk routes were slow, difficult and dangerous. Once take the whole North African coast and our shipping tonnage on the Russian supply route would double since each ship would do two journeys where it had done only one before. Moreover, continuous air cover could be given right down the Mediterranean to the disembarkation ports of Haifa, Beirut and Syrian Tripoli. Not only could we supply Russia rapidly that way but we could build up a great army in Syria and Palestine for an eventual attack on the Balkans. Turkey was another prize. If she could be induced to come in, Allied vessels could ply through the Dardanelles right up to the Black Sea.

It was a bold and attractive scheme and it required much political preparation. That was where Mr. Adolf Berle of the State Department came in. Mr. Berle was in charge of French relations. There was already a chain of American representatives and agents through Unoccupied France and North Africa. Now, the State Department believed that the way of resurrecting France lay not through General de Gaulle and the Communists and the underground Irredentist movements in France but through France's existing leaders who were either in prison in Germany or in the service of the Vichy government in France. True, these Frenchmen were not on the whole well disposed towards the British—the battle of Oran and Dakar had never been forgiven—but at least they were friendly to the Americans. The de Gaullist movement had become pretty well a British movement. It had never been regarded with much sympathy in Washington. De Gaulle seemed to have blundered badly in his Dakar exhibition and it was not at all clear what sort of following he had in France.

To the Americans it was all too painfully obvious that de Gaulle had been repulsed in Syria and Jibuti and indeed almost everywhere he went. Marshal Pétain was still the leader of France, and it was among the Marshal's followers, men like Weygand and Giraud and Georges, that the chief hope of advantage lay. Furthermore de Gaulle was not on the spot and the Vichy leaders were. They had control in North Africa.

There was no frame, no established head of the de Gaullist movement in France and—so one imagines the State Department arguing—there was neither the time nor the means to make contact with those who regarded the Fighting French movement as their salvation. Far better to win over the Darlans and Girauds and once in the Allied camp they could be induced to sink their differences with the British. Moreover, once the Vichy government in North Africa came over you had a working system of government in operation. To put in de Gaulle would mean a political and economic upheaval at the best and a revolution at the worst. You could do very little work for his cause on the inside until the actual landing took place.

Undeniably the State Department was determined to act in the best way for all concerned. Undeniably the British and

American military leaders on both sides of the Atlantic supported the Department's plans for white-anting Vichy rather than raise the standard of rebellion for de Gaulle since the former move entailed the least military risk. It meant that America was going to raise her own French champion to replace de Gaulle, that America, not Britain, was going to take the dominant political and economic role in France not only during the war but afterwards. (Unless of course that very elusive imponderable, the Soviet government, had something to say about it.) At any rate Mr. Churchill gave his assent to the deal, a school of American army officers who were to be the future *gauleiters* of France was set up in the United States and many a mysterious messenger set off for North Africa and Unoccupied France.

So already in the summer six months before the landing took place de Gaulle had lost his cause. He was never informed of the preparations. He only heard officially of the landing after it had taken place. To many it seemed that something else was lost at that momentous conference in Washington. It seemed that the fine clear edge of our policy was blunted. We were prepared from now on to parley with the enemy or at least with those who had been forced to go over to the enemy. We were ready to make concessions. To save the lives of our soldiers we were ready to stretch a point or two in the Atlantic Charter. We still wanted freedom of worship and freedom of race in the world; but if we could gain a short-range military advantage by treating with men who had helped to frame Vichy's anti-Jewish laws then the end justified the means.

People were saying that de Gaulle before this had damaged his own position by maintaining a pretty stiff and intransigeant manner in London. A black mark was recorded against the de Gaullists for allowing out the secret of the Dakar expedition before the ships had arrived at their destination. But for two years his name had gone out over the radio day and night and it stood for the ideals of anti-Fascism, of democracy, of the willingness to fight on for principles. We had yet to discover how deep an impression this had made inside Europe and Africa. De Gaulle himself might not be the ideal leader but his name stood for something. It had become a sort of trade-mark for liberty. Well, from now on the firm was under new management.

All this time, while all these plans were going forward in secret, the Roosevelt administration was under constant fire. Why no second front? Even Charlie Chaplin came to New York and made a speech calling for a second front. Mr. Wendell Willkie, hot from his flight round the world, demanded action. And still people asked, why do we continue relations with Vichy which is collaborating with America's enemies? Why don't we recognise de Gaulle?

On the morning of November 8th all the answers came suddenly together. American troops under General Eisenhower had landed in North Africa. Not Dakar as it was whispered, but Casablanca, Oran and Algiers which were right on the road to southern Europe. The President had sent a letter to the Bey of Tunis and Tunis was expected to fall at any moment. I was in New York when the news broke, and the effect on the people was electric. They snatched at the newspapers and they hung around their radio sets. They were aglow with the news. America was in it at last. At last we had a second front. At last we were hitting back. Hurrah for the American army, Hurrah for Roosevelt and Hurrah for the State Department which in its deep wisdom had kept up relations with Vichy so the boys could make an easy landing.

So it was going to be war in Europe and war from Africa. Knock the Boches out first, than all the Allies would turn on Japan together. There was pride and excitement and strong hope on that day.

A fortnight before the landing I had been urgently summoned to London by air. Unknown to me I had been chosen to go down to Africa with the invading troops as a war correspondent for the British press, but bad weather held up my departure from America until it was too late. Now I had to follow as quickly as I could.

I did not want to go. I had discovered the answers to some of my personal questions but these two months in America had been too rushed, too bewildering and too complicated. I had seen very little really and probably understood still less. I had developed strong prejudices too quickly. As I packed my baggage I found my mind a confused blur of many chance memories.

The livid golden flood of molten metal pouring from the buckets in the steel foundries; the great sheets of glowing metal roaring through the rollers; the new ships sliding sideways into the Ohio River to make their way two thousand miles down the Mississippi to the sea; the bright clatter of the aircraft plants and the uniformed women on the assembly line snatching at bullets and shells and gadgets while all above them and around them the coloured posters shouted, "Don't let them down" "Produce for Victory" "Put 10 per cent into war savings."

There was the monstrous pentagon building across the Potomac at Washington where I walked a mile and a quarter from the front door to the department I wanted; the squirrels playing in front of the White House as the President drove in; the shocking sight of the burnt-out *Normandie* lying like a beached whale under Manhattan's skyscrapers; the overcrowded trains full of plump men hurrying down to Washington with little leather cases under their arms; the Red Birds returning home from their triumph in the World Series to meet an hysterical crowd at the St. Louis railway station; Gypsy Rose Lee doing an act called "I can't strip to Brahms."

Grand Central and the Bronx, that fantastic vision of New York from the Triborough Bridge, and the long beautiful drive home in the evening through the autumn colours of the Hudson River; the hellish underground and the hellish overhead; Broadway at six and dinner at eight, sixty-five stories up, the streets that were German, the cities within New York that were Italian or Jewish, Polish or Czech, Chinese or Negro.

No, it was all much too much. To a stranger there was no cohesion anywhere and the geographical cult of Americanism seemed too new and too superficial to have found its roots. Yet it was there.

I had too a strong feeling that there was something wrong about this sudden universal optimism just as there had been something wrong with the earlier pessimism. I had not been in New York nearly long enough to assess the alternative moods that swept the people from one enthusiasm to another with the regularity of the rise and fall of the tide around Manhattan Island; nor had I had time to probe deep enough and find something as solid underneath as the seabed.

The most conflicting and improbable news was pouring out of Africa and, with the exception of one or two military commentators like Hanson Baldwin, the newspaper strategists were discussing the war in a way that bore no relation whatever to the Mediterranean as I knew it.

Montgomery's victory at Alamein was now complete. Benghazi was about to fall. The current view of the newspapers was that the British forces from the desert would join hands with the American forces from Algeria within the next few weeks—or days.

The Americans would take Tripoli and proceeding out into the desert would scoop up Rommel's retreating Afrika Korps. The meeting between the British and American armies would take place somewhere round the middle of the Gulf of Sidra. Every newspaper published maps showing great arrows pointing across the Mediterranean into Italy, the Balkans and France. Little by little the remarkable story began to come out of how the American fifth column had been organized in France and North Africa, of General Marcus Clark's secret and dangerous landing for a rendezvous with the French leaders, of how the United States minister Robert Murphy had sounded out the

French generals and brought them to our side, of how we had the great good fortune to get Admiral Darlan and of General Giraud's submarine journey from France. More and more it began to look like the biggest diplomatic coup of the war. France was rising again.

Well, at least I was being given a chance of seeing it. I went down to Grand Central station for the last time and took the train northward.

At Montreal the first bitter wind of the coming winter was blowing through the streets. It was Armistice Day and a little procession of old soldiers in civilian clothes and young ones in uniform marched down to the war memorial in the central square. The cold was intense. It was agony to stand still for two minutes while the Last Post sounded and the noise of the city fell eerily away away. For any one of my generation it was almost impossible to respond to a ceremony for a war that was finished and fruitless.

The big Liberator bomber smashed through the iced puddles of the airfield as we took off for Scotland. There were sixteen of us all buttoned up to the eyebrows in helmets, knee-boots, fleece-lined overalls, parachutes, water-wings and oxygen masks. We lay full length on the floor so tightly packed that if you decided to turn over, the men on either side of you had to turn as well. Thus, for ten hours over the Atlantic. A miserable, uncomfortable night. We flew only at eight thousand feet because the weather was good and so needed no oxygen; but it was unbearably hot with all our additional clothing. We were a strange collection—a brigadier, an English peer who had been buying American aircraft, an American armour expert, a Dutch policeman who had escaped from Holland, a fighter pilot and so on. It was the brigadier, if I remember rightly, who was lying on my right side. By accident I pulled the plug in his water-wings during the feverish early morning hours and they automatically filled with air. And there he lay quite unable to deflate himself until we slid down on the green, green coast of Scotland.

Chapter III: London

IT WAS eight o'clock on a bright fresh winter's morning when we landed. Within half an hour we had been helped out of our flying kit, passed through the customs and the immigration authorities, given coffee, a bedroom and a bathroom and told breakfast would be ready whenever we wanted it. An RAF officer said that if we had really urgent business in London he would have us flown down; otherwise sleepers were booked on the overnight train. A girl in WAAF uniform offered to send cables for us. Another changed dollars for pounds.

One blinked a little dazedly at all this. Since the war began I had travelled many scores of thousands of miles but nowhere else in the world had there been such efficiency, such courtesy and precision.

True, we were rather rare birds, coming in by air across the Atlantic and travelling on high priority. But still it was remarkable, this atmosphere. The place was alive. The people looked healthy. They were all busy. They were cheerful and there was something else especially in the faces of the girls, a steadiness, something clear-cut and definite. They were not so pretty as the American women, not nearly so smart, though their complexions were better.

Like nearly everything else in England, from the London underground to the British Constitution, this airport was the result of a series of compromises and makeshifts. The landing fields were once the fairways of a golf-course. The bunkers had been wired off and turned into weapon pits for the anti-aircraft guns. The clubhouse was become the headquarters. There were more aircraft standing about than I had seen in the whole of the Middle East during the first year of war. Every few minutes another military machine swept down from America, from southern England, possibly from France and Germany.

I wandered about in a daze of sentimental memories: Scotland as it was before the war when I had last seen it. That was gone of course, but here was the same wet moss on the earthen walls of the country lane, the same grey-white gulls following the ploughman through the field, the same blurred misty outlines and the incredible greenness of Scotland. For three years, from Gibraltar to New Delhi, I had seen nothing but sharp horizons and strident colours, except very occasionally in the desert at noon when the sand turned into the mirage of an undulating lake. Here every colour was soft and gentle, and one marvelled that one had forgotten this so completely.

Travelling all that night by train to London I had a bedroom to myself, an air-conditioned bedroom with hot water and a proper bed, and tea in the morning; things you cannot get as a rule in America.

London outwardly was no shock. It had been described to me over and over again by friends who had been in the blitz so I knew where to look for the holes in the lines of the buildings and the broken churches and I found them to be just what I expected, bad scars that were healing over. But in the inner workings of London, in its atmosphere and tempo, I found one astonishing thing after another. The buses careered at speed through the blackout keeping to a time-table. There were three or four postal deliveries a day. I took a taxi down to Westminster and within an hour had collected all the wartime documents necessary to live in England—ration book, identity card, clothing coupons (plus some additional coupons because I had arrived by air) and registration certificate. There was no queuing up, no waiting and no hurry. These things were handed out as part of a steady and precise routine.

That night the worst fog in years closed down over the Thames valley. I had accepted two invitations—one for dinner in Battersea, the other for a late party in Kensington—not knowing that most Londoners do not go out at night in winter now because of the sheer difficulty of getting transport. But in my ignorance I set out on this worst of all nights. My taxi got as far as the river before it ran out of petrol and I changed over to a bus that was going vaguely in my direction through the impenetrable gloom. Then I changed over to a tram that ran off the rails on a corner. The passengers with one accord jumped out and lifted the tram back on the rails.

Over dinner—wine, fish and fruit—the conversation was exciting and it was not about the war. Dr. Temple, the Archbishop of Canterbury, had made another speech insisting that the Church should concern itself in government, that the banks must be nationalized and that there should be more equal distribution of wealth and land after the war. It sounded more like the Communist Manifesto than the Primate of England but there it was and that was not all. The report of Sir William Beveridge was about to be tabled in the House. It proposed a scheme by which no man need ever again starve in England or fall ill without medical treatment or fail to get decent burial when he died. It sounded more like the millennium than the British Conservative party at work.

Everywhere in the pubs and the factories people were discussing these things. As they worked on munitions, as they trained in the camps or plodded about on ARP jobs at night they thought about them. The most popular feature on the radio was the Brains Trust. Miraculously the people seemed to know all the place-names of the obscure battlefields in the desert.

By some stroke of good luck a taxi rank sent a taxi for me through the fog and we asked the driver inside for a drink by the fire. He was a wizened little cockney of sixty, scarf round his neck, cloth cap perched across his head. He had fought through Palestine and Mesopotamia in the last war and in a minute he was down on the floor fighting the battles again with empty beer bottles, comparing those campaigns to these, matching Allenby's strategy with Alexander's.

No fog could baulk this old soldier who had his son in the army abroad and his two daughters working in munitions plants. As we drove on to Kensington I walked ahead with my torch to light him through the worst bits of fog or perched beside him while he furiously discussed the theory of fighting a war on long lines of communications.

And so we wandered through London that night and back to the West End. All through November I travelled about the city and southern England learning and learning, trying to catch up with the tremendous upheavals of thought that had been going on since the blitz. There were only about ten hours of these short winter days when you could meet people, but in that time I contrived to be with as many as possible, politicians and journalists, factory girls and actresses, soldiers and airmen, publishers and stockbrokers. I knew I had to go to North Africa very soon and there was so much to learn here in such little time.

I went down for a week to see the new British army in training. There was a day when the air-borne division put on a full-scale exercise. In a bare and frigid building the pilots sat in a semicircle round a relief map of the terrain on which they were going to drop their troops. It was the same room in which they had been briefed for their drops on Bruneval in Occupied France and in Tunisia and Algeria and later in Sicily.

Then we trooped out to the gliders. They were as big as heavy bombers. They carried complete hospitals, lorry loads of ammunition, workshops, motorcycles, water tanks and men. Each glider was attached by a rope and a telephone line to a bomber. The bombers were warming up and as we sat waiting the slack on the rope was gradually taken up. The machines went careering forward across the hilltop. Ours was a beautiful take-off. For two or three hundred yards my glider was bumping and wheezing across the rough ground until we were suddenly being towed into mid-air. After travelling so often in airplanes the sensation I had in this glider was that I had moved from a motor-boat into a yacht. The wind screamed past but it was an easy swinging motion. We rode just above the bomber's slipstream and about two thousand feet up through drifting cloud. Over the objective the bomber increased speed. The two pilots—one in the bomber, the other in the glider—checked their position and then we cut the towrope adrift. The glider banked steeply and sailed swiftly down between two copses of beech trees. We hit hard and ran to a standstill in twenty seconds.

All round us men were tumbling out of other gliders. Parachutists were falling and machine-gun shots began sounding round the ring of hills. One glider landing too steeply had startled the daylights out of a couple of ATS girls on the ground and they raced for cover with the glider in pursuit until its wing hit a brick wall. No one was hurt. Other parachutists lost in the rain fell on the wrong places or failed to jump at all. Things in fact were going wrong just as they always do on the real battlefield and the test was now whether the men could improvise and make good their mistakes.

There were many brass hats from the War Office watching that day and they piled into about fifty jeeps to keep up with the exercise. The men who had landed were attacking a low hill through woodland. A good concentrated mortar fire whistled over our heads and from half a dozen directions men came running with machine guns and hand grenades. They flung themselves prone on the grass every few yards and fired.

At each stage the spectators rushed forward in the jeeps, a wild cavalcade across the fields, and for a time we were hopelessly mixed up with the mock battle. Tracers began skidding past on either side of the jeeps and in their excitement the jeep drivers kept right up with the forward machine-gunners. The advancing infantry had been told to keep hard up against the shifting line on which the mortar shells were landing, a difficult and dangerous thing to do. The machine-gunners were all the time firing through their own men to protect them up to the edge of the wood. At the wood itself the infantry ran in with tommy guns. It was very exciting. I closed my eyes when my jeep ran over a grenade that had been flung out a second before and failed to explode. Beyond the wood a bangalore torpedo tore up a slice of wet turf and barbed wire from the ground and a great smoke ring hung in the air for a moment. Through this the flame-throwers ran to their last objective and the hill, it was judged, was ours.

These things are not so difficult when there is no fire coming at you and when men are not dropping out through injury and death. But what a difference from the plodding infantry exercises of three years before. What months and years of training lived in these boys so that they did in fact, without flinching, keep up with the line of falling mortars. And with only a safety margin of a yard or two they were willing to run up the line of their own machine-gun fire.

I did not then and do not now believe that gliders are an effective instrument except in certain very occasional situations. But these soldiers did believe in them. They did want to fight. They enjoyed it. They believed they were taking part in a great experiment which was to lead to the Wellsian battles of the future.

Another day I joined a battle school. The idea of the battle school was General Alexander's. After their normal training as many NCO's and officers as possible go off on three weeks' special training which duplicates war as nearly as possible. On this wet morning the men made a landing before dawn. With smoke-bombs and hand grenades falling around them they rushed the beach. Then they fought their way inland across streams and through hedgerows and farmyards. I can hardly say I enjoyed that day. Once I went down to my thighs in icy mud. Once I was covered with muck from a near-by grenade burst. When the troops wanted to go through a ten-foot hawthorn hedge they did not hunt for gaps, they walked straight through the thorns. All day until dusk they were at it without food, without rest. They ran and shot and climbed walls with their full equipment until they were tired into speechlessness. At the end of each stage they were called together, told what they had done wrong and then two new students were ordered to lead the next assault. They would simply be given a reference on the map, told roughly what resistance was there and ordered to take the place. Crawling on their bellies they reconnoitred the farm-houses and the barns. Dropping into ditches and swarming over brick walls they went in for the mopping up.

Normally there is something phoney, amateurish and childish about army field exercises, a sort of boy-scoutery that sits oddly upon grown men. But not here. This was tough and uncomfortable and extraordinarily real. It was a tremendous advance since the days of the crushing boredom of route marches and parade-ground drill. The enthusiasm was the surprising thing. By some chemistry these youths had been taken from the suburban milk-rounds and the city shops and made physically bigger and mentally much more alert. They clutched at any information. I once casually said something about the dispersal of vehicles on convoy. A colonel at once shoved me into an aircraft and piloting the thing himself swept me back and forth over his battalion for half an hour to have my opinion on whether they were correctly spaced apart or not. Feeling giddy and far from expert I shouted that it was first class but he continued tree-hopping for another ten minutes before he was satisfied. Clearly these trops were fit for the conquest of Africa and the invasion of Europe.

And so for three weeks I went round England convinced that such a renaissance had overtaken this country as had not happened at least in my lifetime. Just as my first impression of America had been one of confusion and cynicism, so in England it was one of direction and enthusiasm. Both were wrong—at least in part.

Little by little I began to see that. Everything was not all wrong in America nor was everything all right here. It was during the first days of December, while I was waiting in London for my sailing orders to go down to North Africa, that I began to see the gaps and the wastage in this new England.

The people were tired. No victory in Stalingrad, no breakthrough by the Eighth Army and no landing in North Africa could overnight shake them out of the strain of three years' garrison life in England. Casualties were very few as yet but many thousands of families had not seen their menfolk for years. Food was sufficient but it was boring and beyond everything the abiding interest in every one's life was food, food, food, how to cook it and how to get it and how to conserve it. Almost every conversation I had was eventually brought round to the subject of food. (It was strange and refreshing to find that the one cabinet minister who was whole-heartedly approved of was Lord Woolton, the Minister of Food. Woolton had an engaging way of coming on the air from the BBC as soon as some major mess-up occurred like the fish-zoning. "I know the trouble you are having," he would say. "It's an awful mess. But we are clearing it up and it won't happen again.")

More people were getting higher wages than they had ever had before but there was little of any real value you could buy for it. Every one had work but it was high-pressure work that went on in endless drudgery, nine, ten or twelve hours a day, six days a week with fire-watching and other wartime duties on top of it. Women after a long day in the factory had to face up to the difficult journey home in the dark, standing in food queues and feeding their children.

There was enough housing for every one but most people were cramped for space and decent household facilities were disappearing. If the plumbing began to leak you could get no one to repair it. For almost all the little necessities of life there was a day-long struggle that never let up. Since little or no repairs or painting were being done every city in England began to look shabby so that the people were constantly surrounded by ugliness and the atmosphere of neglect and decay. The people themselves were growing shabbier. They were aging. Young girls leaving school who could normally look forward to the gayest and best time of their lives had never known what it was to put on a party frock and a pair of silk stockings. They felt their youth and attractiveness were fading away in the omnipresent greyness of England and the war.

Nor did things seem quite so bright to me in political England as I had at first thought they were. The Beveridge Report was tabled but by no means was it adopted. Huge powerful interests like the insurance companies banded against it. Most of the report was supported by the government but in such a confusing way that half the country had no idea of whether or not they were going to get jobs after the war, which was the real thing they wanted to know. And Beveridge wrote in one of the Sunday papers: "My principles of security and freedom from want have been abandoned."

Dr. Temple was sharply attacked. The Church was the Church, he was told, and it had no place in politics, let alone revolutionary politics.

Since November I had walked each day through a square in London. When I first arrived I noticed that the iron railings round the gardens had been torn down for salvage and that any one in London could now walk across those once private lawns and let his children play under the trees. Now in December a spiked wooden fence had been placed around the park. And after the war? Would the iron railings come back?

Friends began to explain to me the technique of the rackets and the black markets. Every one, it seemed, had some sort of small graft; indeed, half of life was spent in working out just how you could pull a string here and exert a little influence there and get an extra bottle of gin over at the other place.

But it was upon North Africa that the public was now concentrating with growing suspicion and uneasiness. Something was being done down there which they did not understand. Why was Darlan in charge?—the professional Britain-hater, the turncoat admiral, the friend of Laval and the German collaborationists. Why were these de Gaullists who had helped us land suddenly clapped into prison? Were we going to advance on one place after another in Europe raising up Quislings as we went? The Allied foreigners in England like the Norwegians looked on these proceedings with bewilderment. Why stop at Darlan, they said? Why not buy over Quisling himself? Why not the House of Savoy in Italy? And if it came to that why not Goering, even Hitler himself? Much less vehemently but very solidly the British people shared their bitterness.

To some extent the public antagonism to North African politics was hushed by the statement that unless we co-operated with the Vichy French in North Africa thousands of British and American lives would have been lost. To some extent it was diverted by the progress of the war itself or rather the lack of progress. The First Army under General Anderson seemed to be getting nowhere. While Montgomery continued with his great swoops and marches in the desert the First Army seemed to have stopped dead and was likely to remain where it was until Montgomery came to the rescue.

Moreover, the early propaganda on the North African landings had been conducted with the utmost confusion. For some strange reason the authorities in London and Washington had chosen to give the impression that an enormous army had been landed in North Africa. Well, the public began to ask, why doesn't it to do something? Why is it held up by a handful of Germans in the tip of Tunisia?

Still much agitated by these things I packed my bag at last and went down to Euston Station. My personal quest for information was over and I was going back to the war in Africa not much wiser and a good deal sadder. It seemed to me horribly symbolic that my journey of political discovery, begun so hopefully in the American sunshine, was ending in the black and gloomy emptiness of Euston at midnight. I had got the answers to all the things I wanted to know when I set out from Egypt; and now I had a whole cartload of new questions.

In the train I changed back into uniform. I had not worn it for four months. It suddenly felt very warm and reassuring.

Chapter IV: Londonderry

THE life-lines of the North African expedition were strung down from a dozen British ports to the Mediterranean. Each week a new convoy put out into the Atlantic and ran between the U-boat packs into Algiers and Oran. Each day some fatal action was fought in the middle of the Atlantic or along the African coast. These battles were never reported. They were, of course, in the essence of our strategy and unless we won them then everything in Africa was lost; but it was also in the rule of the sea that they should be fought out silently and stealthily with scarcely any one to know about them except those who had taken part in the fighting.

It seemed to me that if one was going to report the North African war one ought to start here, on the sea, so I asked the Admiralty if they could send me down on one of the little ships; not in a big troop-carrying liner where you see very little and hear nothing in addition to being very vulnerable, but in a destroyer or a corvette. And so I went to Londonderry in the north of Ireland two days before Christmas.

The corvette *Exe* (later they called her a frigate) was at her berth in the town and you had to scramble across two sister ships to get at her. *Exe* was brand new and she looked old. There was hardly a day since her launching she had not been at sea and fighting. You could see that from the rust, the peeling paint, the crowded jumble of equipment on her decks and the faces of the men who sailed her.

She was austerely built; instead of planking on her decks she had a chemical mixture that was poured on and set hard and then sometimes buckled under the action of sea water. Even the captain's cabin had been built on monastic and highly economical lines and the furniture was tubular steel that raced about the deck in a storm like a pack of hounds. All the expense and skill in *Exe's* building had gone into the equipment, the Oerlikon guns, the Asdic, the radio-location gear, the depth charges and the instruments that controlled the gunnery, the power and the navigation. She had more power to strike at submarines than anything of her size afloat. She was nothing more than a shell for all these expensive precious gadgets and she was the ugliest and most uncomfortable ship I ever expect to travel in. And because I got to know the *Exe* a little I will irrationally defend that corvette against any other and without reason I will contest any word of criticism I ever hear against her skill, her manners or her company.

Her company at the moment I got aboard was feeling like mutiny. They had orders to sail on Christmas Day. Not only Christmas Day but a Friday. Not only Christmas Day but in lousy weather. Why not Boxing Day? They were bound to be kept hanging about anyway waiting for the convoy. They were due for a spell ashore. They needed repairs. They had just come in and they had more sea days in the past year than . . . The third officer was beyond eloquence. "It's a bloody racket," he said.

I had been made welcome as soon as I slid down the companionway into the tiny wardroom. "Come in. Have a drink," and ironically—"Merry Christmas."

Like the rest of the crew most of these officers were in their early twenties. The majority of the men on that ship had hardly seen the sea six months before. They were butchers, bakers, farmhands, milkmen, bank clerks, students and travelling salesmen. Some had grown beards.

The captain had a beard. He was a round tubby little man and he was Royal Navy with high seniority in this flotilla of corvettes. Earlier in the war he had been mine sweeping. He was born and bred to the little ships and his conversation was racy and gay and often witty.

He came on board with his wife, who had crossed from Scotland where she was living with her two children. She was snatching just these two or three days' leave with her husband and then on Christmas Day she would go back to Scotland again. Her life had always been like that: a series of brief chance meetings with her husband. They had been shopping in the town, buying flowers for the captain's cabin and holly for the ship. The commanders of the two adjacent corvettes came aboard and for a while we sat drinking whiskey and they talked of their last voyages.

Already when we went ashore for dinner in the town the holly was tied high upon the yardarm and the masts.

We had steaks in Londonderry that night—steaks such as have not been seen in England for years. The pavements were crowded with British and American sailors and in the shops you could still buy fine linen and Donegal tweed. I spent my sweet ration on some hard sticky substance and broke a tooth on it as I wandered in boredom round the town next day. As the naval dentist treated me he discoursed mournfully on teeth in the navy now—"Not like the teeth you used to see." In the streets the slow soft depressing Irish rain fell down. There was slush right along the crowded docksides. There were no cinemas to go to, no books I wanted in the shops. The pubs were closed and the cold cheerless atmosphere of war seemed to have reached into the grey houses and choked the feeling of Christmas out of the people living there.

The *Exe* was a drab and comfortless place while she was in port even though I had been given the captain's cabin since he would naturally sleep in a bunk below the bridge while we were at sea. One could not stay aboard or go on shore—there was nothing but coldness and cheerlessness and boredom everywhere.

But in the end sheer boredom drove me back into Londonderry on this dismal Christmas Eve and I met a friend in the navy who was living in the town. As we dined at his home the rain stopped falling and Londonderry was suddenly transformed. A huge and boisterous crowd of sailors on leave had flooded into the streets. They poured off the ships in their best uniforms and nothing could have baulked their determination to be gay.

A clear lamplike moon rode over the town and it had touched everything with a breathless and unreal loveliness. It was frosty and biting cold on the ramparts but looking down you could see how the yellow light had touched the wet slate roofs; each homestead chimney breathed up the smoke of a peat fire and this smoke was turned silver by the moon as it floated over the river and the town. In the streets below there was a wild conglomeration of noise. Since the American sailors had arrived the street boys had discovered a new trade—shoe-shining. They waited at the gates to the docks and shouted to the men coming ashore, "Clean yer shoes for a tanner, mister." As they shone the shoes the boys would sing to the sailors and their girls in their high clear Irish voices. They sang the old laments and dirges of County Antrim and all this sentimental sadness worth a tanner now came piping up over the rooftops to the old stone wall on which we were standing. With it came the caterwauling of many drunken men lurching through the dark streets, the high-pitched giggle of the girls, the crash of thrown bottles smashing against the sides of houses and many other sounds that may have been oaths or tipsy singing or the scraping of trams or the shuffling of many thousands of feet through the slime.

Behind us a narrow sliver of light showed through a chapel door. We went inside and the place was brightly lit and already filling up with the congregation for the midnight service. The organ was playing and as we came outside again into the moonlight this music met the drunken noises coming up from the city and for a little triumphed over it.

There was a naval officers' party in the town and we went in. The guests had been drinking since nightfall and now they danced or swayed or sat about in all the stages of intoxication from hilarity to complete vacuity and moroseness. People shoved drinks into your hand and forgot you. They began portentous conversations and then lost the drift of their talk until it rambled into nothing. One lad kept saying to me over and over again, "Dhrink dhrink dhrink." There were not nearly enough girls there and there were not enough with the sailors in the streets and the pubs.

It is always the same in every British war zone. There are never enough girls and in the end that is probably doing as much damage as anything else in this war. The men drink out of loneliness and a sense of frustration. They lay about in the gutters of Londonderry that night having achieved what they set out to do—to reach forgetfulness.

The *Exe* sailed next day. We sailed alone down the river with the tide and with a weird old Irish pilot at the helm who may have been eighty or a hundred. He came from the Irish Free State and there could be no secret about our going since there was de Valera's neutral and brightly lit territory on the left bank of the river. There was nothing much to stop German agents from sitting comfortably on the bank and reporting the movement of every British warship up and down the Foyle. It seemed absurd that a few yards away on the right bank which was the territory of belligerent Northern Ireland the villages were blacked out.

People passed freely back and forth over the border. Indeed, it was a common practice for the inhabitants of Northern Ireland to cycle across and buy unrationed silk stockings and sweets and liquor, and provided you did not go to excess the Eire customs would wink their eyes at the bundles under your coat.

The river was very narrow and sinuous. Sometimes the old pilot called for almost a right-angled turn. Each time we passed another warship moored on the bank the *Exe's* bosun would sound his whistle and we would stand to the salute on the bridge. Across the water the other vessel's salute would come back and it seemed to me then a most heartening and dignified farewell.

It was cold and the manners of the old Free State pilot were cold until we summoned him a double whiskey from the wardroom. Then his aged flat face and watery eyes screwed up into a smile. "Merry Christmas," he said. The holly was very green and cheerful on the mast. Now that we had actually cast off and accepted the enormity of going to sea on Christmas Day every one felt brighter.

The oiler was waiting for us at the mouth of the estuary and the crew of the oiler was drunk. In some astonishing way the master of the big ungainly barge had communicated his condition to his ship and she lurched about our thin sides like a sailor on a spree. At length we were safely lashed together and the oil began to flow aboard, through the rubber pipes.

We had a turkey for our Christmas dinner in the wardroom that night. It was the last time the captain would leave the precincts of the bridge until the voyage was done and he sat there benignly at the head of the table, a little man in a little ship and he was the feudal master of everything around him. Responsibility seems to lie easily on the men in the little ships. Being so few on board they have a sense of freedom and independence. Transports carrying thousands of troops and much equipment were at that moment beginning to roll out to a rendezvous somewhere and we were to protect them; but just tonight, in the warm and lighted cabin, this was of no account. On this night too, the crew had their last drinks, for they did not take liquor once they were at sea. The sailors were entitled to draw a ration of rum every day but most refused it and accepted instead a payment of threepence.

In the morning the sea was full of savage bucketing rollers. We had company now, sloops, another corvette and a destroyer but of all these the *Exe* appeared to feel the sea the most. She did not even try to cope with the waves. She had a most atrocious roll that pulled up short at its climax and then suddenly swung back the other way. Not for a second was she on an even keel and there were long hours when it was impossible to stand upright without holding on. Every few minutes an extra large wave bashed her on the side she shivered from one end to the other and the green sea rushing along the deck made a deep icy pool in the captain's cabin. This water kept rushing from side to side between the lockers all day and all night.

As a boy I had discovered my own cure for seasickness and I do not recommend it to any one else. It simply consisted of standing on deck until one was frozen to the bone. Then one bolted down to a warm bunk and fell asleep as quickly as possible. Since boyhood I had never been seasick, and I had some pride in my record. The *Exe* upset all that without delay. I felt terrible on the wet and freezing bridge and much more terrible on the damp and heaving bunk. Sleep mercifully came for a few hours at a time but then the thought and sight of food sent me rushing to the side where one at least could be miserably alone and wait to die.

A marvellous sight broke on the horizon on the second day out—the convoy, several great ships, apparently untroubled by the storm and apparently without forward motion. For the next week I was going to look out over the starboard side each morning and always see them there riding majestically and at ease. They became a constant unchangeable backcloth on the western horizon, as though they were painted there, always with the commodore's flagship ahead, the others spaced at just such a distance out astern.

Tiny warships guarded this vital fleet and except when we were chasing submarines or falling into new positions for the night we never changed our stations—ships out in front, ships lying abreast of the commodore's ship, more on either flank and the last bringing up the rear. The *Exe* was posted to the portside of the convoy immediately ahead of a sloop and astern of the destroyer *Loyal*.

All day the escort ships talked to one another in Morse with the lamps. Our orders came from the senior officer aboard the *Egret* which was riding last in the convoy.

Every so often the whole convoy would alter course and speed according to the weather or the danger or the hour of the day. We were a fast convoy and we had one general order—to get through to Oran and Algiers as safely and as quickly as possible.

For days while the sea heaved up and blew itself into a climacteric of sleet and wind, aircraft of the coastal command kept passing back and forth searching as we were for submarines. Then we steamed into calmer seas beyond the reach of aircraft and beyond the hope of aid if we struck the enemy.

I emerged now from my coma and struggled wanly up to the bridge, where I heard with some pleasure that a third of the crew had been seasick as well as myself. It was Sunday morning and the captain said briskly, "We will have prayers on the afterdeck at ten and try out the guns at eleven. Praise the Lord and pass the ammunition." The service went quietly forward among the depth charges and then the men ran quickly to the Oerlikons which had not been tested since the previous voyage. "Fire," said the captain and the gunnery officer shouted down the voice pipe, "Commence, commence, commence." For ten minutes they had the low clouds full of tracer bullets and the din on the bridge was unbelievable.

I had come on board dressed in the battle dress I used in the winter campaigns in the desert, but now like the officers I changed into those heavy padded overalls that keep the wind out while you are afloat and support you on the surface if you are shipwrecked. But still it was cold and two pairs of gloves could scarcely maintain the circulation in your hands.

Little by little, standing on the bridge all day, I learned something of the art of chasing submarines which is probably the most desperate battle of wits that modern warfare has provided yet. I learned that submarines will avoid corvettes and destroyers if they can and aim for the convoy. I learned that they prefer to attack on the surface at nightfall and of the means by which they will try to lure the escort away before making their attack from several different directions at once.

In this fantastic game of chess each side knew roughly where the other was moving and in what strength and at what speed and with what destination. Every mile of this vast featureless sea was plotted and checked, and though the U-boat packs spoke to one another below water and rarely came to the surface before nightfall yet they were discovered. Somewhere back in Britain there was a wall chart, and day by day a little black speck that was the *Exe* was moved on its course along the wall. Equally in St. Lorient or Brest there was very probably a German chart and *Exe* by now was on that too. We never spoke to England lest we should give away the convoy's position, but they spoke to us and day by day they knew each move we were making on a prearranged plan and they kept us informed. Whenever a U-boat pack moved in the Atlantic we were warned. The radio kept buzzing with the news of submarines that moved first towards us then away from us. It was uncanny, this feeling that the enemy was all about us and ready to strike, and yet we could see nothing and hear nothing and our eyes were in some control room on land a thousand miles away.

By radio location and the Asdic we kept peering endlessly into our immediate sea as we went along. The Asdic fascinated me.

Crouching in the dark little cabin there beneath the bridge you had the feeling that your nerve centres were projected out and down into the deep water. Mechanically one grew able to measure the sound of the electric impulses going out—ping-ing-ing . . . ping-ing-ing . . . ping-ing-ing . . . ping-ing-ing. So long as the rhythm kept up it was all right, nothing was there. But once it was interrupted the echo sounded back and there was an interval in the rhythm. It sounded something like "Ping . . . ping-ping. Ping . . . ping-ping. Ping . . . ping-ping." These lacunas showed as gaps in the steady line a mechanical needle was tracing in ink across a chart so one had a double check.

But it took much sensitivity and training to know when in fact one had a submarine.

Our first alarm rang through the ship on the fourth day. For some time we had been enviously watching the other corvettes go tearing off in pursuit of clues, and we had been feeling rather like the fisherman who never gets a bite while his friends keep hauling them in all the time. But now in the dark late afternoon I was jerked out of my sleep by that insistent whistle. One never took off all one's clothes at sea, but still one had to fumble for gloves and overalls and then climb through the lurching ship to the bridge. The men were already on the guns and at the depth charges. The tiny bridge was crowded. Our speed had increased enormously and we had changed direction away from the convoy. A black pennant was being pulled to the masthead to warn the other vessels we were going to attack. In the stern I could see the men knocking back the safety catches on the big barrel-shaped depth charges and getting extra detonators ready.

"Pattern," said the captain, and "Pattern," one of the officers repeated down the voice pipe. In the stern they set the charges to spray out over the sea.

The Asdic at the captain's feet was switched on to the loud-speaker and if one leaned down out of the fierce wind one could hear its broken echo. Suddenly one of the men shouted that he had lost contact. I could tell no difference in the rhythm of the echo but the man kept moving about the direction of his instruments, trying to pick up the contact again.

"Fire," said the captain and he nodded as he said it. The big barrels went out almost lazily over the air. They appeared to poise for a minute in mid-career and then they plopped into the waves clumsily and heavily, and the white wake flowed over them. It was no use tensing yourself for the explosions. They were much worse than you expected. At several points the sea humped itself into shivering green hillocks and on the sides of these hillocks the pattern of foam and spume that had formerly rested horizontally on the water was now suspended vertically and distorted into weird shapes. Then each hillock burst asunder into millions of particles and changed from green into sparkling white so that now it looked like a tall tree after a heavy fall of snow. With the bursting came the noise and a strange rasping shudder that raked the keel from one end of the ship to the other and for a moment you felt she was about to sink.

"Two hundred and ten revolutions," said the captain and he changed course so rapidly a great green wall of water raced waist high across the men fighting to get a new pattern of charges ready in the stern.

"Pattern ready," said the officer at the other end of the tube.

"Fire," said the captain. The barrels floated out lazily again.

Twisting and turning and changing speed we tried again and again to pick up the echo but it was gone.

You do not claim a submarine unless you have something very definite to show for it. A piece of human body preserved in the ship's refrigerator—that is the sort of evidence the Admiralty requires. It is not enough to say that oil rose to the surface or that you saw the submarine go into a vertical dive. So no submarine was claimed here and we steamed back to our station beside the convoy. The black pennant came down from the mast and the men left their action stations.

We were not entirely out to sink U-boats. If we kept them down that would be enough. Kept down and away by the ring of corvettes and destroyers the submarines would have no chance to fire; and the way to keep them down was to depth charge every suspicious sounding.

That night we had news of a U-boat pack in the Atlantic. It had hovered for the past few days in mid-ocean, apparently awaiting information. Meanwhile two convoys were at sea— ours and another slow convoy of small freighters which was making for America with ordinary civilian cargoes from Britain which would keep up our credit abroad. If one of the convoys was to be attacked then it was preferable that it should be the

American one. And now tonight there came word that the American convoy had been spotted by the U-boats.

Hour by hour the news came in. Always the submarines were getting closer to the other convoy. With the slow and paralysing inevitability of a classic tragedy the pack closed in on the freighters.

The Admiralty in London knew they were about to attack, the U-boat command in Germany knew it, we knew it—and there was nothing whatever we could do about it. The freighters had to fight out their battle alone and unaided since no British warship could cross to them in time and no aircraft could reach them. They were remote from the whole world, a private extension of the war.

As we waited the alarm signals rang again through the *Exe*. It was icy dark now and as I groped out of the warmth of the cabin to the bridge the wind seemed to sound more shrilly and the black water was forbiddeng and malicious. Stray U-boats were about us despite the fact that a pack had gone off in the opposite direction. There was a ragged and misty patchwork of blown clouds that sometimes turned silver but never parted enough to let the full light of the moon come through. One could see only the vague outline of some of the other ships in the convoy and no lights showed. Peering around through this silver and eerie semi-darkness you could imagine you saw the shapes of a dozen conning-towers in the waves but then the waves fell back and revealed nothing but the empty and interminable sea.

"Well, I'm damned if I know what's going on," said the captain and he again asked the Asdic and the radio-location crews if they had picked up anything.

"Nothing, sir."

The alarm had come from one of the destroyers, and now without warning a lighted shell of incredible brilliance burst out of the sea to our starboard bow and was followed by another and another. These shells mounted to the floor of the low clouds, throwing off a purple light as they swept upward. At their extreme height the parachute flares were released and above each flare was a propeller that regulated the descent. As the propellers turned they interrupted the flow of purple light on to the clouds so it appeared as though we were looking at some fantastic cinema screen that stretched across the whole sky above. For ten minutes, like the spokes of a moving wheel, the alternate pillars of darkness and light whirled furiously around the clouds, and down below the *Exe* slid through a purple sea.

"My goodness me," said the captain lightly. "Now who did that?" As he spoke the destroyer *Loyal* emerged suddenly from the darkness and began to move across our bows. She was travelling at fantastic speed, the grey foam flying out astern, and she was a lovely silver streak in the black and purple water. She bounded and heaved herself forward almost in the motion of a greyhound, and we cursed her heartily as we changed course just in time to let her by. Clearly the *Loyal* thought she had found something and was shooting flares in the hope of catching a submarine on the surface.

But again while we waited in the freezing wind nothing came out of it.

Twice more that night I bundled out of my bunk as the whistles sounded and I was still on the bridge when the morning broke and one after another the outlines of the other ships took solid shape. I counted the transports quickly. They were all there. On the radio came the news that the other convoy had taken the full shock of the U-boat attack. A few ships were sunk. The rest of the convoy had scattered.

It was too late for the pack to turn back and catch us but from now on we were constantly getting alarms. Sometimes depth-charge explosions would fly up from the wakes of the other escort ships. Sometimes like terriers in a dog-fight all the little ships would scurry across the sea, criss-crossing one another's wakes. Once we raced past one of the great transports and saw the troops in thousands watching us from the high decks. We had a bundle of *Egret's* mail on board and she came alongside us and fired a rocket gun over our stern as we sailed along. But the weather was still rough and only a cylinder of vital documents could be passed across the rope. *Egret* signalled us that she would wait for her mail until we got to port and disconsolately she steamed back to her station.

It was growing warmer now though still the waves continued. We expected to meet trouble at the approaches to the Straits of Gibraltar since that was the obvious place for the submarines to concentrate. I was reading in my bunk when a message came down that the captain wanted to see me on the bridge. For a change he was not very light-hearted.

"I have some bad news for you," he said. "We have just received orders to leave the convoy and go back to Londonderry immediately."

Now this was a sharp disappointment for every one. It meant that the crew was going to miss the excitement of the Mediterranean and the chance of a spell ashore in the sunshine. It meant much more time at sea for them as they would almost certainly have to set out with another convoy immediately. It meant *Egret* was not going to get her mail. It meant they were going to have a lonely and boring trip home and much hard work at the worst time of year. And it meant that my own arrival in North Africa was going to be delayed at least another month.

Typically the captain appeared to be more concerned about me than anything else. "It's too bad," he said. "I am afraid we have let you down badly." He sent off a signal saying he had myself and thirty ratings bound for Algiers and could he not at least drop us at Gibraltar? But no, it was no good, *Exe* had to get back.

"I'll tell you what," said the captain. "If you like to risk it I will ask *Loyal* to come alongside and we will see if we can't get you across to her in a whaler. The trouble is the weather's too bad. But we can try it."

You will never get the men in the little ships to abandon anything so long as there is the ghost of a chance. The weather frankly was outrageously bad for this sort of antic. But off went the signal to *Loyal*, out came the bosun piping for the whaler's crew and down I went to the cabin to throw my kit together.

When I got back on deck *Loyal* was coming up on our lee to make what calm water she could between the two vessels. The heavy whaler was slung out over *Exe's* portside, level with the deck. The mate tied a bulky cork life-jacket round my shoulders and I clambered into the stern-sheets with my baggage. My kit at this time was a thing of pride and joy to me, selected as a result of three years' campaigning—a flat metal typewriter bought in Macy's in New York that winter, a soft cowhide kitbag made in the native quarter in Cairo and stuffed with such things as shirts and a large silver whiskey flask, a featherweight metal stretcher bed and a fleece-lined canvas sleeping-bag just bought in Fortnum and Mason's in London.

It takes years and much travel to design and buy a perfect camping kit, to discover the little things like substituting a light camel-hair dressing-gown for a heavy army blanket; and this was my dream kit, the result of a voyage round the world. Down it all went into the bilge water in the stern of the whaler.

The boat's crew was ready. Each of us gripped a guiding rope with which to ease the whaler down on to the water. But now that *Exe* and *Loyal* had almost stopped the sea appeared really monstrous—or it did to me at any rate sitting in the whaler. At one moment we would be poised twenty or thirty feet in mid-air. Then as the *Exe* rolled and the sea came up we would have the waves rushing about us. The idea was to wait until the sea came up to us and then lower quickly away and so fall back gently with the declining wave. The men of both *Exe* and *Loyal* crammed the decks to watch this unusually diverting sport in mid-Atlantic. Too far off to see what was happening, the convoy steamed on indifferently.

A young mountain of water came lunging up the side of *Exe*.

"Let go," snapped the mate. The men on the pulleys relaxed their grip and it worked like a charm—but only in the stern-sheets. My end of the whaler rushed down to meet the wave. The other end stuck fast, the pulley jammed. This left the whaler and us in it suspended almost vertically down the side of the corvette, and the wave fell back without its burden. In the act of falling with the stern-sheets some ten feet of corded guiding rope had run through my clenched hand removing most of the fingerprints.

The next three or four minutes while the men fought to release the jammed pulley were unpleasant. Each wave that rose half-capsized the boat and the cold sea water poured in. It was certain that we were going to go overboard when suddenly the pulley gave way and, with a rush and a bang, the whaler hit the water. By some miracle we fell only a few feet and hit the sea right side up. The crew grabbed the oars and pulled away.

We had about a quarter of a mile to get across to the *Loyal* but this seemed much longer because we were constantly losing sight of both ships in the hollows of the sea. Moreover, the blood from my hand kept staining the water in the boat a vivid red, making me feel things were much worse than they actually were.

In the end we were washed across and now the full difficulty of our undertaking was apparent. At one moment we would be level with *Loyal's* bridge and then, after a descent at the speed of an electric lift, we would find ourselves almost surveying the barnacles on her keel. We tried approaching from several different directions but it was no good, the deck always slid past too fast and there was some danger that we would be smashed against the destroyer's side and capsized.

"It's bloody well impossible," quoth one of the boat's crew and I fervently agreed with him.

From the bridge of his ship *Loyal's* captain shouted down

through a megaphone at me a remark which I considered down-right frivolous at the time: "I don't see you taking any notes."

The sailors on *Loyal* had now flung a rope net over the side. A lucky wave threw us forward; fright gave me wings; I sprang up and out of the whaler and clutched the net and the whaler vanished below. A dozen hands dragged me on deck. Then the kit. The bedroll and the typewriter came up damply and easily on a rope, but the handle of the kitbag gave stitch by stitch as it was hauled over the yawning sea. I was far beyond caring much, nevertheless it was fascinating to see the last stitch give way just as a sailor made a grab at the bag and missed. Some one else below got his hand on the falling bag and there I was baggage and all aboard the destroyer.

The whaler's crew put safely back. *Loyal's* engine-room bells clanged and she leapt on her course. Down in the surgery the doctor put a strong whiskey in my left hand and got to work on the right. I felt at home again.

That evening a signal flashed across from the diminishing out-line of the *Exe*. She was already miles away. I have kept the signal. It was from *Exe's* captain, and it said simply, "Sorry you had such a rough passage. We all enjoyed having you on board and wish you all good luck in Africa."

Poor little *Exe*. I have not seen hide nor hair of you since that day. Wherever you are sailing, if you still sail—and even if you don't—you carry every good wish which I am capable of wishing. I know I will be welcome in your wardroom wher-ever we meet in this war. And for what it is worth you have my unbounded admiration and respect.

You may remember, Captain, standing with me on the bridge one day looking down at your butchers and bakers and bank clerks who were toiling in the waist of the ship. Watching them, you suddenly said with such convinced pride and without any affectation: "The salt of the earth."

With complete agreement let us have that here in print: "The salt of the earth."

Chapter V: Gibraltar

ABOARD the *Loyal* it was the same routine except that everything was on a larger scale. She was one of the latest of our destroyers. I slept on the bench in the wardroom aft and all night I could hear the propellers wrenching and tugging at the water, making a perpetual battle with the sea. When we were ordered to increase speed and go in Gibraltar ahead of the convoy to oil it almost seemed that the great power in the ship would burst her open.

There were no corridors below deck connecting the forward and the after ends of the vessel, and so to get from the wardroom to the bridge one had to navigate a difficult journey along the upper deck, which was often awash. By day you could hold on to the guiding rope and it was easy enough. But at night when the alarms sounded you could see nothing and you skidded about uncertainly on the slippery decks.

Mostly I stayed aft now, since it was so much trouble to get to the bridge. They gave me an unofficial job of looking after the detonators for the depth charges when we were in action. It was simply a matter of standing there in the wet with the little wooden boxes in my hands while the others did the heavy work of hoisting the depth charges into position for firing.

An aircraft circled round and as we trained our guns on it the watchers shouted it was British. Then a gull came out and swept round the ship. We were getting very near to land.

When at length we passed into the straits at nightfall everything was much the same as I remembered it during the Spanish War—Tangier and Ceuta on the right, both brightly lit, and then Tarifa to left, another beaded string of lights. Then into the harbour, Spanish Algeciras on one side, the Rock on the other side with Gibraltar town clinging on the slopes below. Very little had changed. Gibraltar was not even blacked out. For me Gibraltar had always meant war. When I had first been here six years before, Franco's troops were fighting their way round to Málaga. There had been shooting in La Línea and Algeciras, and the British, sitting on their Gibraltar terraces in the isolation of neutrality, had watched across the bay the pleasant spectacle of the fires and the tracer bullets. Well, now it was the other way about. The Spanish were sitting placidly on the patios and watching us.

The harbour was much the same except it was more crowded, and there were more sailors and soldiers about on the docks, more war everywhere.

Later in the year Mason-Macfarlane, the Governor of the Rock, took me on a day's tour through the defences. For years miners imported from the Rocky Mountains of Canada had been at work driving a vast network of tunnels through the living rock. It is a staggering thing to see, this underground fortress. Gibraltar now, in an emergency, can close up like a clam and live its life underground. I walked along miles of two-way subterranean roads and saw hospitals and food dumps, workshops and railways buried beyond the reach of any bomb or shell. We walked clean through the Rock and coming out of a hole on the face of the precipice looked down into Spain to the north, out into the Mediterranean in the east and the Atlantic in the west.

Caves as big as cinema theatres have been gouged out along the underground roads and sometimes stalactites hang weirdly from the ceiling among the shell-cases and the guns. Great reservoirs of icy rain water lie in the centre of the Rock. It is all built on a much greater scale than anything in the old Maginot Line.

Gibraltar has become a major cross-roads of the war. It is the place where you are quite apt to meet a diplomat from Russia, a general from Washington or a cabinet minister from

London, and every night half a dozen celebrities sit down at
the governor's table.

There are many deep secrets about Gibraltar which I am not
permitted to write about here. One of the strange things about
these secrets is that the Germans know most of them. Enemy
agents sit in La Línea a few hundred yards away and presumably telephone Berlin all the good news about the Rock—
how many ships come in and how many go off into the Mediterranean and so on.

This had once been a pleasant corner of the world where one
could go fishing round at Torremolinos or wander through the
sunshine to Málaga for the swimming. In the *fondas* in the warm
hills you could sit for hours over Valdepeñas wine and Spanish
omelettes, sherry and shrimps. But Spain was hungry now.
Suddenly feeling very fed up with the war I went back to the
wardroom and fell asleep.

When I woke we were already at sea again and trying to
catch up with the rest of the convoy that had passed through
the straits in the night. We were travelling faster than I had
ever travelled at sea before. In clear sparkling weather *Loyal*
was letting herself out with nearly everything she had.

It was an uplifting excitement. At forty miles an hour we
ploughed a long white furrow through the sea. The spray
turned into millions of flashing diamond points in the sunlight
and burst far over the bridge; all the stern-sheets were under
rushing water and as the waves came up we cut them clean in
half and leaped on the waves beyond. On the bridge that morning one felt a sense of tremendous confidence and light-hearted-
ness, a feeling compounded of speed and sunshine and the sea.

When we turned half the ship went under water. It came
racing and bumping in a massive plastic wall against the torpedoes and the gun turrets and it was full of coloured green
lights. *Loyal* shook herself and got free of the burden and the
water streamed away from her sides in cascades.

There was a man, a young bluejacket, standing amidships

working on the torpedoes when we made one of these skating turns. He had his back to the oncoming rush of water. Surely, one thought, he sees, he knows, he has his grip tight on something. At the last split second we realized on the bridge he did not know, he had no grip. Several men cried sharply to him but their shouts, already too late, were drowned in the roar of the wave. There must have been twenty or thirty tons of water traveling at least forty miles an hour in that wave and its force was unbelievable. It picked up two shell-casings from their lashings and crumpled the solid steel, it gathered up a line of steel fittings and flung them overboard, it tore a spare motor-boat engine out of its steel ropes and smashed it through a lifeboat. And it grabbed the boy and tossed him into the sea.

He made one cry as he went through the ropes on the starboard side. Then there was a moment when you could see one arm raised in the swirling waves of the wake.

For half an hour we doubled back on our course and cruised around but the drowning boy was a mile back by the time we had turned and there was never any hope for him.

So unnecessary and unexpected a death quietened the whole ship. A grim-faced little squad of shipmates patched up the places where the boy had fallen through.

An hour or two later we caught the convoy. It had grown much larger by additions from Gibraltar and the sea was full of ships wherever you looked—even ships coming the opposite direction from Oran and Algiers. The fleet was out. Over against the French coast the *Rodney's* great bulk showed against the cliffs and astern of her two aircraft carriers and still another battleship. They moved through a wide screen of cruisers and destroyers, a majestic sight.

We were at the first degree of readiness all this time since enemy aircraft were about and we were in bomber range from Italy. Around the guns we pulled on white anti-flash gloves and hoods so that the ship's company began to look like a gathering of the Ku Klux Klan. Far off to the northeast near the Italian coast we could hear the distant sound of gunfire. Over our sector the protective screen of British fighters flew lazily back and forth.

Some of our convoy turned into Oran that night. Ironically, having come all this way, one of the transports fouled another near the entrance to the harbour and only with great luck and better judgment were the two big ships and their cargoes got to the docks. The rest of us—destroyers, cruisers, aircraft carriers, battleships, freighters, oilers and transports—sailed on to Algiers.

In line astern, this armada rounded the last headland and moved into the channel of the port. Algiers at any time is a beautiful sight from the sea. Today it glistened. Row on row of big white buildings climbed up to the hills above the bay. The white mosques of the *kasbah*, gleaming in the morning sunshine, made a wavering reflection in the transparent sea.

I had seen this vision only once before—when I crossed to North Africa on the Italian liner *Saturnia*, during the Spanish War. Algiers seemed to have grown since then. For two and a half years it had been shut off from the rest of the world behind the Axis wall. Now it was open and free again with a great fleet at its docks. The *tricolore* floated very bravely from the roof of the post office. Two round-eyed English boys who had never been out of England before were detailed to carry my kit ashore.

They stepped very cautiously through the hubbub on the docks. Mounting the long ramp to the Hotel Aletti they gazed with increasing wonder at the palm trees, the flamboyant Algerian cavalrymen, the piled-up fruit barrows, the black boys who wanted to clean their shoes and the Arab women who sidled past with coloured veils over their faces. They screwed their heads round, trying to see everything at once, and drew back in embarrassment when the street vendors offered them necklaces and fly-whisks.

These were two of the boys whom I had seen working waist

deep at the depth charges on the destroyer. In the last few days
they had had only four or five hours' sleep. They had done their
part in fighting the U-boats all the way from England and they
had been quite unmoved and unafraid. I was glad they were
getting ashore if only for an hour or two.

"Look," I said when we got to the hotel, "here are some
French francs. You are not expected back at the ship for an
hour. Have a look around the town."

The elder of the two, the one who actually fired the depth
charge, considered it for a moment.

"No, sorr, thank you," he said. "You never know what will
happen in these furrin parts. I think we better be gettin' back
to the ship."

In the lounge of the hotel I came quite unexpectedly on the
OC troops and the adjutant who had sailed with me in *Zola* to
Canada. It seemed that they too had just arrived in Algiers and
in the same convoy. They had travelled in one of the large
transports.

"Dull trip," said the adjutant. "Nothing ever seems to happen
on these convoys."

PART TWO

The Foreground

Chapter VI: Algiers

IN THE last week of the old year a slim and dark French
boy with a sensitive face, named Bonnet de la Chapelle,
climbed up the steep road that runs from Algiers town towards
the St. George Hotel.

Halfway up he paused before the building which Admiral
Darlan had made his headquarters, and went inside. He asked
by name for a young friend of his who was a junior official in
the building. The girl at the reception desk showed him how to
make out a form requesting an interview with his friend, and
presently he was shown up.

The boy stayed only a few minutes and returning to his home
in the town where he lived with his parents he took from his
room a service revolver of the type that the Spanish arms
makers used to supply to the French government a few years
ago. He clipped the breach open and saw that it contained six
bullets. Then he put the revolver into his overcoat pocket, ate
lunch and returned to the Admiral's headquarters. It was by
now nearly mid-afternoon.

Again the boy asked to see his friend and when he had filled
up another form he was again invited to mount the stairs. This
time he did not go to the friend's room but continued straight
to the Admiral's office, which, apparently, he had discovered
on his earlier visit that morning.

The Admiral's secretary, a French girl, said that her chief
was out.

"Never mind," the boy said. "I will wait."

The girl put a cigarette into her mouth and asked de la Chapelle for a light. He drew a box of matches out of his pocket
and having lit her cigarette he said, "Here, take the box, miss."
This was quite a gesture in a town where matches were rarer

than precious metals, but in no other way was the boy's behaviour unusual. He looked composed and at ease as he strolled up and down the corridor waiting for the Admiral.

Darlan came in with his aide-de-camp, walking briskly. When he had all but passed, the boy touched him lightly on the sleeve and said, "*L'Amiral . . . ?*" Darlan paused and half-turned. As he turned de la Chapelle drew his gun, which was already cocked, and fired three shots diagonally across the Admiral's chest. Darlan slumped on to the floor almost without a cry and died soon afterwards. The boy meanwhile ran swiftly back into the office where the girl had risen in alarm from her desk. The ADC followed him.

As de la Chapelle swung his leg over the office window he took careful aim again and fired three bullets at the ADC's legs. The ADC fell with a crash and de la Chapelle dropped into the courtyard outside.

Many guards and gendarmes had been posted round the building and a group of these, startled by the firing, now rounded the corner and seized the boy before he could escape to the roadway. Only vaguely realizing what had happened from the cries of the girl and the wounded ADC the gendarmes started to beat up their struggling captive and officials came running in panic from all over the building. The boy's friend shouted to the gendarmes from the window to stop their baton play and the captive was brought into the building without further molestation.

When the doctors had done what they could for the two men who had been shot, all the senior French generals and administrators who happened to be in Algiers were summoned. They at once sat as a court-martial—General Giraud, General Noguès and a number of others. No communication was sent to General Eisenhower or the Allies' headquarters at the St. George Hotel, and headquarters, in fact, did not hear of the matter until the late afternoon.

Meanwhile the court-martial decided to sentence de la Cha-

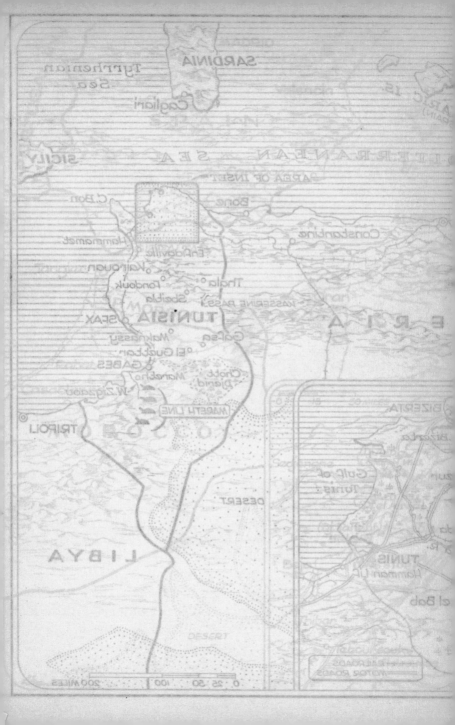

pelle to life imprisonment. A small minority led by General Noguès violently dissented from this decision and forced a re-opening of the case. Late that night the sentence was altered to death by the firing squad.

The boy remained in his cell all night in an exalted state of mind and appeared to be full of reckless confidence, not only in his own fate, but in the rightness of what he had done. He asked to see his parents but this was refused. He then sent a message to the ADC apologizing for having shot him and explaining that his quarrel lay only with the Admiral. Allied headquarters made no real attempt to intervene and the French leaders continued to treat the affair as entirely a French military matter in which no foreigner could interfere.

In the morning a priest was sent to talk to the boy and prepare him for his death. But de la Chapelle's confidence was quite unshaken. "They will not shoot me," he cried. "I have liberated France."

It was in vain that the priest acquainted him with the verdict and sought to make the boy realize that he had only a few hours to live and that the firing squad was even then being assembled.

"They may send the firing squad," de la Chapelle said. "They may go through the whole performance of shooting me, but you will see, the bullets will be blank cartridges."

In the end he accepted final absolution but he continued to protest: "They will not shoot me. They will use blank cartridges." Precisely twenty-four hours after the assassination of Darlan, de la Chapelle was taken out of his cell and shot.

One day there may be monuments erected all over France for Bonnet de la Chapelle but in Algiers that day only the wildest consternation reigned. The military landing had been made on November eighth with extraordinary ease at the three key points, Casablanca, Oran and Algiers, and there was every sign that it was going to stick. Even the fall of Tunis was envisaged for the following week. But the political plot, the plot to win over the Vichy leaders to our cause was now bursting wide open at its seams and giving offence to nearly everybody except the Germans.

Mr. Robert Murphy, the United States Minister, an Irish Catholic of considerable ability and charm, had already lived through a very trying time and now found himself without the machinery or the trained assistants to cope with a situation that was dangerous and rapidly getting worse. The outcry against Darlan had reached full pitch both in America and in England. The friendly neutrals were indignant. The Axis propaganda was making great play with the crisis, and now seized upon the assassination as a proof of the perfidy of the Allies and as a means to turn the hesitating French back into the German alliance. Nazi troops were at that moment flooding through Unoccupied France. Valuable units of the French fleet had been unable to get away from Toulon and were now either uselessly scuttled or at the disposal of the enemy. Moreover, disquieting news came in of more German troops being rushed to Tunisia by air. Mr. Murphy was faced with a situation which was impossible for one man to handle and there was at that time no senior British diplomat on the spot to assist him. Nor was he getting much coherent advice from the State Department in Washington, where such a grave abortion of the Vichy plan had not been foreseen.

And so in bewilderment, confusion and haste and entirely under the pressure of events was fashioned the Allied design for dealing with the French nation and presumably with the other occupied countries throughout the world.

From the first the Allied authorities stuck to the firm official line which has never since been altered: "Darlan just happened to be in North Africa attending his dying son. We had not intended to deal with him but since he was on the spot and manifestly the senior Frenchman, we were compelled to use him. Had we not adopted Darlan thousands of soldiers' lives might have been lost, the landings might have been seriously delayed and we might have been forced to continue for months fighting in Morocco and Algeria."

There was another point that was developed later: "We are not invading or occupying French territory. France is our ally, enjoying equal rights. French politics are the concern of the French alone."

With relief Mr. Murphy turned to the only course open to him. He asked General Giraud to step into the Admiral's place. Now General Giraud was by no means anxious at that time to become the new French leader in defiance of his old friend Marshal Pétain. His flight from the German cell at Königsberg and France by submarine to Gibraltar and his final emergence in this political madhouse in Algiers had left him shaken and uncertain. He was at first without his uniform, the symbol of authority, and he felt uncomfortable and ill at ease arriving in civilian clothes. No great fuss had been made locally of his coming. He protested, "I can't do it. I have no following."

But in the enforced absence of de Gaulle, who was not wanted by the Allied governments, Giraud was our man and no other would do. The minor ex-Vichy figures, Bergeret of the air staff, Yves Chatel, the military governor of Algiers, and others, were rapidly propelled into the breach to persuade Giraud to take over. Reluctantly he agreed and temporarily at least the situation was saved. The British had nothing against the old General apart from the rapidly-being-forgotten fact that he was one of the leaders of the French army that collapsed in 1940. Indeed there was widespread admiration for the old man's indomitable escapes from Germany. At least he was a soldier who had not dirtied his hands in politics as Darlan had.

Without concealment the British cheered the happy assassination of the Admiral and applauded the apt appointment of the General. In America too there was satisfaction.

Since an iron censorship had closed down in Algiers, very few people at home had any clear notion of the most intricate and dark politics that were going on in North Africa.

Having got their new champion in the chair, Yves Chatel, Bergeret and their companions went one step farther. The de Gaullist movement was to them a far greater danger than the Germans. They at once warned Giraud that de Gaullists were dangerously at large in North Africa and that a plot to take the General's life in the same way as the Admiral's was on foot. Giraud acted as any general would act in the circumstances. He gave orders that the dangerous characters should be rounded up and imprisoned. Not without logic the General asked himself, "How can I fight the Germans in Tunisia when I am threatened in my own headquarters?"

And that is how the people who had helped us land, the Frenchmen who were anti-Fascist since the days of the Spanish War, came to be imprisoned. Clearly this was going too far—indeed, the plot at this time was always either stopping short or running ahead of itself. Mr. Murphy protested about the arrests.

"What?" said the General shortly. "Do you not trust me?"

Just about this time I arrived in Algiers and saw the General for the first time. His mere appearance explained a great deal. Of all the graduates of the military academy of Saint Cyr you could scarcely conceive a more polished specimen than this. They were a closed and select group, the Saint Cyr generals— Weygand, Gamelin, Georges, Noguès were all there—men of breeding and strict faith. Of them all, Giraud was by far the most distinguished in appearance. Immensely tall for a Frenchman, he had never let himself go to seed and now in his late sixties he had the slim and graceful figure of a young cavalryman. His greyish uniform with the very long tunic and the broad brown stripe down the trousers was immaculate. In every detail he was precise, formal, stiff and unbending. He appeared to have emerged directly from the barber's shop. His small, birdlike head was beautifully groomed and he held himself with just a touch of arrogance and independence that only comes from having been a long time in command. He spoke in a light, clipped voice, without gestures, very clearly and distinctly.

Perhaps he was unusually icy that morning because he was meeting the press under protest, but on every other occasion I have seen him he had that same unruffled and slightly truculent composure.

Giraud before anything else is a general of the old French school, devout, rigidly conservative, the devotee of a set military code of behaviour, a cultivated and severe man who abhors lawlessness in anything—in appearance, in manner, in behaviour or in thinking. He had been an opponent of the Jews, of the Communists, of all left-wing and untidy movements, but he was never rabid about them, because in his code politics were a slightly shabby form of activity lying outside the soldier's life. He had never been seriously forced to bother about politics; he rather prided himself that he was still no politician and stressed the matter in his speeches. He was, as a result, a little unsubtle, a little narrow and intransigeant and very vulnerable indeed to the designs of the skilled political manipulators who at that moment were flooding into Algiers.

The General was a man with an *idée fixe*. He wanted to destroy the German army. All his long life the French army had been pitted in some way against the Germans. The defeat of the Germans was therefore a technical test of the excellence or otherwise of the French army and of the calibre of its generals. He was physically without fear and beyond corruption. And now in the evening of his life, after a most humiliating setback to his strong military pride, he saw a vision—the vision of General Giraud riding his white horse once again as a conqueror through the streets of his old garrison at Metz. Giraud looks forward to that moment with an almost religious passion. He has stripped off his medals and will not wear them again until he has made good his pledge.

If after this book is published you hear of the General making his entry into Metz you will know that there, at least, is one man on earth who conceives he has made the perfect poetic conclusion to his life.

It was therefore irritating for him to be bothered with political troubles during these bright winter days when it was so necessary to press on with the war. When Philip Jordan of the *News Chronicle* asked him during a press conference one day if he was going to relax the anti-Jewish laws, he answered tartly:

"That is nothing to do with you, monsieur."

When Jordan protested that we had been invited to ask questions and that the Jewish question in North Africa was one of some interest to the world at large at that moment, Giraud snapped:

"It is an affair that has nothing to do with the world. It is a matter for me alone to decide."

I managed to get the question raised again a little later in the interview and the General had in the interval apparently reflected that his remarks were going to create a most unfavourable impression in England and America.

"We must proceed slowly and with caution in these things," he said more amicably. "We will disturb the Arab section of the community if we act over-hastily. I am not anti-Jewish and I will not continue the anti-Semitic laws of Vichy a day longer than necessary."

Indeed, steps were taken after that; the Jewish children were permitted to partake of the distribution of free milk and to attend government schools from which they had been excluded. It was still difficult for a Jew to obtain employment, but the more obvious anti-Semitic measures were abolished.

Presently the de Gaullists and the Communist deputies were released and there followed a general clean-up of the half-dozen concentration camps through Morocco and Algeria where some ten thousand political refugees were imprisoned under conditions that were a disgrace to any civilized nation. A certain relaxation in the censorship was made and the local French papers even published a photograph of de Gaulle.

A prime mover in these improvements was none other than the remarkable figure of Monsieur Marcel Peyrouton, who had come post-haste from the French Embassy in the Argentine to accept the position of Governor-General of Algeria.

Now M. Peyrouton was far from unsubtle. Behind a rather flabby and unpleasing exterior was a witty and charming and most adaptable brain. He had served the French government with distinction, both as an earlier administrator in North Africa, where he had acted with promptitude in the local disturbances, and latterly as Vichy ambassador in Buenos Aires, where he had become a frequent visitor to the German Embassy.

M. Peyrouton had quickly seen which way the wind was blowing on his arrival in Algiers. He was perfectly aware of the animosity his appointment had created in America and England and he set about appeasing it with skill and judgment. He was in fact head and shoulders above anybody else in North Africa as an administrator.

Having carried out a number of necessary liberal reforms, he began to establish a government by committee and Giraud was glad enough to give him a free hand. One after another the committees were nominated and set up—one for the banks, one for the press, another for trade and so on. Each committee contained a government official and was responsible to M. Peyrouton. Above all, good order and efficiency behind the lines was needed at this juncture of our military operations and this was just what M. Peyrouton was out to provide by means of governing committees all comprised of experts who knew their business.

Obviously this new corporate government had to have its army, and M. Peyrouton and General Giraud were in complete agreement in the matter of getting the army together. As in France in 1939, there was a tremendous call-up throughout North Africa. Allied headquarters suggested that things might be done a little less rapidly since there was as yet no equipment to hand over to the French. Even uniforms were lacking. But Giraud was determined to get an army of fifty thousand men into the field, and the call-up went on regardless of the fact that many of the men were much more urgently needed to run the railways and keep the ports and telegraph lines open.

Peyrouton, on his side, needed an army for his new corporate government against the time when the government moved over to France. Moreover, none of the recent converts from Vichy were blind to the fact that de Gaulle already possessed *his* army.

The Duc de Guise arrived in Algiers but the Royalists never got very far. Here Mr. Murphy, who was now joined by the British minister, Mr. Harold MacMillan, put his foot down. The Duke was removed. At the same time the French politicians were losing no point in debate. When they were told to get rid of the Pretender to the French throne they replied to the British: "Well, you have a King, haven't you?" And when some protest was made against Peyrouton's rapidly forming committee government they asked: "What, do you want us to return to the Chamber of Deputies of 1939?"

The trouble was that no one in Algiers seemed to have any clear notion of what he wanted. After two years' slow cooking over Nazi fires the lid had been lifted off the French political stew and it was foul-smelling and unwholesome to a degree. There was hardly an underground or an above-ground political movement of the old France that did not flourish here in the back streets of the big cities. The Cagoulards—the hooded men of the Ku Klux Klan kidney—were there. And the Croix de Feu. And the Communists, of several different hues. The traditional trinity of the Comité des Forges-Banque de France-Four Hundred Families survived in the very wealthy olive oil combine which practically controlled the country financially. There were the Jew baiters and the Royalists, the anti-Italian and the anti-Arab blocs, the outright Fascists and the mild Socialists, the Freemasons and the de Gaullists, the regular army and the Church.

Many political groups of similar views were banded together into uneasy alliances, but suspicion seemed to be the very air they breathed. Down in Morocco the Resident General Noguès was openly derisive of the Americans. "Political children" was one of his lighter epithets. The French Foreign Legion was issued with an order of the day instructing them that they were to stand to their arms, since Marshal Pétain had by no means been overthrown and the alliances with the Axis still held good. There was a constant procession of people back and forth to Vichy by way of Spain where M. Petrie, the Vichy ambassador in Madrid, acted as a sort of official postbox.

From the hoardings and the placards in every street and in every public place the unhappy features of Marshal Pétain gazed down on this unparalleled political mess, and as yet it was a treasonable offence to utter a word against the Leader. The pictures of Giraud which replaced those of the Marshal came along later, and the Vichy slogan "*Travail, Patrie, Famille*" was altered to Giraud's "*Un Seul But—La Victoire.*"

The extraordinary thing was that there was no disturbance to speak of anywhere. Apart from a little restrained knife-play in the streets, a little sabotage along the railways and the ports and a good deal of informing and spying and manoeuvring for position there was no trouble at all. The French went quietly enough into the army and bit by bit they grew to accept Giraud as the new leader. The presence of vast numbers of Allied troops who kept pouring off the transports with their modern arms undoubtedly had a strong influence for keeping the peace behind the lines. The people, moreover, were tired with the tiredness of two years of defeat.

Many odd characters, like M. Flandin, who once used to exchange telegrams with Hitler, and Josephine Baker, who had given up the stage, had come here to find what peace and ease they could. There were many thousands of refugees, and the more astute of them had been able to get into the profitable business of supplying North African products to the Germans.

Algiers fairly bulged with the crowds who pressed along the streets. For two years an automobile had been a rarity in the place. Now the traffic was overwhelming, and it often took a

good half-hour to get up the steep and sinuous road to General
Eisenhower's headquarters. I have known a number of GHQ's
but never one as congested as this. Admirals were working in
sculleries, and as like as not you would find a general or two
weaving plans in back bathrooms and pantries.

Half a dozen restaurants ran a merry black market in food
for a while but it soon vanished as more and more troops came
in by the thousands. The scent and the champagne disappeared.
Prices rocketed. Things like leather goods were unobtainable.
Eggs once sold for a penny a dozen reached sixpence or a shill-
ing each. Prostitutes hovering around the bar of the Aletti
Hotel—the place where the officers went to relax in the evening
—were asking their clients for £10 and £20 and getting it.
Apartments became unobtainable and you had to go twenty
miles out of the city into the hills or along the coast to find an
unoccupied villa.

Guns sprang up round the lovely town, and they made a
brilliant show when the raiders came over at night. Maison
Blanche airfield outside the city became an incredible sight—
dozens of aircraft of every description stood about in the mud
and among the ruined hangars. You could walk into the control
room and book a passage for Casablanca, Tunisia, Egypt, India,
London or New York.

The galaxy of uniforms in the streets made Algiers look like
straight comic opera—Spahis on the white horses and dressed in
their flowing red cloaks, the Goums in their brown *galabiehs*,
the green-uniformed Chantiers de la Jeunesse (The Vichy
Youth Movement) and the various kepis, caps and berets, panta-
loons and cloaks of the Foreign Legion, the regular army and
the native battalions. To these were added the whole remarkable parade of British and American uniforms and the blue and
gold and white of the British sailors.

No, Algiers was far from boring. Yet, like many others I
found myself hating the place soon after I landed. It was not
so much the weather, which was wet and cold, nor our depress-

ing tenth-rate pension, the Regina Hotel, nor the food which was bulk rations, nor even that milling, noisy throng in the press building where the news was handed out each day. It was the overriding atmosphere of suspicion and bickering argument, the endless ferment in the streets, the indigestion created by bad wine, the rows over censorship and transmission, and above everything the feeling that the intrigues of Algiers were a mean and petty betrayal of the men at the front who were fighting for something quite different.

There were many good things, too, of course. I found General Eisenhower's conferences warm, friendly and direct. Both Admiral Cunningham and Air Chief Marshal Tedder went out of their way to emphasise to me that they were delighted to serve under him. Eisenhower, it seemed, had great gifts as a chairman. Mr. Harold MacMillan gave me a very shrewd analysis of the whole situation and one felt a slight return to sanity in talking to him.

I must confess too that there was a certain perverse professional pleasure in baiting such people as Bergeret, who apparently imagined that press conferences were designed for demonstrating that everything in this rank and unweeded garden was for the best in this best of all possible worlds.

Old friends bobbed up in Algiers from all over the world, and it was pleasant to drive occasionally with them into the bright hills at night and dine off wholly illegal steaks and champagne in a wayside inn we knew about.

This then was Algiers, the nerve centre of the North African campaign. But what about the villages? How were they taking it? I got to know one village fairly well—Thibar, just behind the front in Tunisia.

Chapter VII: Thibar

IN THE village of Thibar Brother Mario gathered up his skirts and came running down the main street from the seminary. It was November ninth and he was in a tremendous state of agitation. Indeed, the news he had to tell the villagers was almost too sensational to be believed.

"They have come," he announced breathlessly outside the post office. "They have landed. The Americans."

Some of the villagers had already heard the news but with the heavy suspicion of the French peasant they wanted something a little more definite than gossip. There had been so many rumours since France had fallen more than two years before.

"It's not true," they said; and then, "How do you know it's true?"

"I have been listening on the radio," Brother Mario protested. "Already they have seized the radio station at Oran and I have been listening to the Americans broadcasting. They say they have made landings right along the French coast. They say they have arrived with a huge army, the English as well, and they are calling on the French soldiers to lay down their arms."

There was a great stir in Thibar that day. The district was administered from the market town of Souk el Kemis about eight miles away across the Medjerda Valley, but Thibar was on one of the more important roads that led from Souk el Kemis through the tourist hamlet of Teboursouk to Tunis and thus in a favourable position to watch events in the neighbourhood. All day the prefect of police and staff officers were careering about at mad speed in their chemical-gas motor-cars. There was a company of Zouaves quartered in the district and these men were now urgently summoned to barracks and confined there.

The most conflicting news came over the two workable radio

sets in the village—the one in the seminary and the other in the hotel. From Oran strange announcers kept calling on the people to stay quiet and advising the soldiers to surrender and join the invaders. Radio Mondiale in Paris and Radio Marseilles were saying the most bewildering things. At one moment Radio Algiers was broadcasting that the country was under martial law and that the people must stand firm. The next minute it was playing an endless and meaningless succession of dance records and sugary arias sung by Tino Rossi and Jacques Trainer. Finally it went off the air altogether. Radio Casablanca fell silent too. No newspapers arrived from Tunis and Tunis Radio was simply adding to the confusion by repeating parrotlike all the wild announcements from Paris and Rome. Late in the afternoon three aircraft with strange markings flew very high across the lower end of the valley. Mme Zeni, the postmaster's wife, could get no sense out of the exchange at Souk el Kemis, and when she tried to get through to Souk Arras, the main depot, she was told brusquely that the line was commandeered for military traffic and that no civilian calls were to be put through.

That night it was quiet outside but in the front parlour of the Grand Hotel de Thibar there was violent discussion over the liqueur they called Thibarene and the rough red village wine that also came from the seminary.

Every one was disturbed and apprehensive about the news. M. Delafaine, who had come in from his farm to sell Arab stallions to the seminary, was almost morbidly bitter. He had been a remote but enthusiastic follower of La Roque and the Croix de Feu before the war, and an avid reader of *Action Française* when he could get a copy from Marseilles. His wife was Italian, and more recently his rich wheat had been shipped across in great quantity to German buyers in France and at an excellent price. "We will fight them off," he cried. "We can have no dealings with the traitors who killed our sailors at Oran."

The other well-to-do farmers though less vehement were

inclined to agree with him. Up till now they had not done badly
in the war. Olives, vegetables, sheep and especially cattle had
sold very well in Souk el Kemis, which means in Arabic
"Market Wednesdays," and a little farther off in Souk el Arba,
which means "Market Fridays." Prices were rising steadily.
Moreover, to their minds Marshal Pétain was still the leader, a
man of good sound politics who would bring France out of her
troubles if given time. The Germans demonstrably were un-
beatable. They might have setbacks in Russia and Rommel might
be forced back by superior forces in the empty desert; but
Europe was a German garrison now and North Africa was
indissolubly linked to Europe. Look at the length of the coast
line from Tunis to Oran, they said—thousands of kilometres.
The Allies could not do it. The Luftwaffe would get after their
ships and this thing would end as another Dakar. Why should
France and North Africa be disturbed? They were out of the
war. They wanted peace and a chance to develop their farm-
lands. This mad war had gone on too long, and the quicker the
Americans and the British with their amateur armies were out
of it the better. As for the Russians one knew of old their dealings with the communist deputies in Paris and what a scandal
that had been.

Le Brun, the schoolmaster, was frankly Royalist. The Re-
public was rotten and it was finished, he declared. The only
hope now was to bring back the Duc de Guise with a firm body
of advisers around him, strong men who would settle this communist nonsense once and for all.

The younger members of the group, the farmhands and the
carriers and the young volunteers of Pétain's Chantiers de la
Jeunesse, were by no means of this mind though they were
divided amongst themselves. True, they wanted no war in
North Africa, but it would be pleasant to see the Italians taken
down a peg. The macaronis were grabbing everything in
Tunisia. Moreover, was it not true that the Arabs were every
day getting stronger and more insolent under German patron-

age? Everything was being taken from the French and given to the Arabs. The Americans would bring in gasoline and movies and there would again be cloth for sale in the bazaars.

This last was by far the larger group and as the Thibarene went round the more outspoken of them began to shout for de Gaulle. They were fed up with this humiliation of having the Bouches in France. Maybe now the time had come to strike back.

From time to time the Arab and French women came in from the kitchen and listened anxiously to the debate. "Was the village going to be bombed?" they asked. "Why weren't the men out digging air-raid shelters instead of talking? Should the children be taken away somewhere—to Le Kef perhaps where it would be safer?"

This really was the big thing at the back of every one's mind. Was the village going to be bombed? Were the vineyards and the wheat fields going to be ravaged by terrible war? Were the women safe? Were food and clothing going to become dearer and harder to get? It was already the good God knew how long since they had had real coffee and enough sugar and jam. And perhaps worst of all—were the men going to be called to the colours again and made to fight and die in this never-ending war? If only it would end.

The next day still more planes passed over the valley and now the wildest rumours were raging everywhere. A traveller from the coast came in saying he had talked to a man in Souk Arras who had actually seen the Americans and the British landing at Bougie and there were bloody battles going on in Algiers and Oran. The Algiers radio had come back on the air and now the strange announcer was claiming that the Allies were in possession.

On the other hand the *Dépêche* arriving from Constantine late that night printed a long proclamation from General Yves Chatel saying that the French North African forces were resisting heroically, that men were being urgently summoned to the colours and that all traitors to the Marshal in this hour of supreme crisis would be shot. The Tunis newspapers also revealed a great commotion.

There was a definite swing towards de Gaulle and the Allies in the village that night. If at last the Allies were going to succeed and succeed quickly so that no one need fight, then yes, it might be a great thing for North Africa. France would rise again. There would be more money, more food, more fuel and clothing in the land. One by one the villagers were finding something deep in themselves—some repressed and forgotten hope—coming to the surface again. They grasped at every scrap of news with burning interest and when an Arab lad brought in a leaflet dropped by a British plane they clambered around to read it with tense excitement. Still the dominant thing was to keep this horrible war out of Thibar—let the British and the Americans fight it if they had to. Yet it would be a thing of great pride if the French were to have their own land to themselves again.

All over North Africa such vital swaying arguments were going on while the doughboys and the tommies splashed ashore at Casablanca, Oran and Algiers. Thibar, a remote and tiny little village across the Algerian border in Tunisia only crudely reflected the tremendous issues that were agitating Frenchmen, Italians and Arabs along the Mediterranean, but the Thibar cleavages were the basic ones. Here and in a thousand villages was the Arab in heavy majority and either pro-German or indifferent. And the Italian who sought to score off the French and so supported the Germans. And the prosperous farmer and merchant who was getting good prices on foodstuffs and who felt tired and was willing now to follow the German path since it had for two years been the inevitable path of least resistance. And the petty official who was frightened for his job. That was the opposition. But among the mass of countrymen there was an awakened joy at the idea of freedom from Axis control. The idea of revenge which had been dampened for so long began to take fire again. Fear and lassitude were still for the moment the overruling emotions but the awakened enthusiasm in this sudden change of fate was growing with every hour that went by. However, before they committed themselves irrevocably the people wanted some sure proof that the Allies were there to stay.

Proof, sure proof, began to come in before the week was out. Allied parachutists had dropped at Bône on the coast, only a day's drive through the mountains. They had come down in hundreds out of the winter clouds and they had seized the airfield. Moreover, strange warships had appeared off La Calle and Tabarka. If this went on they would be in Tunis next. But what was going on in Tunis? The city was only a hundred-odd kilometres away to the northeast but every one who came out carried frightening stories. Germans were landing in huge planes on the airfields near Sidi Bou Said and at the port of La Goulette ships were arriving every day from Sicily carrying Axis troops. There had been shooting in the town. The Bey had gone off to the country and the French army had taken control. One man said de Gaullists had sunk a ship in the mouth of the port. Another from Bizerta said that there had been a naval engagement out to sea. And all the time high over Thibar the planes kept passing back and forth.

The villagers were thrown now into a panic more violent than their first shock. If the Germans were going to fight in Tunisia then who knew?—the whole Medjerda Valley might be turned into a battlefield. Was any one going to be safe? The villagers looked anxiously across the hills for the first signs of the advancing troops, and as they debated whether it would be the Americans coming from the west or the Germans coming from the east, Mme Schmée, the hotelkeeper's wife, was kept up half the night serving more and more drinks, to oil the talk.

No one, even now in the dead season in the middle of winter, could have gazed down that lovely valley and remained unmoved. The tourist looking up his copy of the Guide Bleu would have discovered that the banks of the Medjerda River were rated as one of the six most fertile valleys in the world. But there was a great deal more than cold productivity here.

From Souk el Arba right up to Medjez le Bab and beyond the land seemed to pour out every rich good thing on earth. It did not matter from which direction you approached—from the dry fir-covered hills near Tébessa in the south or from the wet cork-tree forests around Tabarka in the north—the young wheat rippled across the valley for mile after mile. In the centre of this richness, on a low spur that ran out towards the river from the surrounding mountains, the village of Thibar stood.

Years before, the White Fathers coming out from France had chosen this as the finest spot in the whole countryside. On the heights of the spur, just at the point where it flattened out towards the river, they built a seminary, a great pink and white storeyed building, the largest seminary in all Africa. To this was added a hospital and presently a pink and white village. The Fathers worked at the land with inspired energy. They tucked up their robes round their waists and ploughed back and forth along the slopes of the spur until every morsel of rich red soil was under wheat or vines or fruit trees or vegetables. As they collected a little money and more and more students came to them, they invested in modern power-driven tractors, and multiple ploughs, in miniature railway lines to feed the piggeries and the horse and cattle stalls, in the latest French machinery to tend the vines.

A gang of workmen came to build a series of huge concrete and steel vats to hold the wine that was now beginning to pour in from the young vineyards. Moved by old monastic tradition they began to brew their own separate sorts of liqueurs—the thick and sticky Thibarene, the yellow curaçoa, a rough brandy. The farm became the wonder of the countryside.

Soon the White Sisters were established in the village and their hand-made carpets began to vie in quality even with those of the famous carpet town of Kairouan to the south. A pink and white church was built and two lines of cottages were spaced down either side of the one broad straight village street. Last came the tiny hotel, just a couple of bare living rooms on the ground floor and a dozen tiny cell-like bedrooms on the first storey. Tourists making the trip from Tunis to the Roman ruins at Dougga would often come on to Thibar to taste the wine and sit for an hour over Mme Schmée's omelettes and *pot-au-feu*. All or almost all belonged to the White Fathers and they kept the mixed population of the village—French, Italian, Arabs and half-castes—to a strict and simple way of life.

Everywhere around them was the incredible changing beauty of the valley. Looking down from the stone balcony of the hotel you would see first the white cottages among the firs and then the almond trees that blossomed in such a delicate shade of lilac that the orchard at sunset appeared to be a cloud floating over the land. Beyond this the vineyards, endless mathematical lines of bare brown twisting stalks that sprouted from earth that was sometimes the colour of chocolate and sometimes vivid crimson. After the vineyards the eye travelled for miles across the swelling green sea of wheat. It flowed across the valley not in a flat pattern but with the gentle undulating contours of a girl's body; every rise and dip in the land was moulded into soft green outlines. Half a dozen farming homesteads were dotted about in this green expanse that poured right across to the foothills on either side of the valley. At the foothills the wheat fell back and wild flowers grew. They grew among the brown and red boulders in startling unbelievable shades of vermilion, canary yellow, sky blue; and in mad African luxuriance. Beyond the boulders lay the last patches of green where the herds of goats browsed with their Arab shepherds right up to the snow-line. Snow gleamed in the sunshine right round the mountains, a sharp white edge against the open sky, a painted frame for the green valley.

Throughout the day at every hour the colours were constantly altering. At night when the sunsets were often of monstrous ragged violence the whole valley was for a little lit with a film of red misty light that made the place seem more unreal than ever.

This then was Thibar in the bright cold days of November when the villagers keeping watch down the valley suddenly saw a line of khaki-coloured vehicles appear on the valley road from the west.

Little Mahmouda, the Arab houseboy at the hotel, was the first to see the strange soldiers turn off the main road and come up the paths towards Thibar. In a sudden instinctive outburst of fear the women in the village ran out and gathered in their children. They bustled them inside and slammed the doors. In an instant the village was cleared. Goats still browsed along the main street. One or two Arab horsemen reined in uncertainly beside the church and a young poilu in uniform bicycled at speed up to the post office and closed the door behind him. There was no sign of the White Fathers anywhere. The nunnery blinds were drawn and you could not be certain whether or not faces were peering through the lace curtains of the other houses. A queer fateful hush settled over the whole village.

Presently the foreign soldiers began to arrive. First a tiny open car with two men in it, both in steel helmets and carrying short stocky guns in their hands. Then more and more vehicles—vehicles with caterpillar wheels that churned up the mud about the cross-roads and filled the air with roaring. Watching from their windows the villagers could see the officers questioning the Arab goatherds. They waited. There was no shooting. The Arab horsemen trotted with elaborate unconcern towards the soldiers. Gaining courage the villagers began to come out of their houses. The gendarme appeared. There was movement up at the seminary and one of the soldiers' cars drove up to the main farmyard gate and disappeared inside.

The children somehow escaped and ran on to the roadway. They shouted, "*Vive les Américains.*" The soldiers waved back. The street began to fill up rapidly. From the tops of their vehicles the soldiers shouted down at the little crowd and they were smiling and friendly. In a sudden release from fear some of the peasants were shouting *"Vive l'Amérique"* now at the tops of their voices and offering up glasses of red wine to the soldiers. The soldiers laughed, drank the wine and handed back cigarettes.

A little group began to gather round an officer in front of the hotel. He spoke French like a tourist but still one could understand him. He wanted to know if there were any Germans in the village.

"No, no," they shouted together. "There have never been any Germans here." Some one ran off to fetch Brother Antonio from the seminary. He came from England many years ago and spoke English. The Arabs began offering eggs to the soldiers and got in exchange wonderful things—crisp cigarettes with real tobacco in them, handfuls of tea, soap, real soap. The village reached a pitch of excitement.

At the hotel Mme Schmée was frying eggs for the officers and handing round wine. One of the officers had had a long conversation with the gendarme and the postmaster and Brother Antonio. It seemed that the strangers were not Americans after all but Englishmen.

The town was full of soldiers that evening. All night the noise of their vehicles passing along the road went on. There were guns too. The soldiers were very dirty and muddy and tired. They dropped asleep on the ground like cattle. On the orders of the English no lights were shown in the village that night.

Miraculously in the morning most of the soldiers had gone. The stragglers could still be seen passing eastward up the road to Teboursouk and Tunis. There was a distant noise of gunfire from somewhere in the direction of Béja in the north.

Then the war fell on the valley itself. German aircraft swooped on Souk el Kemis where the British were trying to fashion an airfield out of the mud. Watching from their safe spur the villagers of Thibar saw the bombs fall and the great

pillars of smoke go up from the houses and from that day onward for the next six months no one in Thibar felt entirely safe.

They grew used to having the war around them. They came
to terms with the noise and the sudden scares. They even grew
used to the Messerschmitts that swept down the valley scarcely
higher than the trees and they accepted that it was dangerous to
travel anywhere abroad in a car during the daylight hours.

Some protective divinity seemed to watch over the little
colony of the White Fathers. The village was only bombed once
towards the end of the war and even though the Molotov cock-
tail broke the windows in the seminary and the hotel, no one
was seriously hurt. The stables were machine-gunned from the
air but the horses recovered from their injuries.

Wild storms of sleet and snow whirled round the mountains
all that winter but nearly always it was fine weather at Thibar.
One after another the surrounding villages were laid waste;
Thibar escaped. All through the spring and the early summer
the front line lay only an hour's drive away but this peaceful
calm in the centre of the maelstrom remained immune.

The war correspondents took over the top floor of the hotel
and as the months went by we grew to know the villagers very
well. There was Mahmouda, the sharp little Arab boy, who
would beg for chocolate as he swept your room, and Monique,
the daughter of the house, who was always surrounded by half
a dozen soldiers in the kitchen, a dark and buxom girl, half-
French and perhaps a quarter-Arabic. Monique was a figure of
considerable importance in the village, at least to the military
quartered there. She had been used to buying her ribbons on
occasional visits to the big shops in Tunis and it was her habit
to croon such laments as *"Je t'attendrai"* as she went about her
work. She had lived in an arch and sentimental world compounded of month-old copies of *Marie Claire* and the movies
and the cracked mirror nailed on the wall of her tiny bedroom.
Already she was engaged to a young Frenchman in the district
but the British troops burst in on this gentle, adolescent love

affair with the effect of an avalanche. With amazing poise Monique accepted it all—the gauche and heavy-handed compliments, the awkward gestures of these men who clumped about the kitchen in enormous boots, the gargantuan efforts they made to speak French. Little Monique, with all her rustic chic and her unaffected gaiety, seemed a very modern girl indeed to us in that monastic world and she enjoyed herself hugely.

M. Schmée, a timid and self-effacing little Alsatian, was the head of the house. He divided his time between helping madame with the hotel and working on the books at the seminary. He was more than a little overwhelmed at the change that had overtaken the village and never at any point caught up with the events that rushed by.

Only two other guests besides the war correspondents and our officers stayed at the hotel and these were a bourgeois couple who had taken possession of room Number One, the best in the hotel. They had fled from Bizerta and were awaiting the day when they could go back. The war had turned their lives upside down and they simply took refuge in their old habits and remained remote from the war. Sometimes I would meet the old man in his shirt-sleeves taking the air on the balcony before breakfast and talked stiffly of the weather and the crops and his Law Suit. He lived for the Law Suit, which was an entirely forlorn and hopeless claim for damages he was making against the government because his house had been damaged in the fighting. God," he used to say wildly, "it's hard e... , I never...

The old lady stole the show that terrible night when five over-excited soldiers pursued Monique's sister through the village. Arriving hot and panting at the hotel they rattled furiously on Honky-Tonk's bedroom door. Heaven knew what visions of rapine and death raged through the old woman's mind, for she collapsed with a loud cry and we had to break in to rescue her. Monique's sister, throwing hysterics in the scullery, was quite overlooked in the general astonishment when Honky-Tonk croaked through her withered lips that she was entirely to blame since she had enticed the soldiery in the first place.

The postmaster and his wife became friends of mine from the day I went to the post office to send a *mandat* for four thousand francs to a Russian family I knew in Philippeville.

"What do you want to send the money for?" demanded the postmaster suspiciously.

I explained. The family had been cut off from their bank in New York and needed the money as a loan.

"Send them two thousand," said the postmaster. "Four thousand is too much."

We argued briskly for five minutes. Finally he called his wife and explained the whole business.

"But this is absurd," she cried indignantly. "Send them five hundred francs. That will be more than sufficient. Make out the forms, Henri."

I felt I was losing ground rapidly. "Please," I said. "This is my money and I want to send it and the people need it. There is a girl in the somewhat she eyed me with sudden coyness. "There is a girl in the somewh...

The postmaster's wit...

"I said rath...

enormous lechery. He took the money at last. All this was before breakfast. Feeling a little dazed I went back to my Spam and eggs at the hotel.

If I was in love with any one at that moment it was with Mme Schmée. The hotel revolved round her. It was madame who rose first at six o'clock and got the fires going. It was madame who cooked all day in the kitchen, sometimes for a hundred. God knew how the pigeon pies and the hot artichokes and the brandy-soaked cakes were concocted on that ancient cooking range but they were. She kept the accounts, she fed the children, she issued the wine, she did the marketing, she cooked and served the dinners, she organized the Arab servants; and she continued doing this every day from six until ten or eleven at night.

Mme Schmée adored children. Since she was not having one herself at that moment she adopted a couple. In the evening sometimes fifty soldiers would form a queue into the kitchen. Each soldier carried two eggs he had bought from the Arabs and these madame would cook with one hand while she handed out wine with the other. Simultaneously she coped with the half-naked babies crawling around her skirts and issued directions to Honky-Tonk and Monique, then flirting in the corner with two dispatch riders. In the next room the radio shrieked at full blast and half a dozen arguments in three languages would be raging over the wine. The uproar and confusion passed description. In the midst of it all was madame, serene, smiling and untroubled. Generosity and kindliness flowed out of her. I never saw her angry or heard her speak sharply. When I was sent as an interpreter to protest at the lateness of the dinner or at the loss of somebody's laundry I found it impossible to maintain the complaint in the face of her distress. Sooner or later dinner would come and the missing shirts would turn up. And then her beautiful face would light up and as a peace offering she would timidly produce a cake she had specially baked or a glass of her precious *eau de vie*.

From the first she never made a serious effort to pronounce my name. I remained "M. Morsel" to the end.

Madame was short and plump and there was Arab and Italian blood in her. Once she had been very pretty. Even now, especially when she smiled, she was as attractive as her daughter.

The seminary had another life of its own. In scores the army trucks would drive into the farmyard and the soldiers would wait to draw wine from Brother Mongo or Brother Antonio. Brother Antonio had been born in Liverpool and I never discovered by what strange route he had reached this haven in Tunisia. But it must have been a long journey for he had forgotten most of his English and what was left of it was a weird mixture of Cockney slang and mongrel verbs.

At first we were the only British in Thibar. But more and more soldiers came every week. First the hospital was taken over. Then another hospital, a vast affair of hundreds of tents, was erected in the valley. Then odd units of the Royal Army Service Corps set up their camps and the main street was crowded with men in battle dress. Then towards the end they gradually fell away. Thibar was practically deserted when I came to leave myself. The vines had come into leaf, the fields had turned yellow and now the crop was already stacked. The vats of wine in the seminary were practically drunken to the dregs and in place of lilac blossom the trees sprouted with full-blown green almonds. The full blasting heat of summer was beginning to oppress the valley. And the German aircraft had vanished from the sky.

Were the people of Thibar typical of the rest of the villagers of North Africa and France itself? I think they were. Beyond everything else they were bound to a routine of the earth and their narrow daily lives. They were frightened when the landing was made. It meant a break in the routine they had grown to trust. But once they accustomed themselves to the change they welcomed it. They accepted the dangers of being at war in exchange for a new feeling of excited hope. They had been

merely existing before. Now they began to live and look forward again. It was only the very old who really resisted the
change and even though they were not prepared to do anything
about it they hated and despised the Nazis and the Fascists.

The Arabs of Tunisia were in a special category. For years
German agents had been among them, buying off the intellec-
tuals of every village. The German policy was, as the young
Frenchman had said, to take everything from the French and
give it to the Arabs. I have never believed that the Arabs were
a major factor in the Mediterranean war and the amount of
sabotage and spying they did against us was negligible.

As for the bigger political issues the majority of people in
Thibar who sided with us were de Gaullist. For years they had
heard his name on the radio and it was the only symbol they
knew for a revived France. Politics and politicians in general
they distrusted heartily. But Pétain counted. The "*mystique du
Maréchal*" had taken hold on their minds, partly because mar-
shals have been pretty imposing and mysterious figures in France
since the days of Napoleon, and anyhow there was no other
mystique at hand.

Nevertheless it was patently absurd to say that these people
would have opposed de Gaulle had he been allowed to come
instead of Darlan and Giraud in the first place. They knew
nothing much of the personalities of these leaders: they simply
knew them as the masses will always know their leaders—at
second hand and by reputation. De Gaulle was the name they
knew as the Frenchman who had sided with the Allies and they
have not yet fully understood what has happened to him.

The French did not hate the British. British and Americans
got an equal welcome almost everywhere, though not unnatu-
rally both sides went about imagining each was more popular
than the other. There would be occasional swings away from
the Americans towards the British and vice versa in certain
regions at certain times but these phases never lasted. I noticed
a tendency after the first few months for the French to regard

the Americans as an innocent, boyish race in contrast to the more Europeanized and sophisticated British. But it was a fairly obvious distinction since the doughboy was a noisy and open-handed visitor and the tommy rather more reserved in his manner.

At all events Thibar accepted us and grew to like us. They did not fear that we would stay to rule and oppress their country after the war was over. We saw, or thought we saw in those early days, great hope for the peace, not through the political leaders but through the common sense of the working people.

Chapter VIII: Djedeida

WHEN I arrived in Algiers it was already the first week of 1943, two months after we had made our landing, and only the wildest misconceptions of what was taking place at the front existed in America and England. It is no exaggeration at all to say that the average citizen in New York and London had not the remotest idea of what the fighting was like, of who was doing it, of what weapons were being used, of the numbers engaged on both sides, of what local objectives were being sought or of the prospects for the future.

All this was due no doubt to a mixture of reasons—the inability of the correspondents at the front to get their messages back, the necessity for secrecy which was often expressed in fretful and overcautious censorship, the strangeness of the theatre, the individual prejudices of the newspapers, the radio and the people, the vast distances involved, the general muddle created by raw staff officers on their first operational jobs, our ignorance of the enemy and—probably most important of all—the fact that the men in charge of the campaign had themselves no really clear-cut picture of a situation that changed from day to day and hour to hour. It was in fact a great experiment, and we had to learn as we went along.

If only to be on your guard in the future, just for a minute throw your mind back to some of the simpler misapprehensions the Allied public was labouring under at this time. The authorities had given the impression that we had a huge army in action, thousands of tanks and guns and aircraft. In actual fact only a few thousand men were fighting at the front and mostly with small-arms and practically no air support at all.

In the States it was believed—as it is to this day—that the overwhelming majority of troops doing the fighting was American.

In fact it was very largely a British operation, and from the start of the Tunisian campaign to its finish the Americans never amounted to more than one-quarter of the troops engaged. (This is not to say that the campaign could have been won without American troops and equipment.)

In England the public either could not or would not understand that the battle was being fought in the mountains and the mud and that northern Tunisia is not flat desert. Almost to the end they continued to make unfavourable comparisons with General Montgomery's rapid advances through Libya.

There was another thing—a thing which will probably continue to the end of hostilities—and this was the fundamental inability of civilians to realize that war is a painfully long, slow business. From the day war broke out people have listened to their radios and read their newspapers and they have always found news of some description: if the Russian front was quiet then something was happening in New Guinea or over the Ruhr. Inevitably this has given them the impression that war is a fast-moving thing. It simply is not. All the seemingly quick moves—the Battle of France, the bombing of Pearl Harbour, the collapse of Singapore—were the result of years of planning and manoeuvring for position. This matter seems childishly obvious, but just try to get it across to any gathering in any pub; to explain just how long it takes to get any division from any base to any front line. Try and explain the fact that up to now only about twenty out of every hundred men sent out from England and America have seen any real fighting, and that the rest are engaged along the vast lines of supply. Try and explain that to keep one heavy bomber with a crew of eight in the air requires about fifty men on the ground. Try and explain that the average ship at sea rarely meets any actual trouble from one month's end to another.

The problems of supply are entirely different from those in the last war. It now takes double or three times the quantity of machines and explosive to kill a man.

But these things I believe are not understood, and so at every stage of the war the people have been impatient for action and irritated by delay.

They were irritated at the New Year because it looked as if the Tunisian campaign was reaching a stalemate. It had indeed. But what a wonderful story these two months had been.

After the first wild rush of landing—and finding everything was all right, the French collapsed—the troops had gone helter-skelter up the coast towards Tunis. It was a difficult journey of six or seven hundred miles, but what did that matter? Get there somehow and get there quick. No one quite knew what enemy if any was ahead or to the flanks but morale was up to the limits and there was an infectious air of excitement and discovery.

Every available motor vehicle was taken off the ships at Algiers and bundled on to the road. They rushed forward to Sétif and Constantine on the inland road through the mountains and still there was no opposition. Others landed from the sea at Bône and started to spread inland. Others again jumped by parachute into the midst of astonished farming communities. RAF fighters swept down on airfields and single-handed the pilots took charge of the surrounding territory, and were quartered there quite happily when the ground troops arrived.

American Rangers and men of their best combat team, British parachutists and battle-school trained infantry from the British Seventy-Eighth Division and the Sixth Armoured Division—these were the men who raced forward into the unknown mountains. They commandeered civilian cars, got the railways working, reopened the telegraph lines, took over farmhouses as bases, cleared the roads; and always they hurried forward until their lines of supply were stretched to the snapping point and huge unpoliced territories the size of half England were spread out behind them.

So great was the area into which this handful of men was running that units lost touch with one another along the empty roads and every company and platoon seemed to be engaged in a private campaign of its own.

At Bône, the forward port, Axis aircraft came over to bomb and since no anti-aircraft guns had yet caught up with the front-line troops the place got cruelly mauled. The interior of Bône became a bad shambles for a bit and from the hilltop basilica behind the town down to the docks at the foot of the green cliffs an angry pall of smoke hung over the buildings. The railway station was ravaged and wrecked. The town cinema fell in on itself. Ships trying to get into the harbour were caught by bombs and the survivors swam ashore through the icy sea. Along the roads the Luftwaffe kept up a dangerous strafing and the men were leaping to the ditches a dozen times a day.

But still in mid-November they were finding no real opposition on the ground. By now they were into Medjez el Bab, which means the Keys of the Gate, and the troops were on the two roads that led straight into the heart of Tunis. And it was then at last that the Germans began to appear.

General Anderson had rushed his headquarters as far forward as Constantine and even Constantine was now a day's full drive behind the front. Going forward the General found himself faced with a very serious quandary indeed. His supply lines back to Algiers were in a hopeless state. The railway was not yet working regularly. Bône was going bombed and very little was coming in there from the sea. His men were wearied and in serious need of everything from bullets to biscuits. There seemed little chance of getting really good supplies up the long mountain roads from Algiers for weeks to come.

But the men were full of determination and eagerness. They were incredibly dirty and short of sleep but they lived now for the hour when they would enter Tunis.

The American consul general in the town had escaped to Constantine and he had a remarkable story. "Hurry hurry hurry," he said. He had gone to the palace in Tunis as soon as the first landings were made at Algiers and he had read out the

President's letter to the Bey. The Bey was non-committal and disposed to wait and see. He would not say whether or not he would give right of way to the oncoming Allied troops. The officers of the German and Italian Armistice commissions were at his elbow.

In the town great things were happening. Some of the French had risen for the Allies. The Director of Railways had sent as much rolling stock as possible out to Algeria. Other gallant men had attempted to block the harbour by sinking a ship there. Work was at a standstill and there were constant brawls all through the night between Frenchmen and Italians.

As in the rest of North Africa, from Dakar to Algiers, no Axis troops whatever were garrisoning Tunisia. There were just the handful of men on the enemy Armistice commissions and these were militarily powerless. The Axis had been caught completely off balance.

But on the third day after the arrival of the Allies in Algiers the Axis had acted, and with incredible thoroughness and speed. A couple of small coasters had put in full of German troops. Others arrived by air troop-carriers on Tunis airport and as they poured out down the main road to the city more and more aircraft came flying in from Sicily.

The German troops raced through the bewildered cities of Bizerta and Tunis seizing every key point—the post offices, the railway stations, the arsenals, the docks, the airfields, the customs, the police stations. They spread through the back streets, cowing those who had been shouting for de Gaulle. The French soldiers and the soldiers of the Bey had been clapped under German orders before they realized what had happened and now they were confined to their barracks. The Director of Railways had been shot, and one after another Frenchmen suspected of Allied sympathies were being thrown into gaol. Any one who resisted was put up against a wall. The people at large were baffled and had fallen back on a sheeplike passivity while the Germans took over.

But still there were only a very few Germans—a few thousands at the most—and they had not yet succeeded in getting in more than a handful of tanks. Scores of Messerschmitts and Focke-Wulf fighters were arriving but they were still awaiting petrol from Italy. Only twenty-five Germans were spared to run down by sea to the big ports of Sousse and Sfax and of these, ten were split off to occupy Gabès on the Tripolitanian border. Kairouan, the big inland market town, had been taken over by a tiny Italian garrison.

If only we could have landed in Tunis at the beginning, the consul said. The pitifully small enemy vanguard could have done nothing. But now the Germans were pouring in. In desperate haste they were throwing up new airfield runways, digging weapon pits, laying mines, mounting anti-aircraft guns and making anti-tank ditches along the roads.

Von Arnim had arrived and seized the American consul's house, which, unfortunately, had just been redecorated. It was being used as German headquarters now. The consul himself had escaped only by a fluke. When he had gone to read the President's letter to the Bey he had told his wife that she should pack and leave for Constantine if he did not return by nightfall. His wife, seeing the German soldiers in the streets, had packed anyhow. That night with some French friends they had driven out of the city. Twice they were stopped by newly posted German sentries on the outskirts. The Germans were under orders to stop all unauthorized outgoing traffic and the soldiers peered suspiciously at the consular party. But the Frenchmen in the car waved nonchalantly and said it was all right and somehow they had got through to the British lines and Constantine.

That was the consul's story. Clearly it indicated that time was precious. The Germans still might not be ready. Anderson talked to his senior generals—the corps commander, and the commander of the Seventy-Eighth and the Sixth Armoured. They were all keen to advance. And so it was decided to go forward with the gamble.

At once in these last days of November there was skirmishing along the roads with the German outposts. This light opposition was overwhelmed but every mile now the Allies were coming under heavier fire. They met Germans outside Mateur in the north and outside Medjez el Bab in the south—these were the two main sectors. The plan was to make the Medjez el Bab sector the main one. The two roads that led thence into Tunis were both in excellent condition and apparently unmined. Both were dominated by an isolated series of bare humps which the troops quickly dubbed "Longstop Hill"—apparently because it bore the same relation to the township of Medjez el Bab as a longstop does towards the wicket in cricket.

The Seventy-Eighth Division swept past this obstacle and reached Tebourba and Djedeida. This was on November twenty-fifth and now indeed the battle seemed almost won. The gamble was succeeding. Tunis lay barely twelve miles off up the valley and British patrols going farther forward held the suburbs in view.

At Djedeida the Germans counter-attacked, and for a moment stopped the British rush. It was one of those moments of high drama in the war when one stroke can finish the battle. This was match point in this tumultuous game of tennis and the Allies had won all the other sets. I had seen almost the same thing happen the other way about in Egypt the previous summer when Rommel was about to fall on Alexandria and the Nile. Just one more tiny little effort he needed and then he had everything—all Egypt, perhaps the whole of the Middle East. Just one more brigade of men, just another couple of batteries of guns and he might have done it.

It was like that here for our men. The Germans held their ground and attacked again. The seesaw was beginning to balance at last. The Allies had gone on and on and deeper into the German opposition until the few scattered elements that we had at the front were not quite strong enough to deal with the increasing enemy opposition. But no one knew that at the time.

Every one from privates to brigadiers did just what he had to do and with what means he had because he was caught up in this game and it had reached the high point of its intensity.

The Germans attacked again, down the Tebourba Road. Useless now for the British to cast around for reinforcements—the reinforcements were hundreds of miles away. Tebourba was given up and then Longstop Hill. Feeling baulked and still determined to grasp their prize before it was snatched away the Allied commanders counter-attacked at Longstop. The Guards fought their way up to the top of that vital hill, and leaving an American unit to hold the place, were retired to strike in another direction. As they were en route marching back to their assembly point dispatch drivers caught up with the Guards' headquarters. They brought the ugly news that the Germans had run through the slender American garrison, and so there was nothing for it but that the Guards should turn round and go back. For a second time that day they swept up to the heights of Longstop but now the physical strain was too much. They could not hold the position. The Allies' line reformed itself at Medjez el Bab.

Even now the allies had an opportunity of returning with a mortal blow. But even as they planned to strike again the matter was taken out of their hands. Rain fell. Not ordinary rain, but the wild torrential rain of Africa. The ground turned to mud, and it was the mud of that same African extravagance, thick, sticky and bottomless. The dead were buried in mud and the living were in it up to their knees. They were wet to the skin all day and all night. They had mud in their hair; mud in their food. When the mud dried it set like iron and had to be beaten off the boots with a hammer or a rifle butt. Before the astonished eyes of the commanders tanks went down to their turrets in mud. A spell of a few fine days made no difference—the mud was there just the same and if you sent out a squadron of tanks you never knew whether or not they would be caught in another downpour and so abandoned to the enemy. The few forward airfields we possessed—at Bône, Souk el Kemis and Souk el Arba—all lay on the floors of valleys. Rain drained down on to the flat ground and for days at a time the aircraft were unable to take off. The Germans had no such disadvantage. Their fields were based on porous sand near the coast. And so their fighters kept multiplying in the air while our were diminishing. Moreover, the Germans were not advancing—they merely sought to hold on to what they had. The rain and mud were for them a godsend. They perched in their foxholes and watched the British tanks come on into the mud-bound belt of fire.

The British foot regiments performed feats of astonishing courage at this time—notably the Hampshires, the Guards and the Argylls. Probably the most ferocious fighters of all were the British parachutists who were grounded and used—perforce— as ordinary infantry.

It was not easy in this bitter, ruthless fighting for the British commanders to realize that the gamble so gallantly taken was now going against them. They persisted for a time, putting in a series of small counter-attacks which got nowhere, largely because battalions were sent out to do what only brigades could have accomplished. But by the middle of January it was clear that a stalemate had been reached. Of necessity we would have to put in occasional limited attacks to keep up our morale and worry the Germans, but clearly we had to wait now until much greater forces were brought over from England and America. At last it was seen that we would have to wait until the wet season was over in March or April.

Eisenhower now had to make up his mind on how he should dispose his forces during the lull. Should he hold on to what he had and make the Germans pay for every yard they advanced? Or should he get clean out of Tunisia and regroup more comfortably and expeditiously in Algeria? He chose to hold what he had.

The stalemate brought all sorts of questions to light. For

example, why had we not landed in Bizerta and Tunis in the first place? The navy's answer to that was it would have meant that the ships were exposed to Sicily-based aircraft and submarines for an extra day of daylight. We were already taking considerable risks in going so far into the Mediterranean as Algiers and Bône.

It turned out that we probably could have got safely through the Sicilian Narrows and then perhaps the Tunisian war need never have been fought at all. There is no doubt that Tunis would have collapsed almost as easily as Oran and Algiers. But whether the High Command was justified or not in taking that risk is only a matter for academic dispute now.

There was another larger question. Had not Montgomery's offensive and Eisenhower's North African landing been staged in exactly the wrong order? Had we gone into Tunisia first Rommel would have fought his desert campaign knowing he had no base on which to retreat and that would have been very bad indeed for German morale and German supply lines from Italy.

The answer to this probably is that the High Command expected to conquer Tunisia with the First Army before Montgomery reached Tripoli—even with the First Army's late start. At any rate the Afrika Korps was scooped up eventually. The only man missing from the bag was Rommel himself.

So then the first phase of the campaign was over at the end of the first fortnight in January. We had not done too badly considering that practically none of the troops or their officers were battle-trained when they started. Every day they were getting more cunning, eliminating waste effort, taking better cover, striking more shrewdly and with fewer unnecessary casualties.

The front had temporarily stabilised on a line running from Tabarka on the northern Mediterranean coast through the sodden cork-tree forests to Sedjenane and the blasted township of Medjez el Bab on the Medjerda River. Thence the line wobbled uncertainly south again over the mountains to El Aroussa and Sbeitla, where the trees became stunted and grounds more rocky. After that with many gaps the troops were strung through Gafsa until the front petered out into an uncontested no man's land in the Sahara Desert.

Roughly speaking the British held the north and central sectors, down to El Aroussa, the newly formed French force was grouped about the Grande Dorsaale Mountains in the south centre and the Americans held from Sbeitla to Gafsa, an uncertainly balanced three-decker cake.

This was the line I set out to see in the middle of January, the line on which I was going to live for the next four months. To the south of Mareth was Montgomery's Eighth Army, which had now flung Rommel out of Libya. The enemy position, manned with about 200,000 troops of Rommel's and von Arnim's combined armies, was a rough rectangle sixty miles wide, a hundred and fifty miles deep.

Chapter IX: Medjez el Bab

IN AFRICA it was always good to be on the road to the front. Once you left the city behind you had a feeling of escape, even a sense of strong freedom as though you were a schoolboy setting off for the summer holidays. You knew that in the place you were going money was not going to count any more. There would be no newspapers, no telephones, no buses or trains to catch and life would be lived freely in the open air. Moreover, you had no idea of how long you would be away or of where you were going or of what would happen.

Even in the desert this was so. When we were in Cairo we would say that we hated the desert. But once we got past Mena House on the road to Alamein and Mersa Matruh there would be a feeling of lightness and escape and expectation.

In North Africa it was even better, because in place of the desert the road wound through a country that looked like a garden and at every twist in the road there was something new.

It was still very early when we got out of the cobble-stone clatter along Algiers Docks and then, a map on my knee—one of those Michelin maps I had not seen since my last holiday through France—I charted the course past the airfield at Maison Blanche, past the village with that perfect name, Retour de la Chasse, and down into the long valley where we would run all morning, keeping the great white range of the Atlas Mountains on our left.

The vineyards were astonishing. They ran on mile after mile, and today the wind coming off the snow blew the white and pink fruit-tree blossoms through the vines. Sometimes through the morning we got involved in long convoys of guns and tanks and trucks that were pushing up to the front. A railway kept winding in and out of the valley and when a shut railway gate

blocked the path and the snorting antique French locomotive
went by you could see that the carriages were full of doughboys
with their outside helmets and tommies sleeping on their kits.
The black tarpaulins over the open trucks revealed the shapes
of more guns, more tanks.

Every few miles Arabs stood beside the road and offered up
eggs and tangerines, chickens and oranges, wine and rabbits.
The sun streamed down.

Towards midday we came to the head of the valley and a
long goods train was stationary on the level crossing, blocking
back the traffic for a quarter of a mile on either side. I was new
to the road then and indeed I had to travel that way half a
dozen times before I realized what a neat job of sabotage the
stationmaster was doing. There was always a train sprawled
across the main road at this place, and consequently always a
traffic block. The army supply lines lost at least three hours a
day there.

We waited on this morning for fifteen minutes. The native
engine-driver hung impassively out of his cab and did nothing
whatever. I walked up to the head of the line of vehicles on
the road and found a military policeman.

"Why can't the train move?"

"I dunno," the policeman said. "It's always happening like
this and I can't speak their bloody language."

He tried again. The engine-driver shrugged his shoulders.
"The signal's down."

"Then who works the signal?" we asked.

With contempt he answered, "The signalman," and no
amount of persuasion could get out of him the whereabouts of
the signal box.

"Divide the train for a few minutes and let the traffic go
through," we said at last. "We can uncouple this carriage here
on the crossing and you pull forward for twenty yards."

"Can't do that without permission of the stationmaster," said
the engine-driver and he had a maddening way of talking.

"Where is the stationmaster?"

"He's gone to lunch."

A sergeant in one of the lorries who was as angry as I was said to the British policeman, "Just look the other way, will you, chum?" and he unstrapped his tommy-gun. The train was parted and the traffic flowed through.

We passed now into the next valley, an outlandish place of slate-coloured boulders and wild cataracts among the firs. Beyond this the road burst suddenly on to the high plains of Algeria, a great steppe where the wheat rolled like the sea under the freezing wind, and here you could travel at eighty miles an hour along the straight and perfect highway.

Near Sétif the air was alive with newly arrived American bombers and fighters, and as we drew petrol in the town we fell in with a platoon of young Americans who had been out on a man-hunt. German aircraft had been over two nights before dropping Arabs and Germans dressed as Arabs, who hid by day in friendly well-paid farmhouses and by night laid charges under the bridges and railway lines. Two of the saboteurs had been brought in.

In the darkness and with no headlights we crawled into the tourist town of Constantine, which is suspended like a spider's web above and around a spectacular gorge, a town on a massive rock from which in the daytime you could see across Algeria for a hundred miles in every direction.

It was a headquarters town now and full of troops who moved curiously among the tourists and the French refugees who had fled here to get away from the war. As at Aix-en-Provence or any of the towns in the Midi in the old days the French sat around in the open-air cafés drinking syrupy *apéritifs* and watching, watching, watching.

At Constantine I began to see just how modern and well equipped this new First Army was. For one thing there was a transit camp and that was something new to me. Instead of pulling in beside the road and sleeping in the vehicles or on the ground you called on the town major and he gave you the address of a place where you could get a bed and a hot meal and food and petrol for the next day's journey. My bed was a wire mattress in a children's nursery school that had been taken over, but there were blankets and the place was warm. Two parachutists who had just come in from behind the German lines lay on the next two beds to mine luxuriating in the comfort. It was their first night out of the mud for a month.

The place was full of odd characters—motor torpedo boat officers who had been making raids on the Italian convoys in the Sicilian Narrows, awkward and lofty young subalterns just out from England with batmen and bright uniforms, RAF pilots who had been shot down and were on their way back to their squadrons, American intelligence officers looking for their units and others who had simply got lost. You could pick up a hundred stories in an hour.

It was all so *new*—that was the thing I could not get used to after the dusty and dilapidated-looking Eighth Army. New uniforms, new guns, new vehicles, new men. There were things that never found their way out to the desert—cases of whiskey, gin and beer, coffee and coffee cups, orderlies to cook and orderlies to clean your boots, china plates and eggs and bacon for breakfast, white bread and hot water. Every one appeared to live in houses or at least in tents. The road was plastered with notices that would have taken the most timid motorist through the wilds of Thibet: "Dangerous curve ahead. . . . Keep your distance. . . . Bumps ahead. . . . Narrow bridge. . . . Steep hill. . . . Rough surface. . . . Beware of slippery surface. . . . Keep clear of the verges (which some soldier had naturally altered to "Keep clear of the virgins")."

Everything it seemed that could keep the army well fed, comfortable and happy had been laid on. If you broke down on the road it was not an hour or two before your vehicle was picked up by a Light Aid Detachment and mended. Every township had a town major and accommodation, the Naafi stores were full of soap, cigarettes, tooth paste, sweets, and even fresh clothing. There was a regular postal service. Every man, especially the Americans, carried around twice or three times as much kit as any soldiers I had seen before. They all looked smart and tidy and well shaven. Generals buzzed about in reconnaissance planes, and jeeps—those jeeps that were beyond price in the desert—were on the road in hundreds.

Now was this a serious army or a luxury parade-ground army? Were these be-monocled young British lieutenants and grapefruit-juice-fed Americans quite tough enough? What was going to happen to them when they hit the German Ninetieth Light Division and the Panzer Grenadiers?

Well, I was scarcely entitled to say much about it, a non-combatant, sitting on a warm bed with a glass of whiskey three hundred miles behind the front. But in a sudden access of doubt and fear I wanted to get forward quickly and see what was happening.

In the morning when hoar frost was still crunching on the road I bought the local French paper in Constantine. There was one little item on the front page that more than anything else abruptly made me realize that France was back in the war again. It said, "A Court Martial sitting in Constantine yesterday sentenced to death the two natives, Mahmoud Aly and Hassan Aly who were found guilty of hiding and assisting enemy saboteurs operating behind our lines. The two prisoners were shot this morning." Only twenty-four hours had elapsed since our American friends had brought the two natives in and handed them over to the French.

We ran down now out of the cold mountains and the snow into the half-tropical vegetation along the coast at Philippeville. If ever one needed a proof of the insanity of war it was here. A superb vineyard that for twenty years had produced the finest wine of the region had been torn out. Soldiers grubbed at the gnarled old roots and stacked them in neat piles beside the road where they would dry and be useful for firewood later on.

An old peasant farmer hung over the fence watching the soldiers at work and though we tried to talk to him his heart was too full for words. In place of the vines they were laying long runways of steel matting through the mud. When I came by a few months later great bombers were already taking off for Italy.

Beyond the lovely palm-tree port of Philippeville the coast road turns straight into the mountains again and this is the region of the cork-tree forests. Mounds of cork bark were piled along the tracks. The cork had been awaiting export ever since the war began. And to this now was added the high explosives that had been brought ashore for the army.

Never before or since had I seen such quantities of ammunition, so many evil piles of yellow bombs. The trains on the narrow-gauge railway were piled with bombs too, and shells. For thirty miles the ammunition was stacked in heaps on either side of the road under the trees, and more was being dumped as we went along. These were the bombs that, in the end, were not all needed in the Tunisian campaign and have since fallen on Italy and Europe.

The port of Bône has a huge square Byzantine basilica standing on a high knoll outside the town, but beyond that the place is purely French. Places like Algiers are hybrid growths, luxury resorts where the millionaires have built their villas. But Bône was almost painfully reminiscent of those Provençal towns we had not seen for years. It was all there—the Saint Raphael advertisements with the hurrying waiters, the signs that read "Dubo . . . Dubon . . . Dubonnet," the gay umbrellas over the tables on the pavement cafés and the people sitting under the trees in the town square, the piled-up barrows of fish and oranges down by the docks, the men in striped sweaters and the women with bright handkerchiefs over their heads, the graceful façades of the buildings with their sloping mansard roofs and window boxes, the red and white terra-cotta cottages by the sea, the cobble-stones and the paper-covered books in the shops, the marionette-like gendarmes at the corners and the mad traffic.

A good deal of all this was blown up. The square was roped off because a bombed wall was about to collapse there at any minute. The church was a mass of black and fallen timbers. There was still running water but no electric light as we groped our way to the town major's office through the rain. He boarded us out for the night with a young Frenchwoman in the suburbs, twenty francs each for the bed.

"I have sent the children into the country while the bombing lasts," she said. She kept running into our room with odd scraps of conversation. We were her first guests from the British army and she was nervous, excited and gay all at the same time. When the syrens howled and German aircraft raced over the housetops machine-gunning she went into the kitchen and baked us one of those sticky caramel French cakes you have to eat with a spoon, and she stood over us until we had finished it. In the morning we found that the cake had taken the last of her sugar ration.

All day after leaving Bône we threaded in and out of convoys trundling through the rain up to the front. The leading vehicle of these convoys travelled about twenty miles an hour, the regulation pace. Yet by some form of mathematics I don't understand the last vehicles in the convoys were always travelling between thirty and forty miles an hour in order to keep up. I watched that phenomenon a dozen times as we ran across the border into Tunisia and back into the mountains.

In the afternoon when wild flurries of snow and sleet were breaking across the road we reached the Hotel Transatlantic, a tiny alpine pension at Les Chênes. We had been travelling three days now and still we had not reached the front. A handful of officers had come back here from the mud for a few days' rest—men who had exhausted themselves temporarily on night patrols and skirmishing through the woods.

They had been up to their necks in muddy foxholes most of

the time with no cover whatever over their heads. There was a Spitfire pilot, the leader of his squadron, who was going home. The other pilots had tried to keep it a secret from the senior officers that the boy's eyesight was failing. In the raids over Tunis he had grown more and more reckless to make up for his deficiency, but it had been impossible to disguise the fact that sometimes, when he got back, he had to make several runs in order to get down. In the end he was ordered to submit to a medical examination and now he was grounded and going home. It had hurt the boy more than he could say, being grounded, for he and his friends had fought together for a long time. He felt he was out of it, disgraced, not good enough any more. The other pilots were giving him a farewell dinner and trying through the conversation to tell him that what he was thinking was not so, that he was still the leader of the squadron. But they made no attempt to disguise the fact that they thought it was bad luck he was not going to have the chance to risk his neck twice a day over Tunisia any more.

In the morning we came down out of the mountains and the storm into the sunshine of the Medjerda Valley. The other correspondents, the veterans who had been on the job since the landing, were drinking gin and lime on the balcony of the Grand Hotel de Thibar. I was introduced to madame.

"*Bon jour, M. Morsel,*" said madame cheerfully. "*Bienvenu.*"

Each day then we travelled out to the most interesting sections of the front from Thibar. You could get to almost anywhere on the line within an hour or two, gather the story and then drive back to Thibar in the evening to write it.

For a month I could not get used to this front. The geography baffled me. The tactics were an endless riddle. It was, I suppose, a kind of claustrophobia, for I could not accustom myself to the nearness of everything, the fact that while you sat on one hill there was the enemy just across the valley sitting on the next hill. Sometimes you could lift your glasses and actually see the Germans walking about.

For years the enemy had been for me some one remote, a red line on the map, a cloud of dust across the desert horizon. A comfortable no man's land dividing the two armies by ten or twenty miles—sometimes by fifty miles—had been the accepted thing in Egypt and Libya. Since the enemy could run across the flat intervening space in an hour or two you would not willingly bed down for the night anywhere within sight or earshot of him. I had never really seen a battle, only bits of battle: all the rest vanished under clouds of smoke and dust and spread for a hundred miles across the desert. You never looked down on any one—or up to them—since there were no hills. Even when the battle joined it was a thing of terribly fast movement that spilled in all directions, so that there would first be firing away to the right, then away to the left, and you might travel for a full day behind the enemy lines and then drive through them back to your own people again.

But here the troops were tumbled on top of one another. They stuck to the roads. They stayed put. They never made great encircling movements. And you could see the fighting. You could climb up on a hill and see your own tanks go out and see the enemy tanks and guns emerge to meet them. The two armies seemed to be for ever clutched in a tight embrace. A ferocious skirmish might be going on in one valley and if you happened to be a couple of miles away in the next valley you heard nothing and knew nothing. If you advanced a thousand yards it was considered a great achievement. Every foot of the front was complicated and dangerous—land mines all over the place, snipers perched in the most unlikely spots, shells and mortars dropping out of nowhere. The pleasure of motoring about the front from one sector to another was gone altogether. You had to keep your frozen head poked through the roof of the car on the look-out, and even then you often got no time to jump out before the Messerschmitt was upon you. And this went on for scores of miles behind the front. At night there was no peace in the forward areas because of the bombing over that confined space.

This compression of the fighting seemed to me to call for much quicker wits and much more vigilance than the desert, except of course when a battle was joined and then perhaps you had to think quicker in the open space. My natural instincts were to seek safety in space—in danger always run for the open desert. Here it was the other way about. Every one dived for cover under a rock or in a wood.

And there was the mud and the rain. It changed everything. Instead of the freedom of shorts and a shirt you were buttoned up to the ears in a heavy kit. Now I began to understand why men lived in farmhouses and caves when they could, why the roads were so well sign-posted, and why the army grabbed what comforts it could when it was not actually engaged. This perishing cold, this all-invading mud and this lack of hot food could exhaust and kill a man just as thoroughly as bullets.

I discovered this around Sedjenane where I began a series of tours down the line. Sedjenane was a wayside railway station in the wet cork forest on the way to Mateur. Whoever held Mateur held Bizerta and whoever held Green and Bald hills outside Sedjenane held Mateur. The Argylls among others attacked those two hills in the early days. They were bludgeoned and broken up by the most terrible crossfire that entirely governed the one narrow road. There was a long railway tunnel at that point too, and the Germans held one end, we the other. At night patrols of each side used to go into the tunnel and lay booby traps. By day the constant shelling went on until the very mountainsides were churned up into craters of red mud. Every time the Argylls emerged from their foxholes and advanced through the mud on foot they were cut up.

Almost to the very end this cruel in-fighting went on and, as in most of the other places along the line, whoever held the high ground held the battlefield. If you won the pass then you won everything. Green and Bald hills were Number One Pass on the line and if you care to drive across the mountains there now you will see by the graves how badly we wanted to get through; how determined the Germans were to stop us.

The road near Sedjenane was so often blitzed from the air by German fighters nipping up from their fields ten minutes away that it was closed to vehicles in the daytime. You had to park your car a mile or two back and walk on foot and under cover to the forward positions.

This was where our parachutists fought when they were turned into ordinary infantry. No prisoners were taken in that terrible skirmishing through the rocks. I called on the parachutists one day and all around the bush was heavy with the sweet and nauseating smell of bodies that were turning rotten in the sun after the rain. In their whole approach to death these young men had completely altered. They had killed so many themselves and with the bayonet. They had seen so many of their companions die. They had become so well acquainted with death they had no fear of it any longer. The fact that that body lying over there was Bill or Jack or Jim who had eaten breakfast with them this morning was not remarkable or horrible: you either lived or you died or you got wounded and any one of these conditions was an accepted condition. It was not that pity or grief had gone out of them, but that they were living in a well of danger and their lives were sharpened and lifted up to the point of meeting that danger directly. It was all very largely a technical matter—whether you got your machine-gun burst in first and with the right direction. These men were soaked in war. They were grown old to war in a few weeks and all the normal uses of peace and the ambitions of peace were entirely drained out of them.

These were the men who were flung into any part of the line that was critical. They led the forward rushes; they stopped the gaps in the retreats. They were feared by the Italians—and by the Germans—as the most terrible animals.

The conditions in which the parachutists lived at the front

were barely good enough to keep life going—bully, biscuits, not much else. Once for four days and nights they were in the rain and under fire and unable to heat any food or drink because the smoke of a fire immediately drew snipers' bullets. Some, in the extremity of their hunger and shuddering cold, said, "The hell with it—I've got to eat," but they were killed as soon as they got a fire going. At length they were brought a few miles back for a spell. Some huts had been prepared for them and a meal. But when the men got off the trucks they did not want to walk the remaining four hundred yards for the meal and the shelter. They fell onto the mud beside their trucks and slept in the streaming rain.

Once on Jebel Mansour a sergeant of these men led his platoon to the top. He himself was still shooting when he got the order to retire, and his companions were dead around him. From down the hill the others saw him suddenly clip another magazine of bullets to his gun and he stood upright facing the enemy and in their continuous chain of fire.

"—— this," the sergeant said. "—— this." He shouted it straight at the screaming sky, his ultimate expression of human dignity and defiant pride. And he walked straight towards the enemy firing as he went, one man against a thousand. It was impossible to see how far he got before he died.

The parachutists were a small brigade—perhaps seven or eight hundred at the front. When the campaign ended they had killed about three thousand Germans and Italians.

Medjez el Bab and Longstop Hill were Number Two Pass leading into Tunis, and the Argylls—or what was left of them—were in the line the first time I went there. A providential burst of sunshine had come through and dried out a thick crust on top of the chocolate mud. Coming down either from Testour or from Oued Zarga further up the Medjerda Valley one found that the township still looked like a township, and the peasants were still tilling their farms round about. Right through this campaign the farmers kept on at their land in the front line.

When everything in their world was crumbling about them they clung tenaciously and pathetically to their peacetime habits. If the farmhouse was blitzed the peasants lived in the cowsheds. If an army headquarters moved in on the homestead then the farmer stayed right on and fed his chickens among the anti-aircraft guns. If a field had to be ploughed then he simply skirted round the shell craters. The peasants and the Arabs went to ground somewhere when a barrage or a bombing was on but they would not leave their homes.

There was one young British artillery officer whose position was overrun by the Germans. He put an Arab cloak over his uniform, hitched a plough on to his gun-towing tractor and spent all that day ploughing round and round the field among the Germans. In the night he coupled up one of his guns and drove back to the British lines.

At first, then, I noticed nothing abnormal in the approaches to Medjez el Bab. But once in the streets one saw a depressing shambles. The old and beautiful bridge had tumbled into the sleepy river and another military bridge had been run up. Every now and then the enemy was lobbing over a shell. For a month they had been trying to hit the new bridge but even today when one shell made a crater at its western end the structure remained solid and it stayed intact until the end of the whole campaign. Post office, church, shops, school and mosque—everything was torn about by the tornado of high explosive and reduced to the same dreary colour of the mud. A magnificent grove of euca-lyptus, only slightly splintered by the shellfire, led through cratered fields to the railway station where the Argylls had their headquarters. These men too had the habit of war. Each night their patrols went out in no man's land rounding up hostile Arabs, laying mines, setting ambushes and getting information. The Germans from Longstop Hill were doing precisely the same thing. Standing behind a low garden wall I saw the trenches and the earthworks of the enemy only a mile away. The fighting now had lost its virulence and it was one of those

frequent moments in war where both sides, as though by common consent, agree not to attack in force because they know
they are too weak.

Equally both sides knew that sooner or later an attack must
come and that again men must go out into the field of oats that
lay between the two armies.

In the meantime the Argylls drank the petrol tin full of red
Thibar wine we had bought and washed their filthy underwear
and wrote letters home and brewed that new solution called
ration tea which is a powdered mixture of tea, milk and sugar
and which tastes, in my opinion, like sweet earth. For the
moment we were content to let this pass, too, stay in German
hands.

Pass Number Three was at El Aroussa, another battered
township in the valley leading up to Pont du Fahs. Something
was usually happening here. The Sixth Armoured Division had
set up its headquarters in a farmyard and from there General X.
(I regret I am not allowed to give his name), knee deep in
ducks and pigs, kept up a sort of red Indian warfare on the
enemy. His division was sent out from England with Valentine
tanks. It is too late now to ask why his division was given
Valentines, which had already proved themselves inadequate in
the desert. The two-pounder gun was simply not good enough
either in the hills or on the plains, and no amount of argument
in either the House of Commons or the War Office or the factories was going to make them good enough. Later on the division was given the American Sherman tanks they ought to have
had in the first place and they lost several valuable weeks making the change-over. However, in January Valentines were all
they had and they made a series of daring but not very decisive
forays up the valley towards Pont du Fahs.

Stubbornly—pig-headedly if you like—we were learning here
the painful lesson that you cannot attack fixed positions with
tanks.

Every day that went by the gun was more and more dominating the fighting in these hills, and the tank was falling into the background. The green floor of the valley looked inviting enough. But send a half-squadron of tanks out and then—crash. Out roared the enemy anti-tank guns from twenty different directions.

You would have thought the Germans would have learned this lesson. After all they were the masters of the anti-tank gun technique—the technique of keeping your own tanks out of the battle and luring the enemy tanks on to the guns. But the day I first went down to El Aroussa the German Mark III's and IV's came charging down the valley. They had the misfortune to choose the day when we had about seventy twenty-five-pounders in the vicinity all carefully sighted.

Traced on the map afterwards the course of the enemy tanks looked like a heart. They came out of Pont du Fahs as one formation, then split and forked off in two lines on either side of the valley. At the same moment both columns ran into our twenty-five-pounder barrage and turned inwards. Those that were left joined in the centre and ran for home. If ever there was a lesson to every tank commander in the war it was there. And now we proposed to follow up our advantage with an infantry attack on a useful rise called Two Tree Hill (despite the fact that the enemy some days ago had cut down the two trees because they believed we were sighting our guns on them).

The Irish went in under a full moon and for the next twenty-four hours the valley was full of crossfire and hot skirmishing with the hand grenade and the rifle through the foothills.

As the fighting died down we came back to El Aroussa village, which was much cut about with bombing, and the usual argument broke out about where we were to sleep. One group favored a great barnlike building in the centre of the village despite the fact that it had had its roof torn off and was now filled with coils of barbed wire. The other group favoured the open countryside away from bomb targets. In the end we compromised with a verandah in a village on the outskirts.

It was an uncomfortable night. The guns kept flashing spasmodically up the valley. Twice I was waked in the early morning—once by a dispatch rider most improbably bringing me a cable from London, and later, by a wounded Frenchman who stood dripping blood over our sleeping-bags until we got up and took him to a doctor.

The morning broke unusually clear and I wandered into the village. In the main street half a dozen tommies were washing in the horse-trough and I fell into conversation with them. They were Londoners, adolescent boys on their first campaign and enjoying a good deal of it. Their backs and chests as they washed were very white but their faces had gone scarlet through exposure. They carried on an effervescent conversation about the only three things that interest a soldier outside his regiment—the mail from home, food and women.

They were friendly and shy and very determined to do well in the war. I declined breakfast with them as my own at that moment was ready.

As I walked back to my camp the Stukas came over. They came very slowly and I suppose about eight hundred feet up, just a dozen of them with one or two fighters up above. There was ample time to run a few yards into the fields and throw oneself into the first available hollow.

It seemed for a moment they were going to sail by the village but at the last moment they altered direction, opened their flaps and dived. The bombs tumbled out lazily, turning over and over in the morning sunshine. Then with that graceful little jump and a flick each aircraft turned upward and out of its dive and wheeled away. It all happened very slowly. They could scarcely have missed the centre of the village but they were very lucky to have hit a large truck filled with ammunition. The truck caught fire and the bullets kept blowing off in all directions, red for the tracers and white for the others. Half a dozen fires were started and the flames struggled to surge upward through the dust and smoke. One of the explosions performed the remarkable feat of killing a dove which flew through the air and struck down an officer who was in the act of talking to me. One of our men had been carrying a tin of eggs up the road and now he picked himself up ruefully from the sticky mess.

I walked over to the centre of the village taking care to stay away from the exploding ammunition lorry. A twenty-foot steel water-tank had collapsed like a fallen house of cards. The barnlike building in which we had proposed to spend the night had taken another direct hit and the coiled barbed wire had threshed about wildly in a thousand murderous tentacles. The blast had carried these fragments across to the water trough and now my six young friends were curiously huddled up and twisted over one another. It is the stillness of the dead that is so shocking. Even their boots don't seem to lie on the ground as those of a sleeping man would. They don't move at all. They seem to slump into the earth with such unnatural overwhelming tiredness. I will never, even if this war goes on another ten years, grow used to the sight of the dead.

That, then, was Number Three Pass as I first saw it and now wish to forget it. There remained Number Four, the American sector about Sbeitla and Gafsa. This was unlike the others. The grass was thinner, the trees stunted, the high ground full of brown bare rocks. Gafsa was not strictly speaking a pass at all— it was a jaunty little oasis sprawling on the edge of the desert— and at this point our front meandered across the open country. We had good positions on which to fall back at Kasserine and Tébessa but the line itself was exposed and could be flanked.

The Eighth Army had not yet come up from the south to join hands with the First Army and plug Rommel securely into Tunisia. A great empty gap lay between the two Allied armies and this empty region extended over the salt lakes called shotts and ran from Tébessa in the west to Mareth on the coast. Beyond that the Sahara rolled on interminably to the Equator.

So at this stage—the end of January and early February—the

stalemate was complete. Our original gamble had failed. Montgomery had still to gear up his army once again at Mareth at the end of its prodigious lines of supply. The four main passes of Tunisia were held strongly by the Germans and they were getting stronger every day.

The fighting along the lines was only a curtain-raiser for the big show that was yet to come. Everywhere we could we wriggled forward on to a hill so as to be in a better position to launch a full-scale attack when the day came. The Germans on their side counter-attacked us off these hills hoping that we should never establish a satisfactory springboard for the great swoop on Tunis. It was an uneasy shifting line and no one was happy about it. But still there was nothing much we could do until Montgomery arrived. Every one in the First Army was now asking, "Where is Montgomery?" "When does the Eighth Army arrive?"

Chapter X: Tripoli

WITHIN four months—from October to January—the British Eighth Army had done amazing things in the desert. It had advanced fifteen hundred miles across some of the most inhospitable country in the world. It had smashed the Italian Fascist empire in Africa. It had fought one major action at Alamein in Egypt and two minor ones at El Agheila and Zem-Zem in Tripolitania.

It had captured 30,000 prisoners including a dozen important generals and killed and wounded something like 40,000 men. In their retreat the Axis lost perhaps 500 tanks, 1000 aircraft, 1500 vehicles, and stores worth many millions of pounds. Three vital ports, Tobruk, Benghazi and Tripoli, were in our hands and in operation. We had failed to catch Rommel but the power of his Afrika Korps was at least halved. Incontestably the Eighth Army was the finest fighting machine in the Anglo-American forces, and the name of its general stood higher than that of any other.

Probably it is still too soon to assess this extraordinary crusade across the desert; but at least now we can make a selection of the most vital events and lay them out for analysis.

If you put the story through a critical sieve a whole mass of things that looked important at the time fall through and you are left with half a dozen hard lumps of military discovery.

First there was the personality of the new general. Bernard Montgomery, as we saw him when he first arrived in the desert, was a slightly-built man with a thin nervous face, an ascetic who neither drank nor smoked, a martinet who could not even endure other people doing these things around him. He was a military scholar who had cut away from himself most of the normal diversions of life, and this left him with a fund of restless energy, part of which he expended in a religious faith in himself and his God and part in a ruthless determination to make battle. Like most missionaries he was flamboyant, and there was in him an almost messianic desire to make converts and to prove his doctrines were the right ones. An unusual man, not an easy companion.

General Montgomery represented central control in the British army as against the democratic ways of most of the other generals—Wavell and Alexander, for example. These last preferred to accept the army and its system as they found it. They tried nothing revolutionary but endeavoured to improve on the existing state of things. They moved on the principle that there is *some* good in every man and every weapon if it were used in the right way. They consulted their subordinates and left a good deal of the actual control to them. They commanded by a system of compromises and make-shifts which were adjusted to meet each emergency that came up. England and the British Empire had been governed on these lines for several hundreds of years and so the system seemed natural enough.

Now Montgomery was just the reverse. He believed in surgery, not homeopathy. If a thing is not going right or is going only partially right then cut it out altogether; don't try make-shifts and slow drugs; sack the man to blame outright. His ideas were a logical extension of the Bedeaux efficiency system in America and the Stakhanov system in the Soviet factories. By the Montgomery method the whole art of war was reducible to a pattern and a series of numbers; it was all based on units of manpower and firepower and so forth. He by no means rubbed out the human element; he simply believed that a correct system and good leadership would inspire the troops and draw out hitherto-wasted resources of energy.

Montgomery had this system and this faith, and he believed in them passionately. He was itching to put his ideas into practice. Suddenly Churchill gave him the chance.

When the General arrived in the Middle East in August,

1942, he had the great good fortune to find a ready-made and experienced army waiting for him. Two years' fighting and training had made many of them wonderful troops and there were plenty of them. The three armoured divisions—the First, Seventh and Tenth—were English and there were in addition two English foot divisions, the Fiftieth and the Forty-Fourth. The Empire had provided five more infantry divisions—two South African, one Indian, one New Zealand and one Australian. There was also the Highland Division. A total of eleven divisions, all ready to go into battle. Moreover, the equipment was pouring in at a rate never approached in the Middle East before—British guns, American tanks and aircraft from both countries.

In itself this huge instrument of nearly two hundred thousand men was ready for anything. But the things it lacked badly were a clearly defined purpose and a leader. They got both in Montgomery. "Follow me," he cried, "and we will smash Rommel." Since the General believed this himself it was not long before the troops began to believe it too. Before their own eyes great squadrons of tanks and guns were pouring into the desert and naturally the new General was given the credit for it. From now on the subordinate took a very subordinate position indeed. Everything came straight from the General. Moreover, the new General was a man the troops could understand. He was very much one of the boys. He painted "Monty" on his tank and he went round wearing a most stimulating array of hats and badges. He harangued the army like a prophet. All this might seem like bad form to the officers of the old school, but the troops loved it. Monty had won them over before the battle started. His shrewdest move of all was to spread the idea that the Eighth Army was an independent striking force, taking its orders from no one. He was their General and he was going to lead them on their own private crusade across Africa.

Behind all this there resided in the General a long and very solid military training. If his battles lacked genius, at least they were fought brilliantly and with good sound logic. Enormous experiments, especially in armoured fighting, were being evolved, and they were entirely beyond the control of any one man, but Montgomery's battles brought the results to light.

Alamein will be studied in military academies for many years to come. The Eighth Army found itself in front of a short line, barely forty miles long, that could not be turned because the sea lay at one end and a marsh at the other end. Consequently it had to be attacked directly.

The Australians had already made themselves a good big dent in the enemy positions along the coast; so clearly this had to be used. But we needed two lines of attack to prevent the enemy concentrating, and a point halfway down the line seemed to be the best second line of advance.

The Germans on their side had mined their ground in great depth and covered it with artillery and smaller guns firing on fixed lines. Both sides held their armour in reserve, ready to rush critical points once the battle was joined. The British out-numbered the enemy in everything except men by possibly as much as three to two, but they needed this advantage since they were going to do the attacking.

The British had one other thing in their favour: Marshal Rommel, whose intelligence staff must have been terrible, was away in Germany and his substitute von Sturma did a thing which Rommel would never have done—spaced his forces more or less equally along the whole line. Whereas the whole basis of his defence should have been to keep his best forces fluid until the battle took shape, he left them lying in static positions, from which they could not be quickly moved.

Most people know the story of the ensuing battle and there is no point in my trying to describe it here, particularly as I was not there. But even a superficial examination of the intelli-gence reports brings out a number of things which are at this minute having a profound effect on our military tactics.

Montgomery attacked by night. He risked the danger of

confusion in the darkness so that he should have the advantage
of surprise and so that his striking units could get right up to
the enemy without being seen. Before dawn each morning the
British dug in furiously in order to meet the inevitable counter-
attack at daylight. Then at night they attacked again.

We struck not with tanks but with men, aircraft and guns.
The tanks for the most part were kept out of it until the guns
and aircraft—in this case mostly the twenty-five-pounder and
the American medium bomber—had softened up the arena and
the infantry had overwhelmed the mine fields and anti-tank
batteries.

Then once a good solid hole was made in the enemy lines the
tanks went roaring through. They fanned out behind the enemy
infantry and panicked them and they forced the enemy armour
to do battle in the open ground beyond.

Rommel, who had come racing back from Berlin, took one
look at this chaos and apparently decided there was very little
he could do about it. Indeed there was hardly a mistake his subordinates had not made. They had been bluffed by a dummy
concentration of vehicles the British had erected behind Alamein. They had confused the position of the real British spear-
head and when they did find it the situation was too late to be
restored. After trying to peg the gaps at one or two places
Rommel wisely abandoned the Italian infantry and got clean
out of Egypt and Cyrenaica with the remainder of his tanks
and his best mobile units.

Montgomery had shown himself resourceful and quick-
thinking in the battle. When his line became too congested he
whipped the New Zealanders and South Africans out. When he
had a final choice of smashing through along the Australian
salient on the coast or farther inland he at once chose the inland
sector because that was where the divided German army was
reuniting and the point of junction is usually the weakest point.

After Alamein began the usual bi-annual cross-country race
across Cyrenaica. It was an especially brisk affair this year as

the Eighth Army fetched up on the finishing line at El Agheila inside three weeks, a record. But there was just this difference from the other two British advances—Montgomery was given the means to plan his supply ahead so that he would be able to hold what he had already won and eventually push on to Tripoli. Nine-tenths of desert warfare is the battle of supply. Whoever first gets up most water, food, fuel, guns and men wins the campaign.

This time the British had engineers waiting to repair the roads, railways, bridges and ports. This time the ships were waiting to put into Benghazi and the port was open for them to unload three thousand tons a day. This time we had American Douglas aircraft to carry urgent supplies at speed with a rapid shuttle service between Cairo and El Agheila. Despite a violent three-day storm which wrecked the ships in Benghazi, despite the foul and bitter weather all over the desert, Montgomery won the battle of supply.

He was planning to attack again at El Agheila on December fourteenth. Rommel neatly anticipated the matter by slipping out two days beforehand. Nevertheless Montgomery very nearly accomplished what he had set his heart on doing—capturing the Afrika Korps—and his plan is interesting because it shows the effect of the lessons learned at Alamein. At El Agheila he developed the tactics which are the distinguishing mark of all Montgomery's actions—a direct blow with the right and an encircling blow with the left. These tactics were more or less forced on the General since he always had the sea on his right and, except at Alamein and his one unsuccessful engagement at Enfidaville, the enemy line could always be outflanked in the empty desert to the south. Like nearly every other innovation in the desert this tactic was first discovered by Wavell; but Montgomery gave the plan incisiveness and additional speed. Wavell's left-right blitz on the Sidi Barrani Line in 1940, his schemes for the reduction of desert strongholds and his general plan of striking straight for Benghazi while his mobile forces cut across the desert behind the enemy have become classic desert lore now and neither Rommel nor Montgomery was able to make any basic improvement on them; but they were supplied with much faster and better machines than Wavell and they controlled very much larger armies.

On this occasion Montgomery sent the New Zealanders off on a staggering march around and behind the enemy positions at El Agheila. The New Zealanders got into position on time and then found they had been asked to bite off far too big a mouthful. They spaced their infantry brigades around Rommel's rear as best they could and stood by to receive the shock of the full Afrika Korps. Rommel, months before on the Gazala Line, had failed to capture a full British division, the Fiftieth, which was caught in much the same position, so now the Germans, profiting by that lesson, escaped in just the same way. They split into small Commandos, each led by tanks, and slipped through the New Zealanders in the dark.

There remained nothing for Montgomery to do but take up the weary chase and the Eighth Army plunged ahead into regions the British had never entered before. Apart from supply, which dominated everything, the chase developed into a battle of wits between the German and British engineers. A great deal of the German mining technique which later was a crucial thing in the battle for Tunis was learned out here in the desert where this one black ribbon of road wound on interminably over the waste of sand. It is a cruel business, mining, a thing that gratifies no one's instincts for combat, for it is a stab in the back and the stabber runs no risks himself.

The German S mine projects three prongs above the ground. When a man steps on it there is a small explosion, a metal ball jumps waist high into the air and then bursts, ejecting small shot in every direction. Its mission is solely to wound and kill soldiers who are off their guard. The German Teller mine is a round metal tin, rather larger than a soup plate, which is buried just below the ground and it contains enough explosive to break a tank track or demolish a lorry. The Italians have a rectangular mine for the same purpose. There are variations of these mines but all of them are either anti-personnel or anti-vehicle. In addition there are booby traps of half a dozen varieties mostly based on the idea that if a string is pulled unawares the pin is jerked out of a hand grenade which thereupon explodes.

The Germans developed this mining to a science along the road to Tripoli. Everything likely or unlikely was mined or booby-trapped. To give you some idea of the complexity of this mining, here is what would happen when the retreating German sappers got to work on a bridge: First the bridge would be blown up. Then the fallen rubble would be S-mined. Then the approaches to the crater on either side would be mined with Tellers. Then the earthen tracks which wound round on either side of the fallen bridge would be Teller-mined by placing one mine above another so that when the British sappers came along and pulled up the first mine they would be blown up on the second. Then, presuming that the crew of a tank or truck would jump out immediately they struck one of these mines, the Germans spread S mines about at the point where they estimated the tommies would land. Then, in case they still escaped, trip-wires attached to booby traps would be strung between the bushes or among discarded ammunition cases or in overturned vehicles. Often the road mines would be varied so that they did not go up until several vehicles had passed over and the drivers believed the path to be clear.

The Germans were wonderful toy makers. They made a neat wooden box in which they enclosed their mines so that they could not be detected with our usual apparatus, which is a flat metal plate on the end of a rod. The mine-searcher wears earphones and the electric device in the instrument emits a high-pitched whine if the plate is placed over metal—but not over wood. Still another device of the Germans was to place the detonator for a mine at some distance in advance of the mine itself.

These savage inventions were the things that held up Montgomery on his long march until at last in January he found himself poised over Tripoli and the Germans once again massing in front of him. The enemy chose a three-pronged wadi called Zem-Zem and mounted their guns on the more westerly of the three ravines. Once more Montgomery struck with a right and a left—the Highland Division leading the frontal assault, the New Zealanders making another forced march through the desert to the south. This time the New Zealanders had to go through country so rough that even the desert veterans were left speechless. Tanks had to stand by all day dragging the vehicles up the worst bits.

Meanwhile a third force was converging on Tripoli. General Le Clerc and a brigade of Fighting Frenchmen had made a fantastic forced march from Lake Chad in the centre of Africa, taking one oasis after another, and now they were ready to strike in from the south. A great book and a great movie must some day be written about Le Clerc's march.

Once again Rommel, after a few sharp rear-guard actions, withdrew his army and the Allies marched into the open town of Tripoli. The Highland pipers went piping into the main square and at last after thirty months of warfare the ragged and dishevelled desert soldier stood with wonderment and emotion beside the playing fountains. If one excepts the entrance of the Germans into Paris, of the Japanese into Singapore and the return of the Russians to Stalingrad, there can have been no moment in the war equal to this one.

In the swaying battle of the desert Tripoli had for two and a half years appeared as a mirage that grew strong and now faded away again, and was forever just beyond the Eighth Army's reach. So many had died or been withdrawn through wounds at a time when the struggle looked futile and endless. So many had recovered hope only to lose it again. So many had aged and grown sick and weak. Only those who had suffered the test of the desert, and for a long time, will be able to understand the emotions of the victors at the end—the constricting excitement of the last few hours when the army was about to penetrate the green suburbs, the bursting elation of the actual entrance into the town and the inevitable sense of anti-climax which followed.

This sense of anti-climax came all the more sharply upon the army because it was suddenly made to realize that its job was not yet done. Tripoli had always been for them the conclusion of the African war, the ultimate reward for the men coming out of the desert. But now something more was asked of them. The majority of the army was not even allowed to go into the town—it was obliged to plunge once more into the wastes and pursue Rommel across the border of Tripolitania, into Tunisia.

With alacrity Rommel nipped into the Mareth Line, which the Italians in misplaced optimism had dismantled a year or two before. His Afrika Korps neatly plugged the southern sector of the German front in Tunisia and a great rectangle of mountain and plain now stood against the combined First and Eighth armies.

The Allied armies, however, had not yet made contact at the end of January. A vast region of desert dotted with tiny oases, rugged stone ridges and salt marshes still lay between the two forces. The area along the Tunisian-Tripolitanian border was badly mapped and except for Bedouins few people had penetrated deep in the Sahara which rolled away in blistering heat to the south.

Philip Jordan and myself now set out from Thibar into this country hoping that we might find a trail through the shotts and make first contact with the outposts of the Eighth Army. For some reason the military press authorities in Algiers were opposed to the trip and managed to stop us from flying across though the RAF very kindly offered us a passage. Even when we made the land journey we were punished by having our messages held up for a month or more.

However, there was a strong personal satisfaction in doing

what we set out to do since I had spent two years with the desert forces and had a strong nostalgia to see them again.

We drove first to the American headquarters in the dismal town of Tébessa in the south where somehow the Roman ruins have been made to look more depressing and uninteresting than any I have ever seen. The Americans, who are always open-handed, gave us food, clothing, an officer and a driver and two pearls beyond all price—two jeeps. We handed over our Humber station waggon in exchange since it would not tackle the rough country and set out. The maps were unreliable to say the least—weird, highly coloured bits of paper drawn by some imaginative Frenchman—but we branched off the main road about twenty miles short of the German positions before Gafsa and struck out across the open country to the south.

It was a fabulous country of stark ravines and crenellated stone ridges that were stained to the colours of pale rose and muddy brown and saffron yellow. A few villages struggled for wretched existence from the bare land and beyond these we sometimes saw a suspicious shepherd clambering among the high rocks. An army might have been held up there for ever; however, the jeeps bumped through and the wild camels stared at us with astonishment and malice.

At Metlouie we ran into a company of French Zouaves who were garrisoning the town in a desultory way and two large doughboys who were roaming unconcernedly about this open section of the front trying to find out if the railway worked. No one had any notion of where the Germans were and beyond Metlouie the earthen track was entirely deserted except for occasional caravans of Arabs mounted on camels. There were no tracks on the road and it was impossible to know whether the German patrols were operating in this area or not.

There is an excitement in reconnaissance like nothing else. For the most part you are in perfect safety as we were here, but you are never sure and you keep looking round the horizon and listening and you have a fine sense of discovery and adventure. And now after all these months in cities and at sea and in the mountains I saw the desert opening out in front of me again and it was like coming home. We ran on through two more oases where the date palm branches had been pegged to the ground to hold the shifting sand back from the miserable crops. The palms yielded almost everything these villages wanted—beams to support their huts, branches for the walls and roofs, shade from the sun and food from the dates.

In the late afternoon, still seeing nothing of any troops hostile or friendly, we came in sight of the Shott el Jerid and ran into the mud and tile village of Tozeur.

Tozeur was made for tourists. It is surrounded by a thick belt of date palms, and clear cold water running from the hot sand makes runnels in the shade where peach trees grow and almonds and rich green vegetables. Squatting at their doorways the Arabs weave baskets and mats from the all-providing palm leaves. Donkeys and camels bray under the snow-white mosque, and through the iron grills of the houses Arab women in brilliant shawls and veils keep peering out.

The Companie Transatlantique had built a semi-Moorish hotel with an inner courtyard on the outskirts of the town and that was where we met my second favourite character of Tunisia.

She was a plump little Frenchwoman with bad teeth and a pretty face and after a series of involved adventures following the collapse of France she had come down here to run the hotel. We had expected to camp out on this trip, but madame was offering an astonishing array of luxuries—bedrooms, baths, food and even wine. A group of Italian officers had been in the town until a few days before and we were welcome to their rooms.

It was a strange situation. We seemed to be poised between the Germans and the Allies in a sort of vacuum—a vacuum that provided most of the comforts of pre-war Europe. Then into the courtyard strolled a British major in full uniform, followed by a captain. They were alone. They had captured Tozeur for the Allies.

It was from the major that we heard we had stumbled on a great piece of luck, and that our journey was a success. By the merest fluke three men from the Eighth Army—the first to come north in search of the First Army—had arrived in Tozeur on the previous day. We jumped into a jeep and hurried round to their camp, in one of the white huts at the other end of the oasis. I thought I knew every unit in the desert army but I was altogether unprepared for the shock of this meeting. The three men who got up to meet us were quite unrecognisable as soldiers. They were black-bearded up to the eyebrows. What was left showing of their young faces was burnt almost henna red by the sun. They wore ragged shorts and shirts bleached white by the sun. On their feet were heavy leather native sandals. In place of helmets—the Eighth Army seldom wore helmets—they had khaki native cloths that kept the sun off the back of their necks. All three were slightly wounded or slightly sick. Two were English boys; the third a New Zealander. They were the survivors of a unit of the Long Range Desert Group which for two years had been making stupendous trips behind the enemy lines.

The Long Range Desert Group were the picked men who set out alone in half a dozen vehicles or more and disappeared for weeks or months at a time. They carried everything with them, including water. They steered for hundreds of miles by compass over a wilderness far south of Tripoli that had never been explored before. They swooped suddenly at night upon isolated German airfields and smashed up the grounded aircraft. They burst into Italian huts and messrooms hundreds of miles behind the front and, like a gang of desperadoes in a Wild Western thriller, shot up every one and everything they could see. They laid ambushes along the coast road and mined bridges. They blew up ammunition dumps and grabbed vital prisoners. They had a hundred ways of catching the enemy by surprise and deceiving him and filling him with panic. And after each raid they slid silently back into the desert again.

If enemy aircraft picked up their tracks and followed them they simply dispersed and faced the music the best they could. If they were badly shot up they had somehow to get their vehicles going again or they knew that their wounded would die and perhaps the whole party would perish of thirst. It was a recurring miracle the way these desperate little parties always seemed to get back even when they had been overdue for days.

If we were going to make contact with any one in the Eighth Army it could not be with any troops better than these, who knew the desert better than any one else. In their speech and their manner and appearance they showed just what the desert will do to white men, how reliant it will make them and how tough. And now this, their last trip, was almost the strangest of all.

They had started, they said, weeks ago, soon after the battle of Alamein and since then they had barely made contact at all with the main bulk of Montgomery's army, which was working further to the north on the coast. Spreading their handkerchief maps on the dust floor of the hut they showed us how they had struck straight across the desert from a point south of Benghazi, mopping up stray patrols of Italians on their route. Their mission was to go right round Tripoli and cross ahead of Rommel's retreating Afrika Korps into Tunisia. They were to wreck as much as possible of the Mareth Line before the Germans got there and to make what hell they could with the road and railway line running from Gabès to Tripoli.

At first everything went well. They got right into the Mareth Line and found the place little more than a string of disarmed and sanded-up pillboxes. They roamed right through that region where a great battle had still to be fought and did what damage they could. Then Colonel David Stirling, their leader, and probably the most resourceful adventurer in the desert war, went off Gabès-way to blow up a railway train.

They waited a week at a rendezvous south of Tripoli for Stirling to return and still they had no news of him. (Stirling, we heard later, had been caught and shipped to Italy where already he had made one half-successful attempt to escape.) Then they were betrayed by Arabs. Two Messerschmitts zoomed down on them from Tripoli and shot up all their transport except one jeep. These three sick and wounded lads were piled aboard the jeep and told to get through somehow to the First Army away in the north. The rest of the party, about twenty in all, collected what water and food they could carry and set out to walk following the tracks of the jeep.

Bedouins guided the wounded men some of the way through the salt shotts. Once they caught and ate a kid goat. At night they stole round Italian encampments, and in the daytime they hid when enemy planes or vehicles appeared. At length they struggled into Tozeur.

They had been living so long in isolation, living on a cup of water a day and the very barest minimum necessary to keep alive, that they were pathetically grateful and astonished at the meagre things we gave them—a few oranges, a book, a couple of bars of chocolate, a bottle of wine.

They loved their life. All their ambitions were confined to the idea of going on, of discovering new places and breaking open new trails.

"I suppose they won't have any more use for us in Africa now that the desert fighting is over," the New Zealander said. "But we got a tip just before we left on this last trip that they may have a job for us in China." It is quite probable that at this moment these boys are in China or the Balkans or the Caucasus or anywhere there are no made roads and the winds blow freely.

That evening, as we were sitting in the courtyard of the hotel, a soldier came in and called my name aloud. "I have letters for you from the Eighth Army," he said. It was an astonishing meeting. This man was with the walking party which reached Tozeur that night. Weeks before two friends of mine with Montgomery at Sirte had given him letters for me. He had carried them through the enemy lines and by sheer luck had stumbled across me in Tozeur.

While I was reading the letters the major came over to us and said quietly, "I have just had a message that I am on no account to go near Gafsa tonight."

This information was official and it had come over the telephone from headquarters. "You say the road was clear when you came down it today," he went on. "Well, it isn't now. It looks as though the Jerries have cut it."

This was awkward. We knew no other way back and it looked as though we were cut off unless we cared to head south over the camel tracks the way the Long Range Desert Group had come. Since we had no compass and it was a ten days' trek to Tripoli if you got through the enemy patrols, we did not care for it much, though the American captain with us was keen to go on.

The major then became a mine of bad news. "I was expecting it, of course," he said placidly. "I shouldn't mind betting the Jerries will be in Tozeur—perhaps tomorrow, perhaps the day after. German patrols have been sniffing round here for the past fortnight. They blew up the bridge on the road down to the shott the night before last. And they have been working along the road you came down on for the past week. Did you see that burnt-out French lorry on the way? They got that. Up till now they have been only mining."

Now to me this was downright alarming. I have no nerves for the cat-and-mouse kind of warfare the major liked to play. He could be up and away within twenty minutes at any time of the night. I was tolerably certain that we could by no means be up and away in anything under an hour or an hour and a half. The jeeps were parked in a remote shed and I disliked the idea of going to bed knowing that at any hour the enemy patrols, who would be very quick on the trigger, might enter the dark streets. The town was wide open without any protection whatever and invading troops would naturally make for the hotel, as we did.

As though to confirm the major's views, a Messerschmitt suddenly sailed out of nowhere, machine-gunning the streets and the railway across the road. We stood under the arches in the courtyard, and he came back for a third run, but this time without firing bullets and obviously taking photographs. The enemy always sent out a reconnaissance plane over a place before they moved in.

The others, however, did not share my qualms and we stayed on a couple of days and nights in Tozeur with the people from the Eighth Army. And indeed it was not for a couple of weeks that the Germans entered the town and Nazi officers took over the bedrooms we had been sleeping in.

Philip and I, with a good story in hand (we did not then know it was going to be stopped by the Algiers authorities), could afford to wait no longer than the second day, and a Frenchman offered to guide us across on a new track to Tébessa through the mountains. I rate this as the coldest drive I have undertaken since the war began. For ten hours we sat in the open jeeps and those beautiful and barbarous mountains flung up at us everything from frozen rain to iced red mud. I never discovered exactly what route we did take—it gave the Germans a wide berth and at times we were running past gazelles in the valleys or looking over cliffs in the mountains. At length we got back, feeling that we had at least seen for ourselves that the junction of the two armies was about to take place and the last stage of the battle for Tunis was about to begin.

Chapter XI: Casablanca

WHEN we were at El Aroussa one day in January the war correspondents received a message recalling them by air to Algiers. Just that, nothing more, no explanations, no reason given as to why we should leave the front at a moment when things were going quite briskly.

I personally had not been included in the summons and so, with deep puzzlement, I watched the others go off until I was left almost alone on the front. For a day or two I moped around Thibar feeling a little like Cinderella and finally, on the third morning, I decided to set off by myself and find out what all the mystery was about.

Flying to Algiers at that time was a rare and wholly unrefreshing experience. The general technique was for the prospective passenger to drive round the front until he saw an aircraft. Then—if he found the pilot and the pilot was willing and the mud was not too deep for the take-off and the air clear of Messerschmitts—he flew to Algiers.

On this morning I must have pursued a dozen different aircraft down the Medjerda Valley and then at last some one gave me a clue about Gaston. Gaston was a French pilot who used to fly a decrepit twin-engined Bloch between Algiers and the front.

Sure enough, just when the white ground mists were lifting from the valley the Frenchman bumped down on a field and I hurried across to the farmhouse in which he had disappeared.

A woman who I can only think was the pilot's mother came to the door.

"Certainly not," she said with decision. "Gaston will not fly again to-day. He has not even had his lunch yet. Anyway I will on no account allow him to fly to Algiers in this weather."

The daughter was more sympathetic. She whispered to me in schoolgirl English that maybe Gaston would fly after all when he had had his lunch. He had several senior French officers as passengers. After an hour or two Gaston emerged, a rotund and cheerful little Frenchman, and he had lunched amply and well on the rich garlic and the good red wines of the valley. By this time there was quite a crowd of us waiting to get away—a couple of Spitfire pilots, a French naval officer and two full French colonels.

"Why certainly," said Gaston briskly. "Let 'em all come," and we bundled inside. It was what I can only describe as an austerity take-off. We shot straight across the potato patch with the wind, and by the time our speed was one hundred and forty miles an hour we had climbed roughly to the height of ten feet. If a haystack or a cow or a camel blocked our passage down the valley Gaston lightly flicked the machine up and over and down again. I will almost assert we could feel the hot breath of the camel on our faces as we went by. Gaston, feeling in need of company, turned round in his seat and conversed animatedly with the two French colonels as we slid in and out of the palm trees. The two Spitfire pilots were full of delighted admiration for this performance and they sat there loving every minute of it. It appeared that Messerschmitts were prowling about the valley that day and Gaston preferred to keep down low "out of trouble"—the phrase is his, not mine. Presently we had to climb over the Atlas Mountains and as we sailed through each pass the tips of the wings had ten, perhaps fifteen, feet to spare on either side. At Constantine something went wrong with one of the engines. When we landed a man came out with a hammer and a piece of wire and fixed it. Finally we arrived at Maison Blanche airfield outside Algiers which was always an aerial madhouse in those days and looked especially bad that afternoon. But Gaston neatly ran under the wings of an American Douglas transport, slid between two Hudsons that were taking off and finished in a line of Flying Fortresses, a remarkable exhibition.

Poor Gaston. He went on flying his old Bloch like a Paris taxi for many days after that but the Germans shot him down in the end.

I hitch-hiked into Algiers on a jeep and went into the tenth-rate pension the correspondents used as a base in the town. The place had certainly picked up while I had been away. Officers were rushing about in all directions. An American correspondent emerged with two movie stars in tow—Carole Landis and Martha Raye, I think they were. "To entertain the troops," the sergeant on the door explained. Major Flood of the Public Relations staff seemed to be the only lucid man in the place. "We have been trying to get you," he said. "You take off at five tomorrow morning." But where for and why? Nobody was very clear about anything.

Even on the wet and gloomy morning when we took off from Maison Blanche there was some doubt about whether we were headed for Gibraltar, Oran or Casablanca. Some twenty correspondents and officers, mostly American, had climbed into the aircraft. Edward Baudry, of the Canadian Broadcasting Commission, and I found places at the end of one of the hard aluminium beaches and we sat there uncomfortably for a while reading *La Dépêche Algierienne* and eating cold bully beef sandwiches. Above the mountains the wings iced over and the big machine suddenly turned and dived for the coast. It was warmer flying low over the sea. Except for a couple of lone tramp steamers the Mediterranean was very empty and it had a blue and solid calmness on that bright morning. Rapidly we swept by Spanish Ceuta, British Gibraltar and international Tangier and then we rounded the shoulder of Africa and turned south.

It was a strange flight in every way. Not only were we doubtful about our destination but we were wholly unable to understand the course the young American pilot was steering. He kept right over the beach where the long swell of the Atlantic was coming in, and the beach was part of neutral Spanish Morocco.

"What's that?" Baudry exclaimed suddenly and I saw the yellow puff of an ack-ack burst in the air behind us, then another and another. We had just passed by three ships and it was difficult to see whether the fire was coming from them or from the shore. At any rate we were being fired on. We did not know at that time that the pilot had not seen these bursts and he continued straight down the coast only a few hundred feet in the air. Every now and then a stray volley came up from the ground and passed harmlessly by.

We slid by two villages and reached the Spanish port of Larache and then things happened very quickly indeed. To our utter astonishment the machine began to descend and circle round the town. This, we thought, could mean only one thing; there was engine trouble and we had to make a forced landing, in neutral territory. We went lower and slower and I was trying to calculate what attitude the Spanish authorities would take—would they treat us as ordinary belligerent soldiers and intern us for the duration, or since we were civilian war correspondents, would they return us to our own territory? One could read the Spanish words on the shop fronts now but there was no one in the streets. And then a bright golden burst of tracer bullets broke through the floor of the cabin. Bullets were flying all round us and now we could clearly hear the rattle of the guns.

I stumbled along to the door of the cockpit and shouted to the pilot, but the noise was too great. As I sat down again another golden ball of fire ripped through the cabin and some one shouted, "Get down on the floor." Useless though it was it seemed to be the only thing to do. Instinctively men under fire will always try and touch something solid with their bodies. Baudry did not get down with the rest of us. With a slight sigh he leaned slowly over backward and his left temple had been blown away. Blood and grey brains were pumping out of the wound and spilling down his cheeks.

I struggled again through to the cockpit yelling for a first-aid kit. One of the American crew had blood coming out of a wound across his head and the second pilot was down on the floor bandaging him. After a minute's confused shouting I got an emergency bandage and went back to Baudry. With an effort we lifted him down on to a rough bed of parachutes. It was useless trying to force brandy through his lips for he was unconscious and we feared that the spirit would choke him. Somehow my friend D'Arcy Dawson got the bandage in place while I held up the dying man's head. There was a great deal of blood.

All this time the bullets and tracers had been coming up at us. Even now when we turned away with painful slowness to the open sea the fire kept following, a deadly rat-tat-tat against the fuselage. The Spanish had learned to shoot in their civil war. One felt so utterly helpless in that plane. Those who had nothing to do sprawled in a confused mass of arms, bodies and legs on the floor near the tail, some of them clutching parachute packs to their chests, some wedging themselves under the benches, others clasping their hands over their heads. A British sergeant found a water bottle and began washing Baudry's face. It was better to be doing something.

We got our bearings now and wirelessed ahead to the friendly French port of Lyautey and an ambulance was waiting there when we put down a few minutes later. From one of the crew I gathered that the pilot had heard nothing of the ack-ack fire all the way along the Spanish coast and had imagined Larache to be Lyautey. The radio operator had sent out recognition signals but had received only a confused jumble in response, then the bullets.

Feeling shaken and distressed we saw Baudry taken off. He was buried the next day. The rest of us continued to Casablanca.

Casablanca was in the midst of a witch's brew of rumour and

intrigue. We were bustled aboard army trucks to a hotel in the town and told to remove our badges from our uniforms.

A grave-faced American general told us that "the biggest assemblage of high dignities ever gathered together since the war began" was then in Casablanca. We were bound to secrecy and warned not even to talk in our bedrooms since the hotel had once been wired and enemy agents were everywhere.

Thus began one of the most portentous and hollow assignments I ever had. The whole thing was most aptly and pungently expressed a few days later when Osbert Lancaster came out in the London *Daily Express* with a sketch of Churchill disguised in Arab dress but smoking an unmistakable cigar. Every one in Casablanca who was not entirely indifferent knew that the Allies were having a great conference up there on the hill of Anfa a few miles outside Casablanca. Roosevelt and Churchill had already been there for a week or more and had been seen driving through the town.

For two days we killed time drinking in the pavement cafés, seeing the sights (which included General Noguès at Rabat), talking to the French sailors and looking at the terrible wreckage caused in the port by our naval bombardments. Two fifteen-inch shells had ripped holes in the battleship *Jean Bart* in which you could have built a two-storey cottage.

On the whole Casablanca had had a good war. There was plenty of food. The shops were still stocked with such things as Moroccan leather goods and cheap scent. There was no blackout and the town had only once been raided. Out on Anfa lived the millionaires who had made great wealth out of the traffic to German-occupied Europe. The town was still run by a core of Vichy adherents and military reactionaries. And the sun streamed down.

On the third morning we were taken through the guards and the barbed-wire entanglements at Anfa. We waited for an hour or two in an exquisite villa that was crammed with sculpture and painting and among other things contained a staggering library of pornographic books bound in the most richly tooled Moroccan leather. Then we walked up the road—about fifty of us—and met the President and the Prime Minister.

That little tableau still seems utterly unreal whenever I think of it. We squatted in a semicircle on the wet grass and Roosevelt, Churchill, Giraud and de Gaulle sat on four chairs facing us. Admirals, generals, diplomats and cabinet ministers perched among the flower beds and the orange trees behind. A brilliant sun flowed down and it caught the fixed bayonets of the American sentries who paced along the flower-hung garden walls around the villa. Aircraft kept passing back and forth overhead. Churchill, a little troubled by the sun, kept his dark hat cocked over his forehead; Roosevelt turned his tremendous smile on to the gathering and with a deal of hearty French tried to instil a little cheerfulness into the two stiff, ultra-formal French generals who sat on his left and right hand.

The photographers jumped and frisked through the flower beds as they struggled to get their angle shots and plenty of them. With Roosevelt's hands on their arms urging them upward the two lean grim Frenchmen rose at last, touched one another's fingers for a second and abruptly sat down. It was all rather embarrassing, like the first rehearsal of an amateur play.

The photographers cried that they had missed the shot and Giraud and de Gaulle painfully got to their feet again. This time a wan smile flickered about for a second under the kepis and the generals grasped hands for a little longer. Then they tramped solemnly away across the flower beds. *"Bon voyage,"* shouted the President. No. It was not a very successful little act. It lacked conviction. It certainly lacked showmanship.

Beckoned warmly by the President we clustered closely round the two remaining actors. The scene now was irresistibly like a Sunday School treat with the children gathered at the feet of their two schoolmistresses. For an hour the President and the Prime Minister discoursed and told us nothing. It had been a most successful conference—the best they had ever had. Every one was here—Marshall and Brooke, Eisenhower and Alexander, Tedder and Arnold, Lord Leathers and Harry Hopkins, Mountbatten, Cunningham, King and dozens of others. They had all agreed. We wanted unconditional surrender. Only Stalin and Chiang Kai-shek were missing. And so on. We scribbled and listened and enjoyed the jokes but no one quite liked to ask the real questions, the only questions:

What sort of an agreement had Giraud and de Gaulle made, if any?

Was the Mediterranean to be made our main theatre of war?

Where was the second front and was there even going to be one?

Had Franco been there and did we have a deal with Spain at one end of the Mediterranean and with Turkey at the other?

Naturally neither Churchill nor Roosevelt raised these points themselves but since they were the only points that mattered there was very little else that was worth talking about. The event of the conference itself was news but after that there was practically nothing that we could write.

Nevertheless we trooped into a large conference room and for the next four hours some twenty or thirty typewriters rattled at the rate of a thousand words per man per hour, a hideous din of noise. The censors sat beside us at a trestle table running through this flood of words until their heads were spinning. That night the messages were flown to London and released a day or two later when the President and the Prime Minister were safely on their way—one back to America and the other off to another of those still mysterious conferences in Turkey.

Yet vast decisions were taken at Casablanca. It marked a major turning point in the war. It settled once and for all a matter which I have tried to make a theme in the somewhat addled structure of this book—that America was to fight in Europe first and in the Pacific afterwards and that in return for this she was to have a fairly free hand in the reconstruction of France (to begin with) and seniority in the military direction of the war.

Again in his conversation with us, Churchill had repeated: "I am the President's ardent lieutenant." The mere presence of the President in Casablanca switched American interest to the Mediterranean.

Given this general understanding—that the Allies were to make their main immediate effort in the Mediterranean—by far the most important event of the conference had been the technical discussions between the naval, army and air staffs.

The plans that were vaguely formed at Washington in the previous July were now given practical and detailed direction. Predominantly as always it was a matter of supply—who should get the aircraft and the guns, where should the men go and how many? It was agreed that while an American—General Eisenhower—should retain the high command the key field positions should go to that seasoned British team which had come to the conference laden with their honours from the desert war—Cunningham for the navy, Tedder and Coningham for the air, Alexander and Montgomery for the army. General Anderson was also retained in his command of the First Army. To these were added a number of Americans of high rank— Smith as chief of staff to Eisenhower, Patton with the American Second Corps (which though technically under Anderson was to operate as a separate army), Spaatz with the strategic air force. And there were a number of others.

We were given no opportunity to talk to these commanders at Casablanca but it was evident that they, being practical men dealing with mechanical problems, had been able to reach a pretty wide field of agreement. Maybe the sunshine and the holiday surroundings had something to do with it. Maybe it was the fact that we could now plan offensives instead of defensives. At any rate there was a very noticeable amount of goodwill about, and the events since have shown that the Anglo-American leaders did genuinely get to know one another at

Casablanca and did achieve a means by which they could fall in with one another's plans. Indeed the whole story of North Africa indicates that at the top at least the American and British commanders did work well together. A great deal of the credit for this must go to General Eisenhower. It was only lower down in the scale of command, and usually through ignorance, that the differences occurred and are still occurring.

The Giraud-de Gaulle issue was treated as a minor affair at Casablanca, or at least of secondary importance to the decision that the war should be fought in Europe. Despite the "we are both determined to win the war" communiqué put out by the two generals under Allied direction, they reached no working agreement. How could they? Giraud in the eyes of the de Gaullists was a reactionary general who along with Gamelin, Noguès, Georges and Weygand was responsible for the collapse of the French army in 1940. These generals were of the school that believed that one must call up a vast number of infantrymen and form them into largely immobile lines of defence.

De Gaulle, in the eyes of the Saint Cyr group, was an upstart who preached much glib nonsense of small, highly mechanised armies and whose political views were dangerously left-wing to boot. And so that gauche and embarrassing handshake in the garden was as symbolic as any forced gesture of the kind could be. It said as clearly as might be—all right, we will try to combine as long as you, the British and Americans, are in control. But we Frenchmen must settle this in our own way. All that has happened since between the rival French groups has been an extension of this unhappy beginning.

Still for the most part Churchill and Roosevelt were justified in coming away from Casablanca well pleased with what they had done. Returning on our plane to the front we knew that every effort was now going to be put into the Tunisian war, and that the Germans were going to suffer such a blitz as they had not yet seen outside Russia.

Chapter XII: Kasserine

ROMMEL still had one last desperate chance of holding Tunisia until the autumn. Already he had fought a magnificent delaying action across the desert. Given another seven or eight months in Tunisia the Allied landing in Europe could be delayed until the following year and in the meantime Germany could launch one more attack upon Russia.

The best that the Axis could spare was now rushed across the narrow eighty-mile sea route from Sicily to Tunis and Bizerta. There were a number of new or almost new weapons, the Mark VI Tiger tank carrying an eighty-eight-millimetre gun, a leviathan of over sixty tons when loaded for battle, with four-inch armour and two-foot-wide tracks. It was also designed to travel under water, which was necessary since few bridges in Tunisia could stand that weight. There was the improved Focke-Wulf fighter and the Henschel tank-buster, an adaptation of the Russian and British fighters carrying cannon with armour-piercing shells. There was the multiple-barrelled mortar and a great quantity of land mines.

Much of this stuff was brought across in the newly designed Siebel ferries. These were vessels that looked like two barges lashed together each with an engine and capable of carrying tanks. They had tremendous ack-ack protection aboard.

Some of the best Axis regiments were then drawn on to bolster up the war-weary garrison in Tunisia. The Hermann Goering Regiments, the German parachutists, the Tenth Panzer Division, the Young Fascists—all these were sent and for the first time the Axis armies in Africa were predominantly German. In addition Rommel had the remnants of his Afrika Korps—the Fifteenth and Twenty-first Panzer Divisions, the Ninetieth Light German Infantry (one of the best formations in Africa) and various other units. Large numbers of Germans who had been wounded in Russia or elsewhere were also rushed across and hurriedly formed into battalions at the front. Many of the old Italian divisions like the Trieste and the Arriete were still in existence as well as odd groups like the San Marco Marines and the Bersagliere Regiments. All through the desert war Rommel had never had more than four German divisions and he had never been able to trust completely the Italians who formed the main part of his array. In fact he was never nominally commander in chief: an Italian held that position.

But now he had a very good army indeed numbering a quarter of a million men, nearly two-thirds of them German, and all in strong defensive positions.

One thing he lacked and that was serious—artillery. Throughout the fighting in Africa the Germans had pinned their faith to the eighty-eight-millimetre all-purpose gun, the Mark III and IV Tanks and the mortar, and aircraft. On his way from Alamein Rommel had succeeded in bringing back a great quantity of ack-ack guns but these could never fill the place of a solid phalanx of field guns worked by a well-trained team. Montgomery alone had five hundred guns and in tanks also greatly outnumbered the Axis. Moreover, Rommel could not hope to compete in the air now that the British Army air force was joined to the North African forces and Malta was engaged in its own private blitz in no small way. German bombers could no longer operate from the last remaining patch of Tunisia held by the Axis and it was becoming increasingly difficult for fighters.

Nevertheless there was a reasonable chance that a defence could be sustained until July or August, and Rommel with all his old resilience prepared to fight. His plan in February was a modern expression of one of the oldest maxims in war: "If you see a superior force approaching you prevent it from concentrating for a knock-out blow by engaging the enemy in piecemeal attacks along his line."

Somehow Rommel had to prevent the British, Americans and French from all getting to the starting line together. He had to throw our offensive off balance before it had begun. The story from February onwards is largely the story of the devices by which the Germans sought to hold off the final concentrated blow.

Looking down the line it was obvious that the American sector about Sbeitla was the weakest. Many of the troops there were not battle-trained and moreover they were spread out in a thin straggling line mostly through flat country. It was not a naturally defensive position and it had been maintained because from the first Eisenhower had resolved to fight an offensive action and make the Germans pay for every foot of ground they won back.

Towards the middle of February, then, Rommel gathered the best of his hard-bitten desert veterans and his new tanks from Germany. On the fourteenth he fell upon the weak American sector. The results were remarkable—probably even beyond Rommel's highest hopes. At Sbeitla and Sidi Bou Zid the American guns were overrun before they could be effectively brought to bear, the American tanks were forced back under a concentrated drive towards the Kasserine Pass and since the American infantry had no proper defensive positions on the open ground they were either taken prisoner or withdrawn. Faid fell in the north and Gafsa and Feriana with its two valuable forward airfields were abandoned in the south. Tébessa, the administrative centre for the whole of this region, was now in real danger despite its protective ring of hills.

For two years Rommel's immediate reaction to any local success had been "Exploit . . . exploit . . . exploit," and the same exultant order again went out to the Germans, who after many weary months of retreat were now experiencing the thrills of victory again. They overran the Kasserine Pass and splitting into two columns made for Thala in the north and Tébessa in the west.

For the Allies this was no longer a local menace—it threatened the whole Tunisian Line. The Tébessa area was the geographical point of junction for the Eighth and First armies and therefore—as Rommel foresaw—our weak point. If the Germans established themselves in Tébessa then they might prevent any junction taking place for months. Much worse results would follow the collapse of Thala for, from there, the Germans could advance straight to Le Kef. They would then be behind the main Allied line in Tunisia and might easily encircle it entirely by running through to the coast at Bône. Something like a hundred thousand Allied troops could be trapped.

General Alexander had just taken over the field command when this critical situation arose. He knew that General Montgomery would not be able to attack for a month. He knew that once through Thala there were no forces at all to prevent the Axis march on Le Kef.

You can judge the seriousness of the situation by the fact that Alexander himself left his headquarters near Constantine and ran along the line looking for some one—any one—to throw into the gap. He grabbed a battery of guns here, a battalion of infantry there, a fighter squadron in the other place and rushed them to the danger point. The Sixth Armoured Division plus the Guards—our finest fighting formation—were asked to bear the brunt of the shock. They hurried down in the night to join the regrouped American forces in the Kasserine area. Commanders addressed their staffs in the field on the eve of battle telling them frankly, "The situation is desperate. We are outnumbered and out of position and your chances of surviving are not very good. But you have got to stop the Germans."

On the very outskirts of Thala the decisive tank battle was fought. It was another of those gambler's moments in the campaign when one side, unknown to itself and its enemy, had reached the peak of its dynamic for the time being—and this time it was the Germans who had reached the end of their tether. Their forward tank units were smashed in pitched battle and before reinforcements could be brought up the Guards and the Americans rushed upon the field and turned the German thrust into a local but headlong retreat. The more slender enemy column directed against Tébessa now found its rear communications being cut and this budding shoot withered on its own stalk. The Allies were left in command of the battlefield and the Germans withdrew to Feriana and Gafsa. It had been a near thing.*

Alexander worked with frenzy during the ensuing lull, which he knew could not last long. He had found the First Army in an appalling mess. Units were mixed up all over the place and all the smooth cohesion that prevailed through long experience in the Eighth Army simply did not exist in this new army. Driblets of French units were under American command and isolated Americans were under British command; a battery of guns would be loaned out here and a squadron of tanks there. A bewildering and overlapping stream of orders was flowing out over the signal wires. The men were willing to fight all right but they were not being given a chance because of the confusion of the staff work at a high level.

* As a result of the Kasserine action and one or two subsequent mishaps an ignorant and malicious controversy sprang up in Europe about the fighting qualities of the American troops. They were said to be "green," which was true enough; but doubt was also thrown on American courage and skill and willingness to fight, which was grossly unfair. It was said that the Americans had boasted before they had seen real action. The truth of the matter was of course that the Americans were at the same stage as the British were a year after they had entered the war—slow, awkward and apt to be thrown off balance on experiencing hostile fire for the first time. There was just this difference—the Americans were much better armed than we were in 1940 and they learned much more quickly. The two temperaments will probably never be the same and it is possible that until the end of the war the British will excel in slogging heavy engagements while the Americans will best supply the speed and dash for the big flanking movements. The best statement on the matter I have seen appeared in a German military magazine we picked up in an enemy barracks in Tunis. It said: "The British soldier is still the best soldier in Africa. The Americans entered this war without any conception of its grimness and hardship. Once they learn this they will become very good soldiers indeed." General Terry Allen's First American Infantry Division provided a brilliant proof of this in Tunisia.

Alexander at once decided that the three very different groups under his command would fight best if they were kept separate and allowed to control themselves in their own way as far as possible. Accordingly he bunched his four British divisions in the north, his two French in the centre and his two American in the south. The Mareth section remained with Montgomery, who had contracted to get four good British divisions up to the line.

Rommel meanwhile was not idle. He struck again—this time in the far north among the rough hills of the Sedjenane sector. Wave after wave of Germans flung themselves on the British infantry and again the enemy achieved a partial break-through, not so dangerous as the Kasserine thrust but still enough to disrupt and delay our concentration in the north. Having achieved this object and having got as far as he could (the key town of Béja almost fell) Rommel suddenly switched to the south for another lightning blow.

He wanted now to throw Montgomery's coming offensive out of gear. On March eighth the German tanks raced forward across the hard flat ground and to this day there is no satisfactory explanation of why such a master in the handling of tanks as Rommel could have attacked in this way. Perhaps he was misinformed about the number and position of the British guns. Perhaps he was over-elated with his two previous successes and he had forgotten how experienced the Eighth Army was. At any rate, he deliberately broke his own strict rule, which we had learned from him at such cost—never attack fixed positions with tanks.

The British tanks were scarcely used at all that day. A trap was laid for the Germans. When the Axis tanks approached they saw British gunners jumping up from their trenches and running away from their guns. To the German tank commanders this was irresistible and they charged ahead—straight into the real British gun line that was waiting for them. The carnage was horrible. Fifty German tanks were blown up in their tracks and the enfeebled remnants drew off in disorder. We lost no tanks and in all about two hundred casualties. The gun line had not budged an inch. Rommel's third attempt to break up the Allied concentration had failed with far greater losses than he was able to sustain. This action, which could not be assessed at its true value at the time, was, I believe, the turning point of the Tunisian campaign. The Germans lost the offensive on that day and they never again recovered it. It is not too much to say that the Battle of Mareth was won in this preliminary tank action and from Mareth flowed all the rest.

Rommel saw what had happened. He gave up soon afterwards. He surrendered his command and left Africa for good. To von Arnim fell the grisly and thankless job of making a Stalingrad on the Mediterranean.

But still the German high command would not give up. They continued to pour troops and weapons into Tunisia and with great skill they devised a new method of defence, which is ideal for hill country and which the Allies must expect to find from now on in Europe. This is the minefield-mortar-gun combination. Every valley was strung with mine fields. On the heights dominating the valleys machine guns and anti-tank guns were sighted so that they covered every acre of the ground in which the land mines were laid. The gunners did not have to aim their guns—the guns were already aimed, and all the gunner had to do was to stay below ground and keep loading and pulling the trigger. (This is in theory; of course there were adaptations in practice.) The mortars and anti-tank gunners were also dug into weapon pits practically invulnerable from the air or shelling, and were free to play their fire where it was most needed. The whole system was most closely interlocked and carried to great depth.

One could not attack such positions with tanks. The sappers had to go forward first and pull up the mines. The infantry had to wipe out the sighted guns. The air forces had to soften up the whole sector. Then, and not until then, could the Allies hope to push their tanks through the gaps into the flat country beyond where they had room to play about. We had overwhelming superiority in tanks but they simply could not be brought to bear in the high passes. Not until we broke through at Mareth, at Gabès, at Sbeitla, at Fondouk, at Medjez el Bab and in the north could the armour operate.

All through the first weeks of March von Arnim concentrated on strengthening the passes with more and more mines. But the sands were running out quickly now. The rains were stopping and especially in the south the ground was drying. As the wheat turned from green to yellow and the first mowers were sent into the fields the Allies struck.

PART THREE

The Assault

Chapter XIII: El Guettar

ALEXANDER'S plan was quite obvious to the Germans because it was largely conditioned by the terrain. He conceived German Tunisia as a cylinder with the First Army forming one wall from Tabarka to Gafsa, and the sea as the other wall from Tunis to Gabès. The Eighth Army was to act as a piston pushing up from the bottom. This plan underwent half a dozen modifications with the changing fortunes of the battle and was eventually abandoned altogether; but that was how the High Command looked at the situation in the middle of March when they were at last ready to move.

I had flown home to England for a few days in a Flying Fortress and on returning to North Africa I continued straight to Tébessa, where the British and American correspondents had congregated for the opening moves of the coming offensive. The Americans with three divisions under General Patton were to strike the first blow. They were to march back into the positions they had lost in the Kasserine action and establish themselves on three key passes leading to the sea—Fondouk, Maknassy and Gafsa. When they had drawn off some of the German units massed in the south the piston would start to shove upward; Montgomery would attack. Then if the Eighth Army was successful in putting the Germans to flight the Americans would endeavour to sally out of their three passes and nip off the retreating enemy.

It was still sharply cold and wet at Tébessa as I drove through the hill forests to see the Americans on the eve of the advance. In the drizzling rain little groups of infantrymen were drawn up to receive their last instructions. They were hardly more than boys, most of them, wonderfully tall and proportioned and looking very forbidding under their Nazi-like helmets. Unlike the British battle dress and equipment, which tends to hold a man stiffly upright, these boys were in a uniform which gave them plenty of free movement. The short and formless weatherproof jacket was scarcely a garment of beauty but it allowed the men to walk in the easy stooping way to which they were accustomed.

Most of the American stuff was first-class, and even as good or better than the German. Their mess tins, water bottles, rubber-soled boots, woollen underclothes, shirts and windbreakers were all superior to the British equivalents and their uniforms in general were made of finer stuff. The Garand rifle and the officer's carbine were already regarded by many veterans as the best small-arms on the front. As for their heavier equipment, it is doubtful if any army went to war so well supplied. The only general criticism might have been that there was too much of it. Every other truck had a machine gun mounted on its cabin. The self-propelling guns and the Long Tom rifles were some of the heaviest artillery along the whole front. The Diesel Sherman was certainly the best tank of its class. The jeeps at the other end of the scale were unmatched and the Germans loved to capture them for their own use, just as we had loved to get hold of a *Volkswaggon*. The weapons' carriers and the command vehicles were all brand new, as were the signalling sets, the bulldozers for road-mending and the electrical workshops. It was the volume of this stuff, the intensity of the firepower that was so impressive. Possibly the troops could have done with a better heavy machine gun and an improved mortar, but in general there was no question that they were the best-equipped Allied army at the front.

By European army standards the American rations were lavish to the point of extravagance—vast quantities of tinned meats, fruits and vegetables. In any American mess you could be sure of getting an excellent hot meat and vegetable stew, a plate of fruit, white bread and a cup of coffee. Things like cigarettes, chewing gum and tooth paste were handed out in a way that made the British soldiers gape. The doughboy was always generous in sharing his good things. As a British war correspondent I personally was given immediate hospitality wherever I went and such things as maps and plans were discussed with me without hesitation.

Lieutenant General Patton selected his best-trained infantry division—the First—to advance on Gafsa. Early in the morning the division surged forward, an avalanche of vehicles bumping over the flat brown country. They had swept through Feriana without opposition and were already on the outskirts of Gafsa oasis by the time my party caught up with the forward elements about midday.

General Patton, a large and gregarious man with a fine weather-beaten face, a pearl-handled revolver strapped to his side, stood on a bare rock and surveyed the village of Gafsa a little uneasily. There was no answering gunfire from the enemy. He decided to go forward at once.

"Go down that track until you get blown up," he said to his ADC, "and then come back and report." The ADC set off in his jeep and soon we were all trundling after him. With every minute it became clearer that the enemy had evacuated Gafsa without a fight. We were travelling on a side track and those of us who were land-mine conscious kept scrupulously in line. One signalling waggon eager to get ahead sheered off into the scrub beside us and by some miracle continued for a couple of hundred yards through a German mine field before it was blown up. We picked our way back off the track to the main road and skirting the big craters the Germans had left behind drove into the township in the early afternoon.

Gafsa, after being occupied by three different armies, was still intact, still a pleasant strip of palm-trees and flowering gardens beside a watercourse. About fifteen miles further east towards the coast is another smaller oasis, El Guettar. At El Guettar two razor-backed lines of hills come down to the main road and run parallel with it and that is where the enemy had dug in. They flung their mortar-machine gun-mine field combination across the valley and prepared to defend. The Gafsa advance came to an abrupt halt.

Meanwhile another American column went up over vile sandy tracks towards Maknassy. There was no real opposition anywhere but the progress was disappointingly slow. The Americans had not quite got into their stride yet and there were many delays along the route. Following along in the cavalcade of vehicles I noticed that whenever an aircraft was sighted in the sky a whistle was blown at the head of each convoy, the vehicles stopped and the troops scattered across the fields. Since the whistles were frequently blown even for single aircraft and before any one could determine whether they were friendly or hostile, many hours were wasted every day.

Most of the vehicles were equipped with heavy machine guns and the men would have felt very much better firing them than they did taking cover among the wildflowers. But at this stage the order to shoot was not given.

We spent hours on that abominable track digging our station waggon out of bogs and sanddrifts, but in the end we managed to get into Maknassy a few hours after it had fallen. Again the enemy had retreated to the hills behind the town and were shooting down on the valley from their safe positions. The Luftwaffe was very active that day. Six times we jumped for cover among the cactus hedges while the Stukas churned up the road in front or behind us. An American half-tracked vehicle caught fire and began shooting out its ammunition all over the fields. Further back at Sened a series of ragged dog-fights was going on in the sky. One of the Germans dived quite unexpectedly out of a strip of low cloud and permitted himself the extravagance of aiming a bomb at my party's one solitary vehicle then travelling on the road. It was, as far as I know, the only bomb which has been aimed at me personally since the war began. We had changed over to a jeep and by then we were much practised in taking cover. By a system of spontaneous levitation I remember rising directly and without effort into the air, and then travelling sideways until I reached the inevitable cactus hedge. The bomb, only a small one, dropped far behind.

We ran on back to Gafsa where we had established ourselves in a comfortable Arab house. It even possessed a wood-burning bath heater which provided the only hot baths we were going to get for the next two months. Since luxuries were to be had in that pleasant place I hired, in the absence of a batman, a bat-woman. Hyah was without glamour. She was an aged and hideous Arab crone who swept the floors and handled the laundry.

It was a strange, rather pleasant life at Gafsa. Each day we drove up to the hills and looked down on the fighting. Each night while we wrote our messages by candlelight German air-craft swooped back and forth across the oasis dropping para-chute flares. Anti-personnel bombs fell through the blinding yellow light. These bombs looked like myriads of big brightly coloured butterflies coming down. They were only the size of a small jam tin and as each one left its container two metal wings painted yellow began to whirl around. When the wings had made a certain number of revolutions the detonator was released so that sometimes the bomb would explode when it hit the ground and sometimes it would lie about until a vehicle ran over it or a man kicked it with his foot.

The doughboys at the front were finding the enemy defence in the high rocks a very tough proposition indeed. Each ma-chine gun had to be surrounded and rushed before it could be silenced and although the American barrage became fiercer and fiercer it was not possible to blow the Germans out of the caves and cliffs.

Then on March twenty-third the Germans forced a crisis. They switched the Tenth Panzer Division west and charged straight at El Guettar. Over a hundred tanks ran along the green floor of the valley directly at the American positions and under the cover of a concentrated air and artillery bombardment.

It requires great nerve and training for anti-tank gunners to meet a tank charge. You must hold your fire until as a rule you are yourself being shelled. You must select your targets one by one and not be disturbed by the fact that some of the enemy may get through. General Allen's gunners fought the Mark IV tanks down to a distance of several hundred yards—indeed, some of the enemy tanks were already abreast and slightly behind the American positions. Then the Germans broke. More than half of them turned back and groped for the paths through their own mine fields. The rest—about forty—were either smashed with direct hits or damaged, and left burning on the battlefield. It was as rounded and complete a victory as you could well hope for; and it was all that Montgomery needed. The Tenth Panzers had been drawn off. The following day the Eighth Army fell upon the Mareth Line.

Again Montgomery attacked by night. Again he began with an intense artillery barrage. Again he struck first with a direct right-handed blow and then with a left-handed flanking move. And again the air force was very closely interlocked with the advancing troops.

Rommel had already surrendered Médenine and the outlying defences without much argument some weeks before. He had established his real defence on the Wadi Zigzaou, a formidable rift in the land with very steep sides and still treacherous with winter mud.

The battle did not go well. The British Fiftieth Division crossed the wadi but only with great difficulty—in places the men were clambering over one another's shoulders to reach the opposite side. A slender bridgehead was made but when morning came the anti-tank guns had still not been got across. When the inevitable German counter-attack came in the British infantry were hopelessly exposed and Panzer tanks charged right in among their positions. In some confusion the division was withdrawn across the wadi again.

This left the left-hand flanking column in an unhappy position. It was again the New Zealanders who had gone round with a brigade of tanks and they had reached their objective— El Hamma—behind the enemy main line. Rommel now wheeled his heavy units on to El Hamma and General Montgomery was obliged to think very quickly indeed. Those who had grown to believe that the General was incapable of anything more than his standard right-left plan now saw something new put into effect and at speed and in a crisis.

A new sector was opened between the coast and the New Zealanders. Rommel was forced then to withhold some of his strength from the New Zealanders and deal with this new threat in the centre. Immediately he saw the Germans splitting up Montgomery ordered the New Zealanders into attack and an armoured division was sent to support them. Again the pressure was applied at the coast and by March twenty-seventh it was all over. The Eighth Army rode into the hamlet of Gabès taking many thousands of Italian infantry who had again been left behind while the Germans retired to their second position on the Wadi Akarit a few miles further north. It was a battle that had begun badly and might have bogged down indefinitely but for the quick change-over in the British plans halfway through.

In the meantime the rest of Alexander's plan was not going according to programme. The Americans were repulsed from Fondouk, the most northerly of the passes. At Maknassy they were unable to make headway towards the coast. And at El Guettar the Germans and Italians were holding more strongly than ever. It was decided then to halt the Fondouk and Maknassy thrusts and concentrate on El Guettar. The American armour was wheeled south and the American Ninth Infantry Division was also ordered to go to the assistance of the First in the El Guettar hills. In the pattern that was now becoming accepted the infantry were to mop up the hills on either side

of the valley while the tanks broke straight through along the
floor of the valley on the Gafsa-Gabès road. It was hoped that
the tanks would make the seventy-mile run down to the coast
and join hands with the Eighth Army at Gabès.

My party had found an artillery spotting post right in the
centre of the El Guettar valley and it commanded the most
perfect view of a battlefield I have had before or since. The
tanks, we knew, were to attack at noon and we got on to our
grandstand a couple of hours before hand.

Sprawling there on the ridge in the sunshine we looked right
down into the enemy positions. In front lay the broad green
plain dotted with the wrecks of the previous week's tank battle.
On either side desultory machine-gunning sounded from the
hills. The valley took a turn to the north beyond El Guettar so
that the plain in front of us appeared to finish in another line of
hills. These last were being shelled with rising intensity.

I crouched in a dugout with one of the artillery commanders
while he gave his orders into the telephone to the American
Long Toms a mile or two behind us. It all seemed so easy; just
a few figures spoken into the telephone, then the air above us
was full of tearing express trains and we grabbed our glasses
to watch the hits. They fell among the high brown rocks first
with a quick yellow flash, then with a snow-white column of
smoke that streamed steadily upward until it was caught by the
cross-wind on the mountain crest and billowed out into grey
and formless cloud. Sometimes when the smoke cleared you
could see the little figures of Germans or Italians running to
better cover. They were only a mile or two away but this was
killing by remote control, without the maddening stimulus of
hand-to-hand fighting. One could carefully assess the targets
and take aim with the same unemotional calmness of a sportsman
shooting grouse on the moors. Almost, not quite. In the intervals
of our firing the enemy fired back and we ducked into our
dugout and hugged the rock.

There was one battery of American medium guns slightly

ahead of us on the plain and they were getting the worst of it. Again and again the German spotters sitting in the hills around us got the range and those four guns and their crews would disappear in immense shellbursts.

Watching from the ridge we would see first one gun then another emerge unharmed from the smoke and the gunners running from their pits would slap the breeches back and take their revenge.

All morning this artillery duel went on with the American barrage growing gradually louder and more persistent as more and more guns were brought in, just as an orchestra conductor will draw in more instruments for his crescendo. My head ached with the noise and the dust and the sight of the leaping smoke and flame in the hills.

It was getting very near midday. Four little Stuart recon-naissance tanks—the ones we used to call Honeys in the desert—came casually down the road from our rear positions and moved past my hilltop towards the enemy.

The artillery major picked up his telephone. "There are four tanks going out now," he said to the commander of his battery. "Get Bill to run out after them in a jeep. He might find some more targets for us."

Presently the jeep came buzzing at speed down the road in the wake of the tanks, three men aboard it.

"Good man, Bill," said the major. "He'll find something."

The Germans now had spotted the tanks and shellbursts began groping towards them making craters among the wildflowers in the plain. Then the enemy saw the jeep scuttling up the road. The first German shell was a hundred yards short, the second fifty yards long. There was a third explosion and the jeep dis-appeared entirely in erupting dust and fumes. Through the rolling smoke two men came running, and they flopped into a ditch as three more eighty-eight-millimetre shells, whining shrilly, slammed down about them. One dark figure lay prone beside the jeep and this was Bill. As the firing eased off the men ran back to him but Bill was already dead.

A dozen such things were happening around us all the time but this little tragedy was so personal and so swift that I separated it in my mind from the rest of the battle and all that day in the dugout we felt guilty for the boy's death.

But there was not much time to reflect. While an ambulance ran out to collect the dead man all the valleys behind us began to rumble and clatter with heavy machinery on the move. From a hundred wadies and ditches tanks began to debouch into the centre of the valley, first in half-dozens, then in dozens and scores. Some, spaced fifty yards apart, headed up the main road and they roared and spluttered and grunted as they lurched past our hiding place and out into the fields beyond. Others turned at once into the pastures to our right. As they took up formation, each tank with a column of dust streaming out behind, it was as though one were looking at a battle fleet steaming into action over a green flat sea, a wonderful sight. Beyond us, all the tanks moved forward together on a mile-wide front and perhaps a mile deep and they made an exact and changing pattern. I looked at my watch and had to brush the fine dust from the glass. It was just twelve o'clock.

Watching from the heights the German spotters caught sight of this frightening array that was bearing down on them at a steady fifteen miles an hour. As they went forward, infantrymen, unseen before, rose out of the long grass and for a little kept pace with the tanks. Long lines of dark figures were rising up everywhere from the plain and creeping towards the enemy. Overhead half a dozen Messerschmitts skidded back and forth over the cavalcade for a moment, little bright shafts of yellow spitting from their wings; but the tanks and the men kept on. A last flight of American bombers swooped upon the end of the valley. One after another the leading tanks topped the horizon and stood briefly outlined against the enemy hills beyond.

"Cease fire," said the artillery major into the telephone. The tanks were in the target area; they had made contact with the enemy.

This was the point in every tank battle I had seen where everything vanished into smoke and noise and whirling dust. In Egypt and Libya no onlooker really knew what was going on because the churned-up sand obliterated the desert. But here in the green wheat it was different. The whole scene was played out in fascinating and terrible detail.

For some reason I concentrated my eyes on the tanks that were fighting on the main road. They had dodged round half a dozen wrecked trucks and were following a line of telegraph poles. Just about a mile away from me they came dead in the line of the enemy anti-tank barrage. You could see the enemy gun positions quite clearly from the flashes that leaped out of the rocks; see where the shells hit around the tanks; and see the tanks belch back at them with answering salvoes. As each tank touched the horizon its gun flared out, a bright flame of yellow fringed with black coming out of a black steel hulk. The third leading tank was hit first. I saw the shell hit the turret and a vivid flame flowered out. The tank went on firing. Then again another hit on the tank's portside. It stopped dead but still its guns kept firing. There were shells now landing every few seconds and the fire had taken hold in the turret. A vast jet-black roll of smoke poured upward and at its base the smoke was red. The tank stopped firing. Simultaneously a new and wider sort of flame erupted from among the enemy guns and another of our tanks was hit and then another. The two sides were only three or four hundred yards apart and all along the road between me and the action little puffs of high explosive were making craters and jagged holes in the macadam. Away on the right flank we were not doing so well. The infantry had dropped out of sight again and a squadron of Shermans was shuttling back and forth in front of a continuous curtain of mortar fire. They probed and turned and manoeuvred but every time they came up to a low brown ridge the mortar shells poured down and there was nothing between the tanks and the enemy but impenetrable bursting shrapnel. In the centre it was better. Our main squadron had almost reached the hills, where apparently a dozen Italian tanks had been dug into pits and were being used as artillery. One after another the enemy gun flashes ceased and where there was flame before now only acrid smoke rose up. Shifting my glass back to the road I saw that the first tank was now completely alight and two others were smoking near by. But other Shermans had passed through and were now fighting out of sight. A steady procession of vehicles raced up the road carrying ammunition. Ambulances began to stream back from the other direction. Over everything sounded the same quick staccato coughing of the guns. And now in the full light of the afternoon the sun was misted over by the battle cloud and the battle itself seemed to be illuminated with its own gun flashes and the flames of the burning vehicles that were running with molten white-hot steel.

For two hours it went on and then, imperceptibly at first, one gun after another fell silent. The fields in front of me began flooding with hundreds of vehicles that were spreading out to take over the newly won ground. A lorry-load of Italian prisoners came back, followed by six ambulances. The dust lifted a little and a shaft of sunlight came through again, turning the hollow in the hills into purple and the dark rocks into yellow. A heavy and unnatural silence began. There was still the noise of machine-gunning, still an occasional explosion. But compared with the uproar that had filled the valley for the past two hours this was silence.

I got into a jeep and went forward down the road. There was a pungent smell, a mixture of burnt oil and steel and clothing and cordite, welling out of the burning vehicles. Odd little things—a toothbrush, a table knife, a charred packet of cigarettes—were scattered over the ground in a jumble of telegraph wires and things too blackened and burnt to be recognised. The burning tanks were still too hot to approach and occasionally a shell came tearing out of the flaming débris. American soldiers were turning over broken bits of Italian weapons with their boots. A major general tore by in a jeep. Two signallers carefully paid out their wire round a crater where a dead man was lying and walked on, chewing gum. A dud shell was upended grotesquely in a pool of sand.

Two or three aircraft went by but scarcely any one bothered to look up. A German newspaper, the *Oasis*, lay on the road beside a pile of empty shell-cases. This was the most forward gun position and now the enemy had gone back five thousand, perhaps six thousand yards. He had broken off the battle and we were not yet able to follow up. There was a tugging weariness over the valley, a subsiding nervous tension. It was oppressive. As the light failed and the shooting died entirely away the fires on the battlefield stood out more clearly. Everywhere the front-line troops were digging fresh trenches and rolling the guns into pits and hollows in the blackened wheat. As we drove back in the evening the rain started again. It extinguished the fires. It left the battlefield cold, and very quiet.

The tanks did not get through to Gabès that day. In the night fresh opposition mounted up before them and for the time being the U.S. armoured thrust was abandoned.

Still it had done its main job by reducing the pressure on Montgomery.

Chapter XIV: Kairouan

IT WAS now the first week in April and Alexander judged that he could safely go ahead with the second leg of his plan—to make the western wall of the cylinder contract a little more and get the piston to shove again from the bottom.

Our attempt to nip off the bottom section of the cylinder by driving down the Gabès road from Gafsa had apparently been halted indefinitely but that did not spoil the general plan. The line was getting stronger every day and indeed we had held off a renewed assault on the Sedjenane position and even captured new ground there. The fighting now was to spread along the whole front. This second stage required that we should clean up a line of hills along the northern side of the Medjerda Valley running from Oued Zarga to Longstop. Simultaneously Montgomery should attack on the Wadi Akarit just north of Gabès. Then we would strike again at Fondouk and attempt to cut off the enemy routed by Montgomery in the Akarit battle.

The First Army's best and most experienced infantry division —the Seventy-Eighth—was chosen to do the job in the Medjerda Valley with the support of about a hundred and twenty-five Churchill tanks and some five hundred guns. This time instead of attacking down the valley we were going to fight across it. Since we held the southern line of hills and the Germans the northern line it would be necessary for our infantry and tanks to surge across the open floor of the valley and fight their way up the slopes on the opposite side. Four A.M. April seventh was given as zero hour.

It was a very still night before the battle, no wind, no sound of firing. We drove almost to Medjez el Bab looking for a vantage point and then ran across a major in charge of the ack-ack and anti-tank guns.

"Come on," he said, "the Brigadier's picked the best look-out on the whole line. I'll lead you up there."

It was a rugged hollow in the hills too rough for farming, and it overlooked the whole length of the valley. We got down into our sleeping-bags early and it was not yet two A.M. when I was wakened by a noise. Not fifty yards away British infantry were filing down to their assault positions just over the brow of the hill. They moved with expert quietness, a long broken line of upright silhouettes winding in and out of the gorse. and there was just the soft rhythmical sound of their boots on the earthen goat track. No one smoked. No one talked. Every so often as they filed by my bed an officer would say, "Companee . . . halt," and the moving shadows stopped dead and melted in the surrounding darkness. Then, "Companee . . . forward," and the silhouettes broke away from the shadow again and vanished over the hill. For an hour they filed past.

Feeling too restless and expectant to sleep we got up into the bitter, stinging cold and clambered to the crest of the hill. The valley below was in purple darkness. Far over to the right the RAF was bombing Tunis and the searchlights or the bomb explosions—we could not tell which—made flickering lights against the clouds. There was no moon.

At ten minutes to four a battery of twenty-five-pounders, some twenty miles away to the west, opened fire; then some one nearer at hand opened up. A clump of bushes a few hundred feet directly below us suddenly lit with flashes and in the brief purplish light we could see the guns jumping with the recoil under the camouflage nets.

"They are a little earlier than I thought," said the major. "They are supposed to have ten minutes' slow, then ten minutes' intense firing. The mediums will come in, in a minute."

They came in with a roar and now the firing made a deep, measured beat right along the valley, a strange play of noise on light, a spectacle that you could not analyse because you could not see where the shells were landing and you had no notion of what was being hit in the darkness. Once or twice there was a steady flare in the distance that indicated something had been hit, a petrol dump perhaps; perhaps a German lorry. There was no sign of answering fire.

A few minutes after four the barrage abruptly broadened and redoubled. More guns came in, hundreds of them. Up to this moment the guns had made a series of flashes that danced along the foothills but now it was almost a continuous band of light that kept renewing itself and seemed to be constantly growing brighter. The noise of single explosions blended into one continuous roar. Hundreds of shells were tearing through the air together and I remember thinking then, "No one can suffer this barrage and still fight."

The first grey shafts of the morning came from over Tunis. As this light steadily increased, the noise of the guns fell away, battery by battery, and in its place the dark valley below was filled with the noise of tanks. The attack had started. The infantry were due on their first objectives at dawn.

When at last the morning came it was an astonishing thing to look down and see that the valley was exactly the same. The farmhouses still stood. The rows of trees were unaltered. The wheat fields still spread out in a neat pattern and there were even Arabs at work about the homesteads. It was in the foothills beyond that the action lay. Already the infantry had rushed the first enemy outposts and we heard the steady rattle of the machine guns. One or two fires had started. In the centre, three lines of soldiers were creeping up to a farmhouse and we saw the men leap to their feet and rush forward over the last hundred yards. They emerged out the other side a moment later, running hard among the outbuildings, in pursuit of escaping Germans. The Churchills on the right were performing staggering feats of hill-climbing. One group appeared to be almost upended in a steep wadi. Every time the leading tank shoved its nose over the top a storm of mortar shells came down and now the tanks were settling into hull-down positions and firing back. Away to the left a line of British trucks was moving slowly across the wheat field when the German gunners got on to them. A squadron of tanks, moving like prehistoric lizards, came crawling back to silence this fire, and presently it stopped and the trucks moved on.

The Luftwaffe, whose efforts had been gradually growing weaker and weaker over the past few weeks (the dive bomber had almost disappeared) made a spasmodic effort to delay the attack. I remember this clearly because of a very ordinary but graphic little incident that happened to my party as we were driving from one part of the front to another. We had run back towards Testour in our station waggon and I think it was Philip Jordan who was keeping watch through the roof—a job we took in turns for about half an hour at a time. The car had run down into a partly wooded valley beside a Bofors anti-aircraft gun when Philip shouted something, and as he shouted pale yellow tracer bullets began to skid down the road on either side of us. The driver automatically jammed his foot down and grabbed the hand-brake. The car skidded to a standstill and we tumbled out. The German aircraft, a Messerschmitt with silver wings, was only fifteen or twenty feet above our heads and as it roared on down the road the Bofors gun fired into its belly. For half a minute the machine continued straight onwards. It rose slightly, executed a graceful half-circle in the sky, and then slithered down to a belly landing among the wildflowers.

We jumped back into the car and drove a couple of miles to the river where we judged the plane had fallen. From many directions troops who had seen the incident were running through the shoulder-high wheat, which was dotted with red poppies and sweet mustard and tall white lilies. In a few minutes we found the Messerschmitt. It had landed practically unharmed on the soft wheat but the pilot had vanished. I clambered into the cockpit and felt the joy stick and the trigger. It was still warm from the pilot's hand, still warm from the grip with which he had fired his guns at us along the road, a minute or two before.

On the bank of the river an Arab peasant was gesticulating and shouting and every one ran across to the direction in which he was pointing. The pilot was hiding in a dung heap under a lip in the bank and he made no effort to resist. He lay there until the pursuers found him and then he got up slowly with his hands above his head and walked back towards his machine with a pistol pressed in his back.

He was a strikingly good-looking boy, not more than twenty-three or -four, with fair hair and clear blue eyes. He wore flying boots and overalls but no cap. The soldiers searched him and took from his pockets his revolver and his belt of bullets and a leather wallet. As they searched the German fumbled for a cigarette and made motions for some one to light it for him. He did this mechanically and without attempting to speak, and the hand which held the cigarette was shaking badly. Some one lit the cigarette and for some reason I could not understand the man with the pistol motioned the pilot to a place in the wheat about twenty yards from the fallen plane. Then quite accidentally every one stepped back from the pilot at the same time and he was left alone standing in the wildflowers.

You could see very clearly what he was thinking. He was thinking, "They are going to shoot me now. This is the end. The one with the pistol will fire at my body." He stiffened and the hand holding the cigarette was tensed and shivering. Little globes of sweat came out in a line on his forehead and he looked straight ahead.

All this took only a moment and then, in the same involuntary way, the British troops moved towards him again and motioned him to march with them back towards the road.

The pilot did not comprehend for a moment. Then he relaxed and drew deeply on his cigarette and it was again quite clear that he was saying to himself in a spasm of half-understood relief, "It's all right. They are not going to shoot me." Then we all walked back to the road. We felt pleased that the matter had ended so well and that punishment had come so quickly to the enemy who had fired at us on the road; but this actual physical contact with the pilot, his shock and his fear, suddenly made one conscious that we were fighting human beings and not just machines and hilltops and guns. Nearly always the battle to us was a mechanical thing and the enemy a sort of abstract evil in the distance. But now, having captured a human being from that dark continent which was the enemy's line, one wanted to talk to the pilot and argue with him and tell him he was wrong.

As it was, we simply drove on again through the hills and the continuing gunfire again brought the war into focus as a thing of maps and calibres and tactics.

In this way then the First Army's attack went in along the Medjerda Valley on the morning of April seventh. It was a successful attack inasmuch as all the objectives set for that day were won. But this was only the beginning. For days afterward that bitter hill skirmishing went on. Yard by yard the infantry fought their way steadily upwards, through mine fields, taking machine guns at the bayonet point, rushing tiny upland villages with hand grenades, always going up and up until at last they stood on the crests. A whole division of men—fifteen thousand— was swallowed up in those hills, and they struggled on desperately among the crags and boulders, often without food or water or even ammunition. There was nothing wildly spectacular about it—no towns to take, no massed formations in pitched battle, no great hosts of prisoners. It was just a painful slogging fight that had to be fought before we could get at the last great obstacle on the way to Tunis—Longstop Hill. It was the slow contracting of the cylinder.

Montgomery meanwhile went crashing in for his last great battle, in the south at Wadi Akarit. This time he charged head-on with his Highland Division, the Indians and the Fiftieth. The Eighth Army was a wonderful machine when it was geared

up to fight. It went forward with a terrible momentum and
in a wonderfully adjusted rhythm—first the bombers, then the
guns, then the infantry, then the tanks. Six gaps were blasted
in the enemy line along the Wadi Akarit and then the First
Armoured Division and the New Zealanders poured through
for the kill. Once again the German line broke under the stroke
of the piston. For one hundred and fifty miles along the coast
north of Akarit von Arnim had no defensive position. It was
every man for himself now, in the enemy camp. If you were
lucky enough to possess a truck you jumped aboard with your
pals and lit out for the north with all the speed you could make.
The RAF fell on that retreat but it was too great to smash
entirely. A vast crocodile of German vehicles filed northwards
day and night. It ran into Sfax and out again. It streamed into
Sousse and still flowed northwards.

On April eighth Alexander made a bid to cut off that fugi-
tive German crocodile. He switched his Sixth Armoured Division (which had just re-equipped with Sherman tanks) and
some of his finest infantry, the Guards and the Hampshires,
into the Fondouk sector for a combined operation with the
French and the Americans. The proposition was the standard
Tunisian thing—the French and the British were to take the
village of Pichon and the high ground on the left, the Americans
were to take the high ground on the right and the British
armour was to drive up the middle straight at Fondouk. Once
through Fondouk the army would enter a broad, cultivated
plain where the tanks could manoeuvre. Once in the plain the
key town of Kairouan would fall and the First Army could
rush across to the coast.

It was strange country, this valley—half-dead and brown, a
patchwork of gaunt red rocks and cactus and broad wheatlands.
There was some quality in the dust, its fineness possibly, that
made it abominable. Running down to the starting line with
the armour was a hot and sweaty business. The lads in the tanks
were full of excitement over their new toys. They had also

managed to get a higher percentage of high-explosive shells in place of armour-piercing shells. For some time the tanks had been finding that it was not enemy tanks they had to deal with but enemy guns. High-explosive and wide-spreading shrapnel was the thing to drive the gun crews away.

These boys went to this bloody business with the high excitement of a troop of Boy Scouts out for a day's hike through the woods.

The Hampshires started the thrust with a flanking attack on Pichon. It was as neat and balanced an engagement as any in the Tunisian war. Following them into the scrawny and unlovely village one could clearly read the story of the assault written in the débris left behind—a gun here that had been rushed, another in the cactus fields that had been knocked out, a Churchill and a Bren carrier that had been caught on the mine field and then the shell holes in the village itself. Already, though it was hardly midday and the attack had only begun at dawn, the regiment was beyond the village and blazing away with mortars at the hills.

The prisoners were Austrian. It was interesting to notice, the deeper we cut into the German defences, the order in which they were prepared to sacrifice their troops. At the start of this offensive most of the prisoners were Italians, not young Fascists but the unwarlike types from the south who made good base troops and not much else. Then we began to pick up Germans who had recently been released from concentration camps in Germany on the condition that they would fight in Africa. These were all (in Nazi eyes) politically unreliable and therefore expendable. There were Poles and Czechs among them. Now we were gathering in Austrians, many of whom had no hesitation at all in saying how delighted they were to be out of it. The hard core of the Germans—troops like the Panzer Grenadiers—still remained at large. They were always withdrawn from tight corners so that they could fight another day.

The general, a lean, tall and quiet-spoken Englishman, in

charge of this operation had one general order from Alexander: "You must hurry. You must get through to Kairouan by the ninth or earlier or the Germans retreating from Akarit will escape you."

He therefore very smartly rushed his Guards up to the heights on the left where the German gunners were in hiding. The job for the Guards was exactly the same as for the Americans on the other side—to silence the German gunners in the hills so that our sappers could pull up the mine field in the Fondouk Pass and let our new tanks burst through.

It was the Welsh Guards I especially remember that day, though there were others in the fighting as well. In a steady, unflinching line the Welshmen went up the last bare slopes on foot, and they faced a withering machine-gun fire all the way up. When a man fell, some one was always there to step in and the line went on until it reached the top.

"You can see them up there now," the general said proudly. He had come into the front to get a first-hand view and more especially to find out what had gone wrong. It seemed that the American troops had not arrived on the starting line and their sector, a vicious line of hills to the right, was still in enemy hands. This meant that the German gunners were still operating across the mine field and the pass. Anything coming in a frontal attack straight down the valley was going to run into murderous fire. But the commander was under orders to press on. He waited twenty-four hours but when the southern hills still remained untaken he decided to sacrifice his tanks. Some would be lost for certain, but there was a strong chance that in being lost the leading tanks would blast a way through. A young squadron leader was chosen to lead the assault. Spaced wide apart the tanks ran forward for a mile over heavy sand. Then as they began to come under fire the squadron leader reported over the radio: "There's a hell of a mine field in front. It looks about three hundred yards deep. Shall I go on?"

"Go on," he was told. "Go on at all costs." The cost in the

end was not too bad—less than one hundred tanks, many of them quickly repairable since only their tracks had been blown off. The bad thing was that as soon as a tank fouled a mine and its crew jumped outside they were caught in mortar fire from close range. Beyond brigade headquarters I came on several little groups of the lads who had set out so bravely that morning. They were badly beaten up, even those who could walk. Their faces were blacked with burnt tank grease and oil, they were half-deaf and their uniforms were cut about in an extraordinary way by blast and near misses.

Then the young squadron leader was carried by. He had lived just long enough to break a passage through the mines and see the reinforcements flow through; and this man is remembered now in his regiment with great affection and pride.

Fondouk fell that night.

It was reported later that the Americans had failed to arrive on time partly because there was some confusion about the zero hour and partly—so American friends later told me—because of the slowness of their vehicular traffic on the road and of getting the men into position. This was the low-water mark of American arms on the Tunisian front and only if one understands and knows about these early mishaps is one able to appreciate the extraordinary change that took place later on. These very units that failed at Fondouk were the ones that swept through to a brilliant victory in the north only a few weeks later. If ever there was proof of the need of field training and the ability of the Americans to profit by it, it was here.

There comes a moment in nearly every campaign when the atmosphere along the front suddenly alters. For days or even weeks or months you go into the line and see the same old things, the same guns firing at the same targets, the same patrols going out; inevitably you give way to the despondent feeling that it will all go on indefinitely. Then one morning you notice everything has changed. First probably you notice the rear workshops and Casualty Clearing Stations have moved from their old positions under the trees. Further down the road more and more trucks are pouring in from the side tracks and there is a general and accelerating movement towards the front. No enemy aircraft appear. Staff cars, ambulances, water carts, lorries, signalling vans are all racing to get ahead. You call at divisional headquarters and find it has moved forward to the spot where brigade used to be; and brigade has moved. Everything is moving and as you run past the procession the troops on the lorries are grinning and shouting. At the danger spots where you never drove in daylight if you could avoid it more and more vehicles are pressing down the road and there is no shelling, no machine-gunning.

It was like this now. The break had come. I found myself in the midst of the most exultant and exciting spectacles a war can offer—a victorious army rushing forward over its battlefields in pursuit of the broken enemy. Every deserted German gun pit, every tangle of broken barbed wire is a milestone on the way and a visible proof that you have won and the enemy is beaten.

A strange, buoyant excitement seizes the army then. Men in their eagerness to rush on do reckless things like running blindly through mine fields. They feel they can't be stopped now, that every gun has twice the power it had before, that every man is equal to a dozen of the enemy. "Get on . . . get on." You hear the order everywhere, and in the dust and the shouting and the confusion the men are laughing and talking at the tops of their voices.

General Alexander pushes by in a big American command vehicle and shouts across at us, "How are you getting on?" He is gone before we can answer. An English officer in a jeep joins us at a traffic block saying, "There's a complete madhouse in the hills over there. The American Rangers, the British Commandos and the French Goums are all stalking one another round and round the mountain tops and no one knows who is supposed to be fighting who. They have just ambushed the general."

Further on the sand is very deep and we can only get by in single file by sticking to the steel netting that has been hastily pegged down through the night. We are in the midst of the burnt-out tanks now—the tanks that sacrificed themselves for this break-through—and lines of white tape laid down by the sappers show where the German mine fields are.

Another friend joins us in the procession and says, "There are a lot of our dead out there and we can't get to them because of the mines. Two of the sappers were blown up half an hour ago."

The scene at Fondouk is quite inexplicable. The Americans have arrived and are marching south while we march north. The two columns cross one another on the cross-roads and there is a most extraordinary mixture of vehicles being straightened out by the military police. Still, it is a great pleasure to be on a good macadam road again—and the road leads straight into the Mohammedan city of Kairouan, the fourth most holy Moorish city in the world, the centre of the Moorish carpet industry and, what is more to the point, the cross-roads town on which the German army is converging.

Realising it was late, the army made a great effort to reach Kairouan that night. As my party ran forward to join the vanguard, others kept coming back with the usual conflicting news: "Kairouan has fallen . . . no it has not . . . we attack tomorrow . . . we attack tonight," and so on. In those circumstances there is only one thing to do—go and find out for yourself.

This is always the most difficult moment for the war correspondent. Shall he isolate himself with the troops at the head of the hue and cry—in which case he will get a better story but be unable to get it back until days afterwards—or shall he stop and get a story off and then resume the chase on the following day? I personally was all for pushing on since this was the First Army's first big break-through after many bitter

months of being stuck in the mud. In the end it was agreed
that we should use two more hours of the precious daylight in
going forward and then return to get our messages away. For
once, it was a sensible decision.

Outside the ruined hamlet of Fondouk we careened across a
flat, soft countryside that was at last beginning to bloom with
the spring wildflowers, a cascade of sweet yellow mustard that
stretched mile on mile into the distance. The vehicles on the
road grew fewer and fewer and already many units had turned
aside into the breast-high wheat to camp for the night. Dark
puffs of smoke began to show on the horizon on either side of
the road and occasionally we caught the distant sound of gunfire. Enemy aircraft were about, travelling very low and fast.

We ran forward to the head of the column, still a dozen
miles from Kairouan, and found the tyred vehicles stopped by
a sanddrift in the bottom of a wadi. Every one piled off the
trucks and got to work with shovels. A huge German troop
carrier, towing an eighty-eight-millimetre gun, had been
knocked out only an hour or two before and the wreckage
still smouldered beside the road. Twice we ran in panic along
the wadi when fighters swooped by twenty feet above the
ground. Then we got through and raced north to find the tanks.
The road was empty now but there was still no sign of the
enemy. A lone British dispatch rider held us up. "I shouldn't
go any further if I were you," he said. "Not at any rate in
that" (a slightly contemptuous reference to our rickety station
waggon) "as there are Jerry tanks ahead."

Content then that Kairouan was not going to fall that night,
we ran back to Fondouk, where we had noticed a particularly
good-looking white villa outside the village.

A group of American anti-tank gunners had got there first
but they did not seem to want the place. Cautiously kicking
open the doors we searched inside with a torch, but apparently
the Germans had left too much in a hurry to mine or booby-
trap the place. From the papers lying about we discovered that

until the previous day this villa had been the Nazi headquarters for the region. The German general's breakfast things were still lying about. A lamb had just been skinned and cleaned for him and was hanging up in the kitchen. In the bedrooms there were packets of "Louse powder" and they were marked for use in Russia. The villa shook a little that night as the Germans bombed our end of the valley and we bombed their end but it was a pleasant night and we were on the road early next morning. On a slight rise that commanded a view of the white walls of Kairouan shimmering in the distance we found General X. (again I regret that I am not allowed to name him), the commander of the British armour.

General X. can give a more lucid and entertaining account of a battle than any field commander I have met. In ten minutes he told us the position. Sfax, the big port to the southeast, had fallen without a fight and the Eighth Army was now pushing up the coast road to Sousse. The First and the Eighth armies were therefore running parallel with one another, but unfortunately the Germans had put on an additional turn of speed. We were too late to catch them at Kairouan. We had nipped off one of their rear columns an hour or two before but the bulk of the enemy had got away. Kairouan was declared an open city and our patrols would enter it within the hour.

At that we hurried down the road again. Ahead of us a Stuka with the most improbable good luck dived on a Sherman tank and put a bomb through the turret. After that we drove peaceably and cautiously into Kairouan. At first there was no sign of life among the glistening white tombstones that surrounded the town. Then, penetrating past dozens of German notice boards into the central square, we were surrounded by a crowd of mingled Jews, French and friendly Arabs who gave themselves entirely to hysteria. They did all the things the crowd usually does when a town is taken. They gave the *V* sign, they shouted and waved flags, the girls kissed the soldiers and the men ran out with bottles of wine and fruit. But here the demonstration was so spontaneous and so genuine it was somehow most moving and most gay. It was the first glimpse we were going to have of the delighted relief that swept the whole countryside at the departure of the Germans.

Not every one welcomed us, of course. Indeed, that evening I had this shattering experience. A Frenchwoman ran up and said that her two baby girls wanted to kiss me. I had hoisted the first one up on my knee when out of the corner of my eye I caught sight of a little Arab girl watching the proceedings. And with elaborate malice she slowly pulled the back of her hand across her throat and disappeared.

It took me a day or two and much enquiry to find out what had been going on in Kairouan since the Germans occupied the place four months before. Then I sent the following message to my paper:

KAIROUAN, Wednesday.—This is the story of what happens when the Germans take a village. I write it just as it fell out here—and at half a dozen places I have been in the past two days.

First Messerschmitts come over very low and very fast and two Arab ARP wardens run to the roof of the town's tallest building beside the mosque. They turn over the petrol motor that works the town's one syren, but by then the people in the earthen streets below are already slamming their doors, picking up their children and running blindly to the rough trenches they have dug in the main square. Twice more the Messerschmitts go by but it is quiet towards evening.

Rumours are passing everywhere around the souk and the bazaar, where the men sit cross-legged at their doorways. Eventually the French Civil Controller gets his counsellors together. They order the people to be calm. They warn them to hide their flags and anything that might anger the Germans. None is to carry weapons lest the Germans should grow suspicious and start shooting . . . and what are half a dozen long barrelled rifles from the Berber wars against German tanks?

Presently there is dust on the empty road leading into the

town, and from the north a German armoured car slowly edges its way through the outer streets. A German officer stands in the open turret with a pair of binoculars round his neck and a revolver in his hand. All his men are at their machine guns.

Arabs in the doorways smoke, look up and do nothing. A few excitable children run into the street, shouting and cheering at the big strange motor car. In their doorways and from behind their lace curtains the French watch and wait. In the main square the car stops, and as the crowd gathers round the German officer asks in broken French for the Mayor.

The Mayor is there in his best suit, and he tries hard to understand the German orders: "No lights at night. . . . Hostages and immediate death if there is any trouble. . . . Are there any British here?"

More and more armoured cars come into the square, and as the crowds gather round to stare, the officers flock into the little tenth-rate hotel. They want wine. They want dinners. Madame does what she can. The wine is sour, the eggs hardly fresh—but, they will pay.

The Germans have a great deal of money. They pay thirty francs for four eggs apiece, which works out at ninepence an egg, a fantastically high rate in this land of chickens.

The tension breaks quickly in this hotel as the Germans eat and drink. They start making jokes with Madame and her daughter.

All this time more and more Germans are coming in, infantry-men in dusty green gabardine uniforms, who start pitching tents on the outskirts of the village and digging holes for their guns. They park their vehicles carefully under the trees and hedges, and throw branches over the guns. A few gather round a pump with flat five-gallon tins and they try to talk to the Arabs as they draw water.

By the morning quite a lot more Germans have arrived. Some go to the town hall and tell the Mayor that he must be out by noon, for his offices are requisitioned. Half a dozen other buildings are taken over through the morning, and the Germans are asking questions everywhere around the town. And they are very busy talking to informers. Always they have plenty of francs for information. In the afternoon the arrests begin.

First the Mayor. It turns out that he is a de Gaullist. Then half his counsellors, just to be on the safe side. Then the corn merchant. Apparently he has been saying things about the Nazis recently. A Jew, of course. There seem to be quite a lot of Jews. An informer obliges with a list.

The Germans are very correct and very methodical. In all the surrounding farms they ask: "How many sheep, how many pigs, how much grain?"

It is all paid for at high prices. The villagers find that prices have doubled overnight. Next day they have tripled. It is no longer possible to buy wheat.

But why worry? There is plenty of work. The Germans are offering Arabs up to five shillings daily to work on their new airfield, three miles outside the town. The Jews get work too. Not in return for money, of course, but still they are not killed so long as they are willing to work a ten-hour day digging drains. They can keep going by buying vegetables with their savings. Frenchmen, too, find it difficult—all favours seem to be going to the Arabs.

It seems to get tougher every week. The wine vanishes. Meat is unobtainable. The bread goes brown and then black.

But the young German officers are tremendously good-looking, and tremendously full of confidence. They have a series of good jokes about how the English ran away, first in France, then in the Far East, and then in the desert; and if any one suggests they are not about to run away again in Tunisia—well, then, that is another good joke.

And here are newspapers to prove it—newspapers in French, German and Arabic appear by magic, filled with the latest news of the U-boat war and raids on London. The bazaar gets a free gift of two strong radio sets so that the villagers can hear special broadcasts from Berlin.

As the days go by the village slips into the gradually tightening routine. Each Jew has his badge of David pinned to his coat. Each day he struggles a little harder to get food.

Even the first RAF raid fails to shake the boyish high spirits of the Germans. But they grow irritable when eggs and wine fail to appear at the hotel. Nor are the local people so pliant. They have plenty of francs. But now there is nothing to buy. An Arab will work for a full day for just one handful of tea.

There is no great Axis advance, but instead rumours begin to fill the bazaar—rumours that the British are approaching. There is a second air raid, and then a third. More than one hundred civilians are in hospital, and the women in their grief grow recklessly critical of the Germans. The Germans themselves stop making jokes, and there is much movement of Wehrmacht traffic in the village. All trucks seem to be headed north, and that is not the direction of the front. Ambulances keep passing through. The atmosphere grows sullen and morose and apprehensive.

There is no more talk of what Marshal Rommel is going to do.

A Jew dies of weakness. A Frenchman is knocked down in the street. A German is shot for trying to desert. Bazaar rumours go on and on.

Then one night there is the distant sound of artillery, and as it grows louder, and more and more dusty vehicles rush through the village, no one can pretend that this is a great German advance to throw the British out of Africa.

Suddenly German gunners who have idled for three months around the village walls pack their guns and vanish. Flares keep showing on the southern horizon, and there is heavier gunfire.

Only a few Germans are left now, and it is hard to believe that these tense, drooping men are the boyish officers who arrived laughing and shouting only a month or two ago. The Colonel drives away with his staff. Work ceases on the airfield.

Odd parties of Germans, looking exhausted and dishevelled, walk into the village and snatch bicycles, carts, horses—anything that moves—and depart. They do not pay now.

Suddenly the villagers find they are alone. A single Spitfire rushes across the white, flat roofs, and presently is back with ten more fighters, weaving back and forth just above the mosque.

The Mayor gets his counsellors together. "There must be no excitement . . . Wait until we are certain it is all right . . . Get the flags ready."

As he talks, two armoured cars burst through the dust in the south and make towards the town. An ARP warden on the roof shouts "It's the British"—and the people rush into the streets.

This is not an imaginative short story. It has happened. It is being made to happen, more and more, as every day goes by.

Chapter XV: Sousse

BEYOND Kairouan the good hard road ran straight to
Sousse on the sea. All my instincts now made we want to
meet the Eighth Army again. I had left them eight months before at Alamein and at a moment of indecision and defence.
Now they rode on a great victory and I was curious to see if
my friends had changed. Sousse lay only eighty kilometres
away from Kairouan but the road was empty and no one had
yet passed along it. The First Army's tank battle had veered
away to the north and west and the general had told us that
he yas not going to the coast at all but continuing inland. On
the seaboard Montgomery was presumably about to take Sousse
if he had not already done so, and the patrols of the First Army
were too busy on their own sector to take a joy ride and find
out. Meanwhile it was known that odd groups of Germans were
still straggling northwards across the Kairouan-Sousse road between the two British armies.

My party was as keen as I was to reconnoitre across to the
sea by ourselves, but on the first night we turned back after
going only a few miles. A patrol leader of a group of Valentines
told us firmly that German tanks were reported down the road,
in addition to mine fields, and it seemed stupid to go on.

Next morning we set out again and it was all plain sailing for
a while. Humps that appeared from the distance to be tanks
turned out to be haystacks or Arab huts. The road ran over
gentle hills and dales and it was deserted except for odd civilian
cyclists who gabbled incomprehensively in Arabic and could
give no accurate information.

After an hour a jeep and an ambulance overtook us. They
were searching for one of our armoured patrol cars which had
fouled a mine field and we followed on. The broken car lay in

the fields near a place where the enemy had blown a series of craters in the road. It was the old story. The car had turned off along a side track to get around and now it was completely capsized over an exploded mine and the dead driver was stretched on the turf.

We picked our way past cautiously. The country here had burst into a wild fantasy of colour and that overworked cliché, "a carpet of flowers," became a proven fact. It was just that, a rich deep Persian carpet woven of bluebells and poppies, of sweet peas and tulips, of daisies and lilies; and these grew so thickly that for miles you could not see the ground or the grass, only flowers. They made patterns that swept over hilltops, hilarious shouting bands of colour. Partly to rationalize our astonishment and partly because we were unable to express our delight we fell back on our old game of out-cliché-ing one another.

"A veritable carpet of flowers."

"A regular Brock's benefit." And finally:

"Good enough for *Punch*."

It helped to relieve the tension of travelling in an open vehicle into enemy country. As we talked we always kept watching for strange vehicles on the road ahead or out in the fields on either side. Then quite unexpectedly we had a great stroke of luck. A British artillery officer whom we had known in the Middle East casually drove up in a truck from the east.

"Yes," he said, "Sousse fell an hour or two ago. I have just come across country from the coast and as far as I know the main road is clear."

After that we came on scattered villages where the people ran out and waved flags as we went by. Twice we ducked into a wood and hid from aircraft. The country began to break up a little into hills and then at last we turned into the town of Msaken and saw the Eighth Army. We had come in off a side road and just for a moment it seemed that we had made a bad mistake. The vehicles running up the main road were all German or Italian. Then drawing closer I saw the British troops in the lorries. The British desert soldier looks like no other soldier in the world. He looks at first sight like a rather rakish and dishevelled Boy Scout, the effect, I suppose, of his bleached khaki shorts and shirt and the paraphernalia of blackened pots and pans and oddments he carries round in his vehicle, which is his home. He practically never wears a helmet and he has a careless loose-limbed way of walking which comes from living on the open plains and which is altogether different from the hill troops weighed down by heavy battle dress. The desert is a healthy place, especially if you can camp by the sea. These youths were burnt incredibly by the sun and they had that quality of brimming health that made them shout and sing as they went along.

Very content to be among them again I struck up conversations with the troops as we bumped along in the cavalcade. It seemed that they had taken over the enemy vehicles when their own had broken down. Montgomery's forces had split into two halves, one going directly into Sousse on the coast, the other splitting off northward here at Msaken because the main bridge was blown by the enemy.

For an hour or more we coasted along over a rough and filthy track and after many months I felt almost pleasurably my lungs filling up with dust again. It was much warmer here on the coast and the palm-trees still gave the flavour of the desert. The progress was very slow and sometimes we ran into traffic blocks, for ten minutes or more. The Eighth Army was swarming through the countryside and every side road was choked.

At last we cut around a field of cactus and joined the main road north of Sousse. With the main road we hit the New Zealand Division coming head-on towards us—in the way the enemy would see it coming. They rolled by with their tanks and their guns and armoured cars, the finest troops of their kind in the world, the outflanking experts, the men who had fought the Germans in the desert for two years, the victors of half a dozen pitched battles. They were too gaunt and lean to be handsome, too hard and sinewy to be graceful, too youthful and physical to be complete. But if ever you wished to see the most resilient and practised fighter of the Anglo-Saxon armies this was he. This wonderful division took a good deal of its fighting morale from its English general, Freyberg, the VC who through two wars had probably been more critically wounded more often than any other living man.

After Freyberg had defended Crete and carried his gospel of the bayonet through half a dozen campaigns in the Middle East the Germans very nearly killed him at Mersa Metruh. By continuing to conduct the battle with a wound through the back of his neck, the general practically threw away his chance of survival, but somehow he had been patched up. And now the old gentleman himself rode up the road standing in the open turret of a tank and he looked a good deal younger and tougher than I had ever seen him before.

Against this tremendous flood of vehicles, all painted a brilliant light desert yellow, we rode into the blasted town of Sousse. For months this place had been attacked by the RAF and the United States Air Force; now driving in through the target area along the docks it was a frightening sight, a vision of what we are one day going to see in the Ruhr, in Germany. It was not so much the general devastation, it was the violence with which everything had been done. A grand piano had been picked up from a basement and flung on to a housetop. The roof of one apartment building had been flung bodily on to the next building. The palm-trees on the waterfront looked like those photographs one used to see after a hurricane had passed across Florida. The ships in the bay were set in a frame of blackened warehouses and they were in all stages of decomposition—the ships that had been merely hit and sunk, those that had been beached by a near miss and subsequently broken up by the waves, those that had been entirely disintegrated. Bits of cork, broken scraps of lifeboats and rope and spars were mingled with the tangled mess of the railway lines that ran down to the docks. The walled Arab section—the kasbah—had been split open and the midday sun poured in over all its tawdry and shabby secrets: the labyrinthine brothels, the sweet-vendors' shops, the miserable foetid courtyards where the Moorish women wasted their obscure and furtive lives.

Beyond this, away from the port, the modern city had been untouched and now the civilians were in the excited high tide of their relief that at last the hell of bombing was over. And so they made the soldiers welcome. A day or two later when Montgomery drove through the town in a jeep a great crowd saluted him, *"Vive Mong-goum-ree, vive Mong-goum-ree"*; and an unusually attractive little French girl offered a bouquet and flung her arms round the general's neck.

But to-day they were still a little stunned.

I hunted about through the ruined streets looking for my friend Alexander Clifford. I was quite certain he would turn up. Long before all this, even before Italy had entered the war, we had met in Athens and flown across to Cairo and the desert. For two years we had covered all the campaigns together as correspondents, until finally we had both got fed up with the war and managed to get leave, he to go to England, myself to America. Then he had rejoined the Eighth Army and I had gone to the First. I had failed to get a rendezvous in Tripoli and now I felt sure he would turn up in Sousse.

He had of course entered the town within an hour of its fall and we met in the main street. With him came the other two men with whom we always played bridge in the desert— Geoffrey Keating and Russell Hill. I had had many journeys with these three. We had camped alone for long periods in many difficult places and there had grown up between us quite unawares a network of tacit understandings and little habits. Within the hour we had broken open and entered a comfortable villa by the sea; one man had gone off to ferret for wine, another to clean the house, a third to cook. Each one fell naturally into the job he had always done. I would no more have dreamed of interfering with Clifford's cooking than he would have thought of instructing me on the lighting of the stoves or the unpacking of the trucks. Keating always procured the petrol and the rations, and so it went on. I do not know if we were efficient or not, but our personal lives were made easier and pleasanter by these naturally formed habits and when we worked as a team we seldom missed any vital incident on the front.

It was only after many months of mistakes and errors that we had learned how to live on a campaign, how to interpret a line of rising dust on the horizon, when to go forward and when to stay back, who the key men in each division were and how to recognise the certain feeling that told you whether the battle was going well or badly.

And now on this night, sitting back after dinner with my friends, I began to understand the differences between the First and the Eighth armies. Already there was a good deal of superficial jealousy and fundamental misunderstanding.

In Kairouan a friend of mine from the First Army had gone up to a sergeant from the Eighth Army and said, "Hullo. Pleased to see you. I am from the First Army." To which the desert sergeant replied lightly, "Well, you can go home now. The Eighth Army's arrived." Again, a young officer from Montgomery's staff who joined us on this night was full of derision for the First Army. He asserted that the Eighth Army would have to take Tunis since the First Army was incompetent.

Such obvious boasting usually came from men who had only recently arrived in the desert but it antagonized the soldiers who had been struggling all winter in the mountains and the mud of northern Tunisia. They regarded the desert soldiers as noisy and over-confident, an army that was sunning itself in publicity, and they looked forward with grim and unfriendly relish to the moment when the desert fighters struck the mountains.

In the same way the First Army men themselves were not

understood. They appeared to the veteran soldiers in Montgomery's forces as a parade-ground army, beautifully equipped
but not much good at fighting.

I do not say that these feelings went very deep, but the antagonism was there, and it continued until the troops went into
action side by side. Then they began to know one another.

The fact was that the Eighth Army was not a European army
any more. To a great extent it had become an overseas army,
an army based not on London but on Cairo. For months and
years it had been cut off from Europe and in their isolation the
troops had developed a complicated set of private habits, and
even a slang language of their own.* Any one who did not fit
into these habits, who had not shared their adventures, was an
outsider. They had been encouraged for the past few months
by Montgomery to regard themselves as invincible, as an independent and private expeditionary force knowing no law except
their own. It was irksome, therefore, for this vigorous and victorious force to learn, following the Casablanca conference, that
it had been placed under the command of Algiers. They felt a
little aggressive about it and showed it. In other words they had
a superiority complex just as the First Army at that time had
an inferiority complex.

But the thing went deeper. The Eighth Army was very
largely an Empire army comprised of Australians, South Africans, New Zealanders and Indians. The settlers who had gone

* For a long time the desert soldiers had been using Egyptian Arabic terms
such as *Moy-ah* for "water," *Shufti* for "look" and so on. They used the
Western Desert Bedouin expression *Say-eeda* (which means "Go with God")
as a form of greeting. These Arabic words were perverted or lost entirely
in the passage of the original Moorish invasion around the Mediterranean from
Arabia to Spain. The word "wadi" for example had become Oued. In Thibar
I found some of the older Arabs knew a word of greeting, *Seeda*, but it was
obviously not in use. The Eighth Army troops now imported the bastard
Nile Delta Arabic into Tunisia. The Tunisian Arabs naturally thought these
expressions were English words, and began to use them as such. When a
soldier saw an Arab he at once shouted *Say-eeda* and the Arab after a little
began to say *Say-eeda* in response, thinking it was the English for "Hullo."
Within a few weeks of Montgomery's arrival *Say-eeda* was in pretty general
use in southern Tunisia.

out to Australia in the nineteenth century learned and earned their interdependence. When they returned on visits to England the Australians appeared to the English as aggressive, boastful and a little uncouth in manner. To the Australians the English appeared as more than a little effete and soft. Yet the Australian was very often aggressive solely in order to hide his sense of insularity. And the Englishman very often admired the virility of the Australian. Then when the tommy demonstrated his toughness in Flanders the English and Australian troops got on very well indeed.

Something of the same sort happened in Tunisia. When the Eighth Army saw the fine equipment, the new guns and tanks and uniforms of the First Army, a slight sense of insularity was forced upon Montgomery's men and to stifle it they boasted a little. In other words an inferiority complex existed inside their superiority complex.

This was the argument I developed over dinner that night and the others would not agree. They asserted that the bulk of the Eighth Army—the part that had existed before Montgomery's arrival—were simply veterans who were sure of themselves. They had come through much fighting to a seasoned maturity and they sought no one's good opinion but their own.

Either way we agreed that the Eighth Army, despite the fact that its fighting had mostly been in the desert, was the better force because of sheer experience. This dispute, which was at that moment a favourite topic throughout Tunisia, was happily going to be settled in the best possible way before the end of the month.

For the next ten days or so I hunted with the Eighth Army. It was to me a never ending pleasure to see again the units I had known so well. Fundamentally nothing had changed but on the surface there were many differences. Montgomery had given the men a tremendous eagerness and there was always a stir along the road when the General drove past, a black beret on his head, his lean ascetic face looking always intent and preoccupied. Driving up to the three caravans he used as a travelling home one day I heard that he had got his Flying Fortress, as strange a story as any that came out of the campaign.

It seemed that after his conquest of Tripoli the General was dining with some American officers and for some reason the conversation turned on the subject of the town of Sfax.

"What will you give me if I take Sfax by April fifteenth?" Montgomery said suddenly to the Americans. He had still to fight his battles of Mareth and Wadi Akarit and the distance alone made it unlikely that the Eighth Army would get there so soon.

"We'll give you anything you like," the American said lightly.

"Will you give me," Montgomery said (I am paraphrasing his words), "a Flying Fortress for the duration, its crew to be on the American pay roll?"

"Sure," they said, and forgot about the matter. Montgomery did not allow himself to forget. He gave Sfax the code name of "Fortress" in his message and when he duly arrived there two or three days ahead of his bet he sent a signal to Eisenhower in Algiers: "Fortress please."

Now this was distinctly embarrassing. It was not quite in the province of American generals to go betting in American government Fortresses. So it was suggested that Montgomery should wait for the machine until the campaign was over. The General however was adamant. He insisted on the Fortress at once and after a somewhat brusque correspondence it arrived. The crew was delighted and at once set about flying Montgomery between Algiers, Tunisia, Cairo and subsequently London.

Meanwhile the fascinating spectacle of the desert army entering the mountains was going on. The enemy had halted about thirty miles north of Sousse around the village of Enfidaville. It was an obvious place in which to make a stand, for at that point the mountains came down almost to the sea.

The attack began long before dawn an April nineteenth. Feel-

ing our way forward in the darkness to the New Zealand headquarters we heard enough to know that it was not going too
well. Enfidaville itself fell quickly enough but beyond that the
enemy were dug into fearsome hills, hills that had to be as-
saulted directly. For an hour I watched them sending down
concentrated mortar fire and the Eighth Army's guns bayed
back in force until the hills were full of teeming smoke from
the shellbursts. The Indians, the New Zealanders and the Guards
went in and soon found themselves obliged to swarm up sheer
cliffs. The enemy above had merely to fire their guns straight
down on the climbing men. The Ghurkhas were in their own
country here and when they did get to grips with the Italians
they did terrible things. They used the knife. There were even
hand-to-hand struggles where men sought to throw one another
from the heights.

For the rest of the men their first contact with the hills was
not easy. Some confessed they even had that same feeling of
claustrophobia I remembered on arriving in Tunisia, the feeling
that one was being constantly overlooked—as indeed one was.
Clifford and I were involved in one little antic by the sea. We
were travelling into Enfidaville when the troops in the lorries
on the road suddenly began to dismount and disperse across the
fields. They split up into platoons, the Bren gun crews out on
the flanks, the stretcher bearers drawing up behind. It was a
tense little scene. The men crept forward yard by yard taking
what cover they could. They held themselves ready for the
command to rush forward with the bayonet and the hand
grenade. Suddenly a major jumped up and hurried to the main
road. "Damn it," he shouted, "we have debussed two miles too
soon. Get back into the vehicles." Rather tamely every one filed
back to the road and the cavalcade rolled on through the peaceful landscape.

It is doubtful if any army could have broken through that
Enfidaville position without support from the left flank. Unit
after unit was sent in. Some reached the caves where the enemy

were in hiding, but there were always more caves higher up, more mortars, more open slopes to cross against machine-gun fire. By the end of two bitter days of many casualties it was evident that the first attack was not going to break through.

Tanks could not operate in this congested space and it was at this point—about April twenty-first—that Alexander diverted the First British Armoured Division away from Montgomery's army and attached it to Anderson's forces in the Goubellat Plain.

Again and again the desert fighters thrust forward, always making a little ground but never forcing a decisive action.

Most of the trouble concerned a hill feature known as Garcia. The fighting turned on this spot and whoever held it was in possession of the battlefield. A fresh division of British troops was called up to assault Garcia and it was agreed that once they had taken the hill the New Zealanders and Indians would again go forward for the kill. There was bloody fighting. Each time we got on to the hill the enemy counter-attacked us off it. The commanders of the New Zealand and Indian divisions both agreed that it was entirely impracticable to go ahead until the feature was definitely won and they told Montgomery so. Montgomery was inclined to agree, and the matter went to Alexander.

There followed a number of rapid conferences among the generals. Clearly now we were in sight of Victory. The enemy was compressed into the last tip of Tunisia. We dominated the air—it had been a wonderful sight seeing our machines flying out all day over Enfidaville. We out-gunned the enemy and we out-tanked him. But still he stood on the vital passes—Green and Bald hills in the Sedjenane sector, Longstop Hill in the Medjerda sector, Pont du Fahs further south and then finally Enfidaville.

It was no longer a matter of friendly rivalry—who should get into Tunis first, the Eighth or the First Army. It was a question of whether we were going to get in at all and of how to do it with the least loss of life and machines.

There were three known centres of interior enemy resistance

which were capable of standing even when the outer passes had gone—Bizerta, Tunis and Cape Bon Peninsula. No one at that time exactly knew von Arnim's intentions though it was fairly clear that Cape Bon was going to be used as an evacuation area. Our reconnaissance machines had brought back many photographs of the jetties that had recently been built round the Cape.

Standing on the coast one day in the purple and white village of Hergla I looked across and saw the heights of the Cape Bon mountains, but that did not mean we could get there. Already by April twenty-first it was becoming pretty evident that we were never going to break through on the coast. The Medjerda Valley still appeared to be the best way in. But the Medjerda Valley was blocked so long as the Germans held Longstop Hill. On April twenty-third Alexander attacked the hill.

Chapter XVI: Longstop

WHAT a legend Longstop had become. We checked it on a dozen different maps. We explored the roads and tracks around the hill. We talked about it: "Once we are on Longstop . . ." The veterans who had mounted the hill before we were thrown off in the early days declared that on a clear afternoon you could almost see Tunis from the heights.

In the German ranks too, Longstop was a great thing. When an officer of the Panzer Grenadiers was taken prisoner he declared, "You will never take Longstop. It is impregnable now."

For five months it had lain right in the front line, the fortress of the Medjerda Valley, the locked gate on the road to Tunis. We climbed the surrounding hills and looked down upon the hill and it always appeared darker than the surrounding country and more sinister, a great two-humped bulk that heaved itself out of the wheat fields like some fabulous whale beached on the edge of a green sea.

All through April the Seventy-Eighth Division had been edging its way along the heights towards Longstop. One after another the mountain peaks had been cleaned out. Toukabeur village and Chaouach had fallen and while the donkeys and the mule teams dragged up ammunition and food the men crept forward on to Jebel Ang. At last, on April twenty-second, the men in the forward platoons could look right into the German defences of Longstop itself.

To launch his final assault the general commanding the Seventy-Eighth Division established his headquarters high up in the mountains and very close to his operational brigades. To get to this place you had to turn off the main road just short of Medjez el Bab and take a winding earthen track through Toukabeur. The track began in a field of poppies that spread in a blood-red pool across the floor of the valley; it finished in miraculous alpine fields where a flower of the most delicate lavender bloomed among the rocks.

We called on the intelligence major we knew best. "It's started," he said. "You can have a look at it if you go round that corner. Don't go on to the top of this hill because there's a lot of red flannel up there."

"A lot of red flannel" presumably meant that General Alexander and his staff, who usually wore their red bands at the front, had come to watch the battle; so we took a lower track and moved through the stunted mountain trees looking for a good commanding point. The British twenty-five-pounders were making vicious cracking echoes through the rocks. Heaven knew how the guns had been dragged to those heights. Beyond the last battery we crept around the crest of a steep hill until we were in view of the enemy in Heidous village across the valley and Longstop lay below us on the right.

From that height everything appeared to happen in miniature. The Churchill tanks climbing on Jebel Ang looked like toys. The infantry that crept across the uplands towards Heidous were tiny dark dots and when the mortar shells fell among them it was like drops of rain on a muddy puddle. Toy donkeys toiled up the tracks towards the mountain crests and the Germans too were like toys, little animated figures that occasionally got up and ran or bobbed up out of holes in the ground between the shell explosions.

Most of our shells were falling on the near slopes of Longstop. The barrage kept rushing over our heads and falling among the black gorse on the hill; at times it was so heavy everything disappeared in grey-black smoke and the hill became a cloud of fumes and dust.

On Longstop the Germans had dug trenches which had a horizontal shelf deep below the surface. During a barrage such as this the Germans lay under this shelf and waited in safety. Their guns were fired from below the surface so that it was only in the very last stages of an assault that they had to put their heads out. They had ample stores of food and water and ammunition. The Germans knew that the British infantry would have to cross the mine fields first and that they would have to expose themselves as they climbed upward. It was no use our ignoring Longstop by going around it. The Germans would still be able to shell the two roads running into Tunis. They would break up our convoys. They would launch counter-attacks from the hill. And so it was necessary now, even at great cost, for the Seventy-Eighth Division to make a direct assault.

On the second morning of the battle, when the British guns had done all they could, I went with my party down on to the plain before Longstop to see the infantry go in. The brigade in charge of this operation had taken over a farmhouse in a little grove of trees. The command vehicles were drawn up against a wall close to a ruined tennis court.

The enemy seemed to be aware that this was a headquarters because they kept firing at the place, occasionally with eighty-eight-millimetre shells, occasionally with mortars that sent up puffs of black or white dust according to whether they landed on rock or soil. It was never quite clear until the last minute whether the shells would fall over the farmhouse or short of it. As we came up the road a padre said to us, "It is very difficult at the moment. I have been trying to get to some of our dead but every time I go out they can see me and they start mortaring. I shall have to wait until it is dark." The padres were very brave on this front and some had been decorated for it. They were armed only with their helmets and their faith and often they went forward with the attacking infantry to be at hand to help with the wounded. At these times they did not pray or preach on the battlefield; they dealt out brandy to the dying and they administered morphia and helped bind the wounded and get them back in trucks and Bren gun carriers to the dressing stations. They carried food and water and medical supplies.

In return for this the men looked on the padres with an affection and respect which they had never felt at home.

We could see the lower slopes of Longstop quite clearly from brigade headquarters and even here, only half a mile off, the hill looked dark and uncouth. Zero hour for the attack was 1:30 A.M. but the Germans above could see our infantry massing and they were already firing very heavily upon them with mortars. The West Kents, the Surreys and the Argylls were making this attack, each taking a separate part of the hill, and they had a few Churchill tanks in support as well as the artillery that kept banging away at the places where the German mortars seemed to be hidden.

At 1 o'clock the artillery increased and for the fiftieth time the hill disappeared in dust. At 1:20 the guns fell silent. There was a long pause. The shell dust lifted slowly off the hill. At 1:30 a flare rose out of the foothills and at that signal the attack was on. In little quick ripples of noise the machine guns sounded first from one side of the hill then the other. Sometimes the bursts went on as long as a full minute and always the machine-gunning would be drowned eventually in the crump of the enemy mortars. The mortars fell in sprays of half a dozen or more, and watching from behind a cactus hedge at the farm-house you would see roughly from the mortar fire how far our men had advanced. At 2 A.M. little dark figures appeared spas-modically on the skyline at the crest of the first slope. They stood silhouetted for a second and then dropped away. Near the top there was a patch of open yellow rock. Men were run-ning across this, always going upward. Then they disappeared for a moment until they were on the skyline and dropping down over the other side.

In a calm, reasonable voice the brigade major was calling over the telephone for a bombing raid to help the advance. His phone was ringing all the time now. Little scraps of coded information were coming back from the battalion headquarters. They were map references, jumbles of figures. You could not tell from the faces of the officers whether the attack was going well or not but it was obvious that we were advancing.

It was hot and presently through the dust Bren gun carriers came rattling down the track that led from the hill. The wounded were piled on the carriers just as they had been lifted there in the midst of the firing. They lay quite still on their backs, staring upwards, and the blood dropped down among the instruments inside the carriers.

The drivers sat fixedly in their seats and said nothing. They brought the vehicles to a standstill beside a line of ambulances sheltering under the cactus hedge and the stretcher bearers lifted the wounded on to stretchers and slid them into the ambulances. Then the Bren gun carriers turned and went back through the dust into the battle again.

One of the officers who came back took his helmet off and let it drop on the ground. "The men are very tired," he said. "It's not the opposition so much, it's sleep. They have been going for a long time now."

"How long?"

"I don't know, a long time." The officer himself was very tired. He had been in the line for a week and during the previous night some of his men had just fallen on the ground and cried. They cried because they had no strength any more, not even the strength to stand up. They had continued without sleep for two days under the compulsion of their brains and beyond the point where the body will normally function. But now when their minds would not work any more they discovered that the strength had already gone out of their bodies and that, in fact, they had no control of anything any more, not even of tears. The tears came quite involuntarily and without any sense of relief because the body was incapable of feeling anything any more and what became of the body now was of no consequence. And so they had lain about the hill for an hour or two in a stupor. The cold and the dew bit into them through the night and brought them back to consciousness. Then they stumbled about in the darkness until they found their platoons. They ate a little cold bully without tasting it and took swigs from their water bottles. By morning their brains were operating again—not their bodies but their brains—and they were able to contemplate themselves and consider what still had to be done. Some of them slept in the sun through the morning and this brought back a little strength into their bodies—enough to co-operate with their minds and give obedience. At noon then they had regrouped and they mechanically registered the order that they had to attack again and they assessed their strength against what was required by the order. These were the men we had seen running across the top of the slope and the men who came back in the Bren gun carriers.

The wounded were not just yet in great pain because the shock of the bullets in their flesh was still taking effect. They were very dirty and the dirt ran in lines in the sagging hollows of their faces. Their hands dropped over the edges of the stretchers, lumpish hands, coloured a greyish yellow colour that was inhuman. No one could look at them without protesting.

The German prisoners came next. Black jack boots, green gabardine uniforms, wings on their chests, cloth caps with the red, white and black badge, the Afrika Korps. They marched stolidly in columns of three, the officers in front. They were not so tired as our men since they had been lying in provisioned dugouts and they marched mechanically but well. One of the officers started to argue. He wanted to see a British officer. A Scots sergeant waved him on bleakly with the tip of his bayonet.

The Germans stood stolidly beside the ambulances, waiting their turn to go into the cowshed. In the cowshed British military police were running their hands over each prisoner, taking away from him his combined knife, fork, spoon and tin-opener, a neat gadget, also his pocketknife and any weapons he carried. The Germans submitted to this, automatically raising their hands above their heads. The pile of knives and forks got larger and larger on the floor. Some of the Germans started smoking after the search and they sat quietly on a fallen log. There was something in their faces that registered not fright or fear but deep tiredness, a sense of relief. Only the German officer was still arguing. A British captain who had been tending the wounded came over to him.

"You bastard," he said. "Get back in your place." The German, not understanding, offered the British officer a cigarette.

The British officer said again, "Get back." It was quite clear that having come so recently from the fighting and the wounded he wanted to shoot the German.

There were many such scenes that day. The Germans were firing their machine guns until the British got within thirty yards or so—near enough to kill. And then the Germans surrendered. This meant that we were taking many casualties but not killing many Germans and the physical presence of the prisoners did not entirely satisfy the desire of the British troops for revenge.

That night they took three-quarters of Longstop Hill. As soon as it was light in the morning I drove to brigade headquarters. A young signals officer was going up to the hill in his truck and he offered to take my party with him. We got only half a mile in the truck and then, leaving it under the cover of the high wheat, we began climbing on foot, keeping to the right-hand side of the hill. We followed the line of the signal wires so that we could check for breakages. Every few yards the wheat had been torn up and blackened as though some sort of plague had blighted it; this was the effect of the mortars, which were fused so that they exploded immediately on contact and were therefore more likely to kill men. It was very hot. The dust rose up out of the wheat and when it had coated one's face and body little runnels of sweat ran over one's cheeks and under the armpits.

Now we were on the hill I saw that it was much more thickly

covered with scrub than had appeared from the distance and it did not consist of two big humps, but a whole series, seven in all, with many subsidiary ridges. As soon as we pulled ourselves to the top of one slope another appeared above us. Over all this ground the troops had fought the day before and now the carriers were bringing up water cans that had to be lugged the last half of the journey by hand.

On the lip of the third rise we came suddenly upon a scene so dramatic, so complete in itself that I recall it now, detail by detail, almost as I would remember a painting or a play in the theatre. It was a front-line trench. The Germans had dug it but our men had occupied it the day before. It was a shallow trench and it made a zigzag suture through the blackened grass on the slope of the hill. On the piles of freshly turned yellow soil the men had thrown their battle-dress jackets, the tin mugs and plates from which they had been eating, the empty salmon and bully beef tins.

A profusion of things lay about all the way up the trench— empty packets of cigarettes, both British and German, water bottles and hand grenades, half-used boxes of cartridges, German steel helmets, bits of notepaper, discarded packs and torn pieces of clothing. Through this mess the rifles and machine guns were pointing out towards the next slope but the men were not firing. The sun was shining strongly and they sat or leaned half in and half out of the trench. Some smoked. One man was mending a boot. Another was sewing on a button. But mostly they leaned loosely on the earth and rested. Every time an enemy gun sounded they cocked their heads mechanically and waited for the whine that would give the direction of the shot. It was only a slight movement and you did not notice them doing it at first. Sometimes the shells landed short three or four hundred yards away, sometimes very near, perhaps only fifty yards down the slope, but anyway not on the trench. No one commented on the nearness of the shells. They had had much heavier shelling than this all night and these spasmodic shots were only a nuisance that still had the power to hurt unless one watched.

There were several old London papers lying about. One, the *Daily Mirror*, had its last page turned upward and its thick head-line read "No more wars after this, says Eden."

Seeing me looking at it the soldier on the end of the trench said bitterly, "They said the last war was going to end all wars. I reckon this war is supposed to start them all again." The others in the trench laughed shortly and one or two of them made some retort. The men had greeted us with interest but without enthusiasm. When they read the war correspondent badges on our shoulders they were full of questions and derisive comments. "Why weren't you up here yesterday? You'd have seen something." Then another, "You can tell Winston Churchill we have been in the bloody line ten bloody weeks already." Then a third, "Are you the bastard that wrote in the paper that we're getting poached eggs for breakfast every morn-ing?" And a fourth, "Where's the Eighth Army? Aren't they doing anything?" And several of them, "How's the war going, Mister? Is there any one doing anything besides us?"

They were hostile, bitter and contemptuous. Every second word was an adjective I have not quoted here and they repeated it *ad nauseam*. They felt they were a minority that was being ordered to die (a third of them had been killed or wounded in the night) so that a civilian majority could sit back at home and enjoy life.

It is useless to picture these men who are winning the war for you as immaculate and shining young heroes agog with enthusiasm for the Cause. They have seen too much dirt and filth for that. They hate the war. They know it. And they are very realistic indeed about it. Instead of sitting on an exposed hilltop in the imminent danger of death they would much prefer to be on a drunk, or in bed with a girl, or eating a steak, or going to the movies. They fight because they are part of a system, part of a team. It is something they were obliged to do and now that they are in it they have a technical interest and a pride in it. They want to win and get out of it, the sooner the better. They have no high notions of glory. A great number of people at home who refer emotionally to "Our Boys" would be shocked and horrified if they knew just how the boys were thinking and behaving. They would regard them as young hooligans. And this is because the real degrading nature of war is not understood by the public at home and it never can be understood by any one who has not spent months in the trenches or in the air or at sea. More than half the army do not know what it is because they have not been in the trenches. Only a tiny proportion, one-fifth of the race perhaps, know what it is, and it is an experience that sets them apart from other people. If, after the war when the men come home, you find they do not want to talk about the fighting or what they have done it will be for this reason only—they want to forget it.

We went higher on to Longstop to join the Argylls, and as we moved off, the men shouted at us to keep down so that we would not draw the fire on to their position.

The Argylls too were resting after the bad night and their eyes were red-rimmed with fatigue. The commanding officer had been killed. His deputy, a tall major who was a Highland farmer, had been drinking wine with us at Thibar only a few days before, but now a great gulf of experience separated us. He was still as hospitable and level-headed and kind but there was something he could not communicate. We were very near the top of Longstop here. From the surrounding caves Germans were still being routed out. We overlooked a German gun pit, empty now of men but the black snouts of the gun still pointed towards us. In every direction the rocks were chipped with shell blast and the camel thorn was rooted from the ground. A light heat haze hung over the far end of the hill where the Germans were still hiding and shooting.

Below us the Medjerda Valley spread out majestically and we looked for miles across the enemy lines and deep into our own.

At that moment, surprisingly, half a dozen enemy shells whistled over our heads and landed on the brigade headquarters we had just left at the bottom of the hill. The cowshed where the prisoners were was enveloped in great billows of smoke and all that part where the ambulances lay appeared to be in the range of fire. There had been so much killing all around here that the only emotion I felt was: "I'm glad I'm not still in the cowshed."

It was a shock then to look across the valley and see that an entirely separate battle was going on. Longstop had for the past forty-eight hours so absorbed our interest that we had begun to think that it was the whole battle. But now I remembered Alexander had sent two armoured divisions into the Goubellat Plain and other formations were working up from Medjez el Bab to the villages of Crich-el-oued and Sidi Abdallah in the centre and southern side of the valley. Tanks were moving about very briskly and firing but from that distance we could not see exactly what they were doing. Bombers kept coming in low and adding to the turmoil on the plain. Crich-el-oued (inevitably the troops called it Cricklewood) was having an especially rough time and it was surprising to see the minaret of its little mosque survive the constant salvoes.

As we watched another officer of the Argylls came up, a major named John Anderson. Just before he introduced us, our friend whispered, "Here's the man who did the whole thing. Don't say anything about it but we have put him in for the VC."

It was not much good asking Anderson how Longstop had fallen. "Oh, I don't know," he said vaguely. "I shouted 'Come on' and the boys jumped up and ran forward shouting at the top of their voices. We found the Germans cowering in their trenches—it was probably the noise that made the Jerries give in."

Anderson, to look at, was not very different from the other officers in this battalion except he was still alive and most of the others were dead or wounded. He himself had been slightly wounded. His uniform was in a bad mess and his beard was matted with sweat and dirt. What he had done was this: He had led the frontal attack at night up the first slope. With so much fire coming from every direction and so many confusing explosions and flares the only thing that was clear was that the enemy was somewhere above. Anderson, armed with a revolver, did the thing that sounds so mundane in words. He stood up in the fire and shouted to his men. They swarmed up after him as men will when they find a leader. He ran straight through the mine field and up through the darkness to the points where the yellow streams of bullets were coming out. He and his men yelled and screamed as they flung themselves upward. They got caught in barbed wire and clawed it aside. Some were shot down. The others jumped down into the dugouts on top of the Germans, firing as they jumped. That was one hill. There were still men left and Anderson jumped up again. Sheer rage carried them up the next slope and again they broke through the wire and killed with the bayonet. Even then there were a few of the Argylls left who had not died or been wounded and a third time Anderson ran on and upward until he had achieved this height.

Many such things happened on Longstop during this terrible three-day battle but this was one of the great charges. When the third day came it was evident that the enemy defences were pierced and as we stood near the summit that afternoon new units were going in to mop up the rest. Longstop was taken in the only possible way, by men going in yelling with the bayonet and meeting the enemy face to face.

Anderson got his VC.

Chapter XVII: Mateur

I CAN imagine something snapping in General Alexander's mind when he heard of the fall of Longstop. At all events he went to work in a tornado of energy as one who has suddenly seen the light. Just as a player of bridge or chess will parry and thrust for position here and there and then suddenly see the way clear before him, so now Alexander moved forward with a touch and sureness that had not been apparent in the battle before.

He ordered a wholesale regrouping of the armies and at urgent speed. All the Americans, three divisions, were swung into the northern sector around Sedjenane. The French with their new Valentine tanks and American vehicles were wedged into the Port du Fahs gap. On the coast Montgomery's forces were ordered merely to maintain a series of holding attacks. This left only the Medjerda Valley and upon the Medjerda the General concentrated all his great hopes for a knock-out blow. He wanted only the best of his British forces here. Already the Seventy-Eighth Division, the Fourth and the First Infantry divisions were in position. To these were added the Sixth Armoured Division from the First Army and the Seventh Armoured Division and the Indian Division from the Eighth Army.

These last two desert divisions were obliged to make a spectacular forced march from the coast in order to reach the Medjerda Valley in time. They were unable to pause even long enough to camouflage their vehicles from the desert yellow to the mountain blacks and browns.

The scene on the roads during these days was bewildering. Tens of thousands of vehicles crammed the passes day and night and when, after darkness fell, we were sometimes caught in the mountains away from our base at Thibar it was an unnerving thing to drive past the immense convoys of blacked-out trucks and tanks. Not infrequently vehicles tumbled headlong into the valleys and ditches below and the strain upon the drivers was intense.

The battle plan was quite simple. Now that the line was barely a hundred and thirty miles long we were going to apply severe and continuous pressure along its whole length—the Americans striking towards Mateur, the British along the Medjerda Valley, the French at Pont du Fahs and the British again at Enfidaville. As soon as the pressure was applied in force then the blitz would go in up the Medjerda Valley, a needle thrust aimed straight at Tunis. Two infantry divisions, the Indians and the Fourth, were to break the crust of the German line. Then the two crack armoured divisions, the Seventh and the Sixth, would pour through and continue until they reached the sea.

A sector only three thousand yards wide was chosen for this thrust and it was to go directly up the road from Medjez el Bab through Massicault and St. Cyprien to Tunis.

That was the broad plan. Although surprising and unpredictable things occurred and the plan had to be altered and extended its essential structure remained the same to the end.

No one man could hope to watch the whole of this spectacle. During the first week in May my party found itself buzzing about agitatedly all over the front, never quite certain that we were in the right place, never quite sure that if we went to the Mateur sector something more important might not be happening in the Goubellat Plain, never able to resolve whether or not Bizerta would fall before Tunis.

In the end I suppose we did not do badly. At least we got a superficial view of most of the preliminary moves and we were in the right place when the final blow fell.

One day we drove on to the hills south of Medjez el Bab and all the Goubellat Plain spread out below us. It looked like a bright flypaper with thousands of black flies stuck on it. Two whole divisions were dotted across the valley and sheltering on the edges of the mountains. They had run through Goubellat village and spread in a flood of armour and guns across the plain. At the spot where we sat there was a burnt-out German Tiger tank. The Tigers were a failure in Tunisia. We even stopped them with two-pounder guns. They were too cumbersome, too slow, too big a target, too lightly armed to meet modern anti-tank weapons. And yet as I clambered over this vast wreck I found it frightening in its sheer enormity. It was the biggest and the ugliest vehicle I had ever seen on land. Like a London bus or a sixty-thousand-ton liner it had that quality of largeness that never diminishes no matter how familiar it becomes.

A little group of British tommies seeing battle for the first time had put up an exemplary defence here, on the edge of Goubellat.

They had been surrounded in the night by a great weight of German tanks and infantry—it was one of these final desperate efforts the enemy made to disorganize our coming attack. The hilltop where the tommies were defending disappeared in shell-bursts. In the morning when our reinforcements drove off the Germans a column was sent up to the hilltop to see if any of the defenders had escaped death or imprisonment. As the rescuers appeared the defenders bobbed up cheerfully and unharmed from their foxholes. They had fired off all their ammunition. They had flung back successive waves of German infantry all night long. They were greenhorns no longer. It was a perfect demonstration of what you can do with really tough training in the battle schools at home.

Across the other side of Goubellat where our tanks had touched the lakes things were not going so well. A jagged and precipitous ridge of rock called Kournine rose out of the plain beside the lakes and it bristled with German guns. Every time our tanks approached they were caught and from our eyrie we could see them burning. Every time the infantry tried to infil-trate they were swept back with small-arms fire. Across the plain itself the Germans were using their new Henschel tank-buster—the fighter with the cannon—with devastating effect. Just as at Enfidaville it was obvious that we were going to do no more at Kournine than keep the enemy busy.

The sappers at this time were completing a job which had the importance of a battle. They had to prepare a series of springboards from which the final offensive would be made. With bull-dozers, with dynamite and with pick and shovel they ran roads right out into no man's land. They worked in pitch darkness and under mortar fire throwing up new steel bridges, making fords across the streams, driving cuttings through the rocks. The sappers were in the forefront of everything. They were out ahead of the infantry making passages through the mines. They went out on patrols to plot the country. They made tunnels and set new mine fields right under the German guns. From the days of the Abyssinian War I had seen the sappers getting more and more expert, taking on bigger and bigger jobs and often working under fire without the time or the means to protect themselves or hit back. In this last week they reached a climax of effort.

One day we got ourselves entirely out of position. We knew the final assault was some days ahead and the front seemed quiet. We decided to take a few hours off and we ran up to Cap Serrat on the northern coast. It was a beautiful day, no sign of war. Nightingales were piping in the bushes. We plunged into the sea among the washed-up wrecks of invasion barges and rusting guns. We loitered over lunch—the lunch which I had designed as the best and easiest for these long day trips when we were often twelve hours on the road; a bottle of Thibar wine diluted with water, a chunk of American cheese from Vermont, a loaf of madame's white bread, a tin of margarine and a slab of chocolate. Easily and pleasantly we drove back towards Thibar in the evening. On the road we all got an attack of conscience through staying away from the war for so many hours and we turned into an American headquarters near Sedjenane. And that was when we first heard the astounding news about the Americans. In defiance of every one's predictions they had made a full-scale break-through towards Bizerta. You might wonder how on a narrow front like this we could not have known about so big an event beforehand. The truth was that no one expected the Americans to break through. They were faced with some of the roughest country in Tunisia. Moreover, we did not know then that two major events had happened. First, the Germans were already beginning to draw back from the Bizerta area towards Tunis and Cape Bon; and secondly the Americans, profiting by what they had learned in the south, had suddenly become some of the most adept and determined fighters in the whole battle.

There was nothing much that we, as correspondents, could do about the break-through that night. We could only gather the astonishing story at headquarters—Green and Bald hills had fallen, Mateur had been entered. The Americans were on the borders of the Bizerta lakes and had the city itself in view.

We drove hard next day to catch up. The Beja-Mateur road was one long hue and cry of army vehicles pushing forward. We ran over the old front line—a graveyard now of dynamited German tanks—and then into the great hills we had never been able to reach before. Others turning back said it was hopeless— the traffic was jammed all the way to Mateur—but we edged on, often being bawled out by the military police for getting out of the single line of traffic but more usually sneaking past when nobody was looking. The enemy gunners were still firing out of the line of hills to our right but somehow they could not get on to this perfect target, these thousands of vehicles jammed on the road.

Near Mateur the traffic thinned out at last and the town itself appeared dramatically through the hills. It lay at the mouth of the valley on the edge of Lake Achkel. Between the town and the lake Jebel Achkel rose up, a fabulous mass, dark, precipitous and isolated, a rock skyscraper that made an island in the sky. Beyond this, in the narrow causeway of land between

Lake Achkel and Lake Bizerta, the clean bright town of Ferry-ville was clearly in view and beyond that again the haze that was Bizerta.

As we looked most of this area was under fire of some kind. A Messerschmitt dived on Mateur, blew up a jeep and then, caught by anti-aircraft fire, it dived in streaming yellow flames to the ground. Shells were bursting steadily round Ferryville and the German fire, both from guns and from dive bombers, fell heavily on the outskirts of Mateur. They were aiming at the one bridge we had to cross to get into the town.

An American doughboy was sitting on that bridge as we made our dash across between salvoes. God knows what he was doing there. He just sat grinning on the rails with smoking bomb holes all around him and more shells due any minute. Decidedly the American soldier had got his teeth into the war this time.

Mateur was devastated and deserted. A few stray dogs and cats ran among the tottering walls, a handful of gendarmes and a plucky French girl had taken refuge in a cave decked with the *Tricolore*. In the streets jeeps and Sherman tanks were milling about. Shells were landing haphazardly round the town and we drove out quickly to the north following the shores of the lake. It was hard to make out what was happening and nobody had any accurate information. Some said there were Germans on the Jebel but we rode under the mountain without interference. It was much softer country here in the north, well cultivated with large prosperous homesteads, more European. We were now entirely alone and I did not like it much. But of my two companions, one, A. B. Austen, seemed to derive a strange satis-faction from being fired at, and the other, Christopher Buckley, had for years been quite unable to resist a craving to explore anything and everything whether it lay inside enemy territory or not.

And so we rode on round that lovely lake until we came on an American reconnaissance unit. They had taken cover in a farmhouse which had been vacated by six hundred Germans the day before. There was a touching domestic scene going on in the French family circle in the house. Mme Verdier, a charming woman, half-English, drew us into the parlour to act as judges in the matter. It seemed that her husband had escaped to England two years before and joined the Free French. In the meantime his son, Robert, had grown up and now at seventeen was determined to set off and find his father and then join the RAF, for which he had conceived an intense admiration. He had wanted to pass through the German lines at night and with difficulty his mother had dissuaded him. She had been forced to promise that as soon as the Allies reached the farmhouse he could set off. Now her son was holding her to her promise. The boy, a thin sensitive lad, stood tensely in the corner while it was all explained.

We said the obvious things. The front was in a turmoil at the moment. He would be lost for days, even weeks, if he tried to find his way without passes through the army to Algiers and then to England. If he would just wait until Tunis had fallen then everything would be easier. The French authorities would be able to help him then.

I don't think we made much impression. The boy was keyed up to a state of excitement that could not have been brooked. I was sorry for his mother. All the time we were talking the guns were going outside but she had no thought for these, only for the boy. She was gripped with her anxiety to do the best she could for him. Already she had faced up the fact that she was going to lose him anyhow. I never heard what happened. We were swept back at once into the prodigious moving spectacle outside that little farmhouse parlour. But still the incident sticks in my mind for, just as in the case of the German pilot who had been shot down, it forced one for a moment to see that all the machinery of war, all the organization and the outward show, was in the end based on such little family matters as these—and the spirit of them.

Beyond the farmhouse we took the empty road again, and

at last caught up with the front on the banks of the Sedjenane River. I call it a front but in reality it was a quaint little pocket of the war. A column of Frenchmen had come through the thickets along the coast and had been stopped by mortar fire outside Bizerta. We were unable to join them because the bridge across the river was down, and the enemy were shelling the river. Shells fell now among a group of frightened horses, now around an American doughboy who was trying to build a ford across the river with a bull-dozer, and now close to a French poilu who was squatting on his haunches and throwing hand grenades into the river. Each time a grenade exploded a few muddy-looking fish floated to the surface and the Frenchman dragged them in with a stick. A line of American shock troops sat under the lee of the bank watching with interest. Nobody seemed to be paying the least attention to the shelling or the war. Clearly we were not going to get into Bizerta that night and we turned back.

We had had such a day of reconnoitring on our own that we decided to push our luck a little further. Since Green and Bald hills had fallen it was reasonable to presume that the road linking that pass to the lakes was open, so we turned up it. As we climbed into the mountains I saw through the back of the car that there was a battery of German guns firing out of the hospital in Ferryville. The shots kept falling in the lake and sending up columns of water that were pink and shining in the sunset light.

We were now approaching Green and Bald hills from the enemy direction, and we ran full tilt into a vast crater across the road. Beyond that a stray American colonel told us the road MIGHT be clear of mines. But then again, he said, it might not. We pushed on cautiously, and then at the crest of the pass saw something that made the driver jam on his brakes. A party of American sappers with mine detectors was approaching us from the opposite direction. Walking in front of the car and studying every foot of the ground we got through to the

Americans and continued home. When we passed that spot on the hills the following morning two of the American sappers lay dead beside the road. They had been killed by a mine which our car had harmlessly gone by the night before.

It had been a curious thing passing through Green and Bald hills and seeing the dugouts of both sides where so many had died in the winter in the mud and the cold. At the end the Germans made no attempt to hold the two bastions. A handful of Americans had struggled up both hills and reported back the astounding news that the enemy had decamped in the night. It seemed an anti-climax that the great battle of the Sedjenane sector which had cost thousands of lives should finish so quietly and without display. The little wayside graves, some with swastikas on them and some with British or American helmets, are practically all that is left to mark that terrible battlefield now.

For three days we hunted in the Bizerta district, hoping every hour that the town would fall. Enemy troops and civilians we knew were pouring southward out of the town along the one road that lay open to them into Tunis. But a rearguard fought bitterly. To every one's astonishment it turned out that there was a garrison of Germans perched on the black heights of Jebel Achkel. A lavish French homestead stood on the slopes opposite the mountain, and we drove up there to watch the battle.

It was quite a set-piece, this affair—the infantry spread in lines across the wheat fields, the guns and the tanks closing in, the shells bursting on the heights of the Jebel, and the enemy hitting back, sometimes by casting shots off the heights, sometimes by dive-bombing and strafing along the roads. In perfect safety we looked down on the arena from this homestead, and then the bizarre figure of M. Louis Roderer appeared. He came out on to the verandah, an elderly Frenchman, a cosmopolitan who contrived to look like an English country squire by wearing riding breeches and a voluminous tweed jacket. M. Roderer was one of the champagne family. He had come to Tunisia years ago and apart from his town house in Paris and his estates in France he had devoted most of his life and his great wealth to this farm. He had built himself this lovely home. He had drained and cleared the land with the cheap native labour and now his neat and orderly fields spread away to the Jebel.

"That is my land you are fighting your battle on now," he said. "I hope they don't do too much damage."

He spoke in English, almost as well as he spoke French and German.

"Come inside," he said, "and I will show you General Mann-teufel's room."

It was a charming countryman's study. The walls were lined with books in three languages. There were many sporting prints, a collection of stuffed game birds and a shelf crowded with the stocks of old Moorish hunting guns. Here, among the fishing nets and the sporting prints, the German General Mannteufel had conducted the defence of the whole Bizerta area until he had been forced to leave hurriedly two nights before. "He did not appear worried," M. Roderer said. "He remained very correct and charming to the end. I used to have breakfast with him every morning, but of course we never discussed the war or politics—we just talked about fishing and shooting and sports. He was very correct. I was sorry in some ways to see him go. The Germans paid for everything during the four months they were here, and did far less damage than your troops have done in a single morning. Just look at this"—and he led the way out on to the verandah again. Pointing down to a grove of trees he said:

"Ruined—all ruined—by your tanks when they broke in here and sheltered this morning. When I protested the American officer in charge said that I was pro-Nazi. I replied that it was only because I was friendly to your cause that I could be so frank and open with my complaint."

A good deal of M. Roderer's conversation ran like this. We

were to meet more of his kind among the wealthy people of
Tunis later on. It was not so much that they were pro-Nazi, it
was that the sole consuming interest of their lives was to safe-
guard their property. They gave hospitality to the Allies and
the Germans with an equal mind. They were prepared to talk in
German, French, Italian or English. Before the war they had
divided their lives between London, Paris, southern Europe and
New York, always with one eye on their investments. They
were simply not interested in the war. They were waiting with
impatience for the day when they could enter into the full use
of their frozen wealth again.

To M. Roderer the spectacle of wounded American soldiers
being brought into his house from the fighting on the Jebel was
more of an inconvenience than an appeal for his assistance. He
did everything to help, of course, in a perfunctory way, but he
was glad, profoundly glad, when the battle of the Jebel was
finished. What a difference between this cultivated and cynical
old man and the burning enthusiasm of the young French boy
who wanted to join the RAF.

By May fourth it was clear that Bizerta was not going to fall
at once, and since Tunis was fifty times more important we
returned to the Medjerda sector to await the zero hour. Alexander had wheeled the main bulk of the American forces eastward
directly toward the coast and away from Bizerta. His object
was to bottle up the German army in the Medjerda Valley,
which was now being invested from all sides including the sea.
It was ferocious country the Americans entered now, but still
they forged on and finally got astride the road between Bizerta
and Tunis. Simultaneously the last obstacle in the Medjerda
Valley was mopped up. This was an ugly Jebel called Bou
Aoukaz, just outside Tebourba. In a series of hectic rushes the
British infantry swept on to the crest. On the night of May fifth
the enemy's last battle line around Tunis lay exposed to immediate assault. At dawn on the following day the British blitz
went in.

Chapter XVIII: Tunis

AS I SAY, we had taken a sector of only three thousand yards for this last assault. This cauldron seemed to us at that time the whole battle and the whole world but in reality it was a tiny piece of the line, not 2 per cent of its entire length. Like the arc of a bubble now the German line stretched round Tunis, and Alexander proposed to prick it in this one place.

Von Arnim was issuing printed orders of the day to his men: "Behind you lies the sea; before you lies the enemy. You must go forward. You must fight to the last round and the last man"—the sort of pamphlet they issued at Stalingrad. But the German position was not desperate. The minefield-mortar-machinegun combination still stretched like a web around Tunis and Cape Bon. There was still a quarter of a million Axis troops on the field of battle. They had petrol, food, guns, tanks and ammunition. Only the Luftwaffe seemed to have packed up. Most of it had already gone off to Sicily and there were rumours that a dispute was going on between the Luftwaffe and the German Army Command.

For the rest the German morale was not bad. I glanced through some letters we had taken from prisoners. One sergeant wrote from Tebourba. "We are all right here. We can hold them off for months if need be. It's only those bastards back at base and on the lines of supply. The cowards are already making jokes about 'Tunis-grad'. Our lieutenant sent for a gun replacement and the fellow at base workshops sent back word 'What do you want replacements for? All the guns are going to be spiked in a fortnight.' We will know who to deal with in our own ranks when we have won the victory here." There was another letter addressed to a soldier from his father in Berlin. It described street by street the damage done by the RAF in Berlin and it ended, "Be pitiless for the English know no pity."

Up to a point this was true. The Allied army had no pity now. It was a machine, a great mill pressing down and now a blade was going to come out of the press.

Alexander made his last reshuffles behind the lines. The corps that was going to deliver the first blow leap-frogged over Number 5, the one that had done all the serious fighting up the Medjerda Valley until now. It had fine infantry divisions and two heavy armoured divisions. One-half of the force was from the Eighth Army and one-half from the First. That was right. Both armies should share in this honour. The corps commander had been borrowed from the Eighth Army because he was a veteran, an aggressive man, a successful commander with three or four recent victories to his credit.

In the same way Air Marshal Coningham bound his two air forces together, the one from the desert and the one from the mountains, and it was an instrument of air war such as Africa had never seen before. Thousands of aircraft. They had three jobs—to smash the enemy in Tunisia, to prevent what was left taking to the boats, to knock out the enemy ports and airfields in Sicily and southern Italy. The navy likewise was ready with hundreds of motor-boats, destroyers, corvettes, cruisers and even aircraft carriers and battleships to deal with the Italian fleet if it came out (it never did).

It was the air force that started the battle and the air force which brought back the first indication of the way the battle was going to go—though we did not at the time fully understand the indication. On the morning of May sixth one thousand sorties were made on the enemy lines before breakfast. That is to say some of the squadrons were used twice or several times but in all one thousand trips were made before 9 A.M. They rose in swarms out of the clearings in the vineyards and the cork-tree forests, out of the beaches and the sandy plains to the south.

Before 9 A.M. the pilots were coming back with extraordinary reports: "We have nothing to bomb. The enemy have dragged all their remaining aircraft off the airfields and hidden them under the trees. There are no enemy aircraft in the sky. There is no movement of vehicles along the road. There is no sign of German activity at the front. There is practically nothing we can see to hit, nothing to strafe."

The Wehrmacht had gone to ground. It was dug into its trenches and weapons pits and heavily camouflaged. From the air the ground appeared dead, and deserted. It was one more demonstration that you cannot accurately bomb a stationary army in the field because you cannot see it. I do not say that some of the pilots did not find targets but for the most part the bombs had to be dropped at places where the enemy was believed to be but where no enemy was visible.

Coningham did not change his plans. He went right on bombing. From the opening of the battle to the end I saw something I had never seen in a campaign before—shoals of Allied fighters patrolling back and forth protecting the ground troops every hour of the day. You must certainly give a good deal of the credit for this Tunisian blitz to the fact that the army was not bombed as it went forward.

The corps commander had spaced one gun about every five yards along his tiny front. The actual spot for the break-through was just to the southeast of Medjez el Bab on the southern side of the Medjerda Valley. The land was gently undulating at that place and between the scattered villages the wheat was now breast high and beginning to turn yellow.

The guns had begun bellowing soon after midnight on May sixth: one shell landing every five yards every few seconds. It is simply not possible to explain the effect of that. Even if one is there the full enormity of the noise and the brilliance of the light does not persist in the memory; and the Germans receiving the barrage do not speak clearly of it because each shell that fell near them was every shell; they could see nothing beyond their immediate trench and hear nothing except the monstrous noise of the explosions near at hand.

Under this roof of shells the sappers went forward at 4 A.M. In the flickering light of the explosions they cut the barbed wire and felt on the ground for the mines. Then the Indians and the British infantry charged through. In the midst of the web of mines and mortars and bullets the battle was on.

All this time the Germans had never been sure of the precise point at which the main shock of the British assault was coming. They expected it somewhere in the Medjerda Valley but just where they could not foretell because the whole front was in an uproar. And the men in the direct path of our onslaught never had time to realize what struck them.

In that triangle of villages around Sidi Salem, Sidi Abdallah and Peter's Corner the Germans were manning their positions in the usual way when the British fell on them. While it was still dark the Indians and the tommies came creeping through the wheat. Over the last few hundred yards they rose to their feet and rushed the enemy positions. They swarmed into the enemy dugouts. They yelled their war cries, each man taking courage from the excitement of his neighbour, and they poured a hail of bullets across that three-thousand-yard front that was more terrible than the earlier barrage.

By sheer weight of numbers and the exhilaration of the charge the British infantry swept through the German outposts and got up to the main chain of machine-gun posts. As dawn broke they were leaping from one German weapon pit to another, shooting as long as the German's shot, and killing so long as they had to kill. When a group of Germans round a machine gun gave up the British ran on to the next knot of opposition without waiting to collect prisoners or wounded—some one coming on behind would do that.

The German line was perhaps a mile to two miles thick— that is to say, there was a loosely connected series of trenches and defended positions of that depth. At daylight the British

were right in the midst of this line and our penetration was being
measured in thousands of yards. And still it went on, the hacking
and thrusting, the hand-to-dand fighting, the overwhelming of
the enemy positions one by one. It was scarcely noon when the
leaders of the forward companies were reporting over their
portable radios that they were meeting reduced opposition.
They had burst clean through the German line and come out
into the vacant space behind.

It was only a narrow breach but that was all that the General
wanted. He had pricked the bubble. He was behind the German
line. He was through the mine fields. For seven or eight hours
the tank crews of the Sixth and Seventh armoured divisions had
been waiting. A few tanks had gone in the infantry but the
bulk of them were waiting in the rear under the cover of the
trees. He now turned to these vital reserves and said "Go."

The tanks charged ahead. They went straight at the gap the
infantry had made for them and they passed through practically
unscathed. It was like releasing the floodgates of a dam. In
scores, in hundreds this vast procession of steel lizards went
grumbling and lurching and swaying up the Tunis road. Tunis
itself lay barely thirty miles away, the line was pierced. Visors
down, dust streaming out behind them, they shot ahead straight
for Tunis. They took no account of the Germans on either side
of them, no account of the fact that the road behind them might
be closed. The line was pierced and that was enough. They
roared on. With them flowed the artillery and the anti-tank
guns, the fuel and the ammunition waggons, the workshops and
the recovery vehicles, the jeeps and the command cars. Out in
front and on either flank rode the armoured cars on reconnaissance. When night came they were all on the road to Tunis.

On the morning of the seventh the Medjerda Valley had become a hateful place. It had turned from green to dirty yellows
and greys. The fields of wildflowers had withered entirely. The
ripening wheat was flattened. The dust was appalling. Nearing
Medjez el Bab visibility was barely two hundred yards and on

the dozens of newly made side tracks it was much worse than that. Huge trucks lurched suddenly out of the gloom and we turned aside fifty times at the last moment to avoid a collision. General Alexander, driving a jeep, shot past us over a culvert. He was travelling at almost reckless speed, both his hands tight on the wheel, and his face was whitened like a baker boy's with white dust. We felt our way on to the general's headquarters but it had vanished. A solitary redcap simply said, "They moved on two hours ago. They've got to Furna." To Furna? Furna was behind the enemy's old line. It scarcely seemed possible. If corps headquarters had gone as far as this where then were the front-line troops. For the first time we thought, "Can Tunis fall today?" No one said this. No one liked to say it. But we all thought it as we raced down the side tracks towards the main road.

Inside half an hour we were on yesterday's battlefield and no enemy anywhere, just empty trenches and gun pits. Past the villages which the Germans had held for months, past Sidi Salem and Sidi Abdallah where there had been nothing but death and killing the week before. Over a ruined bridge and round by Peter's Corner that was once an enemy stronghold. Nothing there now. Nothing but the rusting broken tanks around which the wheat and flowers had grown tall, as if the earth itself wanted to hide those hideous machines.

And then on the main road, there it was again, for the third time in one month—the army careering forward in pursuit of the enemy. But this made the other cavalcades look puny and of no account. Miles before Furna the vehicles were touching almost bonnet to tailboard. They stacked themselves two and three deep along the road. The infantry lay sprawling on their kits on top of the lorries and their rifles lay stacked together as though the war was over. At Furna still the procession went on; it was not so thick now but still it stretched away in the distance. Only twenty miles to go. It was there on the white stone—"Tunis 33 kilometres."

We wanted no part of corps headquarters now. We wanted only to get to the head of this incredible race. Brief scraps of information came to us on the road: The troops were through Massicault. The tanks were moving into St. Cyprien. Where then were the enemy? Who was on either side of this narrow thrust? We asked and asked and got no reasonable answer. Only "God knows." "Who cares? It's Tunis we want."

In Massicault the traffic had definitely thinned out but the village was entirely ours. Two Tunisian girls hung over a wicket fence talking to a group of tommies as though the army had been there for weeks. There were only a few shell scars on the white buildings along the single street. The tanks had blitzed clean through. Sixteen miles to Tunis.

Presently a mosque and another group of white farmhouses showed up across the plain, St. Cyprien. We ran into the village and stopped at the first farmhouse. That was a pleasant moment. We had found the front—if you could call it a front. Standing there were the men and the guns of the Royal Horse Artillery, the Desert Rats, the original Desert Rats. The men I had seen in Syria and Abyssinia and the desert. The guns that had fired from the very beginning of the African war for Wavell and Straffer Gott, for Jock Campbell and Alec Gatehouse. The twenty-five-pounders that used to accept and turn back the German tank rushes in the desert though they were never meant to fire at tanks. They had come all the way from Alamein and they had been through everything, young cockneys and Lancaster boys in shorts and shirts and burnt by the sun, men of the Seventh Armoured Division who had fired first shots in the African war, some of the finest gunners in the world.

They were excited. "We're going to get into Tunis somehow."

But as we turned back to their brigade headquarters for information my spirits sank. German shelling began. There was resistance still. It was already midday. We could hardly round up those enemy guns before dark. Even as we stopped in a wheat field to gobble a quick cold lunch the shells began coming in our direction. A line of German prisoners was marching into the camp and each time a shell cracked into the field they broke ranks and went to ground, not in panic but mechanically and automatically as men do when they have been shelled too much, too often, too recently. After each burst they formed ranks again without bidding from the guards.

There was more firing away to the right, where it was said a tank battle was going on. All this time, while we ate cheese and bread on the steps of the car more and more desert vehicles kept flowing into the fields behind St. Cyprien and dispersing. We decided to go forward again to the hills outside the town to get a better view of the fighting before we turned back to Thibar to send our messages away.

It was there on the hilltops in the early afternoon that we saw for the first time what a wonderfully professional thing this advance was. All around us the army was flowing forward—first the tanks in squadrons of fifteen or twenty nosing up to the hills, then splitting and going around into the next valley, then lying stationary and hull-down for a bit and firing. Behind them the guns came up and settled into positions on the newly won hill. In fifteen minutes they were firing. Up the road came the ack-ack guns and the supply waggons and they too dispersed, waited and then went forward again. It was all most professional, this weaving in and out of the hills. Every commander seemed to know exactly what to do. There was no rushing, no overstraining. Everything worked. Each hill was checked on the map, invested, surrounded and passed by.

A thin rain came down and it made no difference except that it settled the dust a little. We ached to see Tunis but we were too far off. A mountainous column of black smoke was going up from the sea, that was all. As we watched we saw other vehicles going ahead of us down the road. Was it possible then we were going to get a little nearer? The trail was very warm as we followed on. Outside St. Cyprien there was a German cemetery, row upon row of neat graves divided by flower beds and gravel paths. You could read the history of the Tunisian campaign there.

Near the ornamental gate were the old graves of the past year, Oberleutnant Hans this and Corporal Fritz that from the Hermann Goering regiments killed in the early skirmishes at Green Hill and Tebourba.

These graves had elaborately painted swastikas. Then others, Stuka pilots, with their black emblem of the diving plane, the laurel wreath and the German eagle. Further inside the cemetery the graves were increasingly newer, the paths ungravelled. The last graves had crosses but these had not been erected or painted; just little tabs lay on the ground giving the dead man's name. Beyond that a series of gaping holes in the ground waiting for more bodies. At the end of the cemetery a Mark IV tank had taken shelter behind the cactus hedge and it had been destroyed an hour or two before. It still smouldered. I looked inside the smoking wreck and saw the nauseating sight of the dead crew. The war had caught up with and passed this cemetery too quickly for the recent dead to find a grave. Across the road two French children were playing with an ack-ack gun and a British reconnaissance plane that had just put down.

As we drove on and still there was no impediment on the road our hopes began to rise again. Perhaps it would be Tunis tonight. I felt a twinge of conscience about Clifford and Keating. For the past three years we had entered most captured towns together. We had always been together at the last. Clifford was definitely out of the running. He had gone off with the French down at Pont du Fahs miles away across the mountains. Keating I had not seen for days. It was hard on them, I thought, to miss Tunis after coming two thousand miles from Alamein.

We were getting very close. Kilometre 14. The Village of La Mornaghia. A notice in German: "Danger—typhus in village." The villagers were standing on the steps of the Café aux

Délices de Mornaghia in the Place des Carnières and cheering. Out ahead there was a series of new explosions—tanks fighting possibly; perhaps the enemy blowing up dumps. Smudges of smoke crept up through the rain on the northern horizon.

The first man I recognised in the village was Clifford. He was standing on a bit of raised ground watching a fight between Shermans and a Mark IV's on the next hillside. "I hitch-hiked up from Pont du Fahs," he said airily. "I got a tip Tunis was going to fall." It must have been a monumental bit of hitch-hiking in that traffic jam, experts though we all were in getting lifts from the army and the air force.

I saw the corps commander arrive in the main street and made a bee-line for him. Except for the crown and crossed swords on his cap you would never have recognised this slight thin-faced man as the controller of the huge machine that was fight-ing around us. Like every really able general in the British army he had time to talk and patience to explain. I believe that he had genius that day. You can never attribute success in battle to any one man or any group of men. It is the system and train-ing of an army that takes it forward, not the general, since not one per cent of the army ever sees or hears from its general once the action is joined. But this general at this moment was the ultimate and essential cog in the machine, the governor from which the machine took its rhythm and its pace. And what was important to us, he had more information than any one else.

I believe he had genius because he not only planned this thrust and sent it in, but he now made it clear that he understood the significance of what he had done.

"We have captured the headquarters of the Hermann Goering Regiment and eighty staff officers, though the general got away," he said. "We have penetrated right through the enemy line. It is simply the blitz method confined to a narrow space that has paid us here. The Germans along our line of advance were paralysed by yesterday's shelling and bombing and they have been overrun by the tanks before they could recover. Speed was the thing. There was one moment last night when they could have held us by counter-attacking at Frendj but we broke through again before they could muster. They might have erected gun positions in these hills if they had had a little more time. We have captured a great number of 88's and vehicles. The prisoners are demoralized. It is the blitz. After the shelling and bombing the first thing they saw was hordes of Churchill and Sherman tanks coming over the horizon and they gave in."

He added unemotionally, "The Eleventh Hussars signalled me at 2:25 P.M. that they were on the outskirts of Tunis. I have given them as their objective for the day Tunis Central Railway station. They may be there now. The Derbyshire Yeomanry are also in the suburbs."

This was electric news. Could we go in?

"I don't see why you shouldn't try," the General said. "But don't blame me if anything happens."

We hurried into the vehicles. Ten miles to go. We were standing in the cars now, poking our heads through the open roofs and terribly anxious not to miss anything. This moment had been a long time coming.

Presently on the wet and winding road we fell in with a group of armoured cars reconnoitring the road. That was good; our cars could not even stop a rifle bullet. They were travelling fast and we went with them, each vehicle spaced about fifty yards away from its neighbours. I counted the kilometre stones. Only eight miles now. It was gentle country, almost market gardening country. The Arabs stared out of their huts without comprehending. The smoke ahead got heavier and heavier.

At kilometre 9 all Tunis broke into view—the wide bay, flanked by mountains, the spreading town, one of the largest in Africa, not much harmed by bombs but smoking now with a score of large fires. We stood poised on the summit for a moment before we dipped down into the suburbs. I remember thinking over and over again as I stood in the rain, "Tunis has fallen." That simple thought seemed to be quite enough in itself,

A German with blood pouring down his leg popped out of a doorway in front of me and surrendered. We waved him back towards the British prisoners. Two more Germans came out of a house with their hands up but we were intent on getting to the car and took no notice. At the corner of the brewery two sergeants, one American and the other British, who were staff photographers, ran across the open road to their vehicle, grabbed their tommy-guns and began firing. They were enjoying the whole thing with a gusto that seemed madness at first. Yet I could understand it a little. This street fighting had a kind of red Indian quality about it. You felt you were right up against the enemy and able to deal with him directly, your nimbleness and marksmanship against his. The American was coolly picking his targets and taking careful aim. The young Frenchman with the Sten gun turned up and I realized now that he had been warning us about these snipers in the first place. He led the two sergeants into the brewery kicking the door open with his foot and shooting from the hip. They sent a preliminary volley through the aperture. Presently the three of them came out with the two snipers who had been shooting above our heads. They had wounded one.

The sergeants then offered to cover us while we ran for our car. My driver was quick. He whizzed it backwards up the street and we ran to the point a quarter of a mile back where the rest of the British column was waiting.

Clifford had been having a busy time at the cross-roads. He had stopped one car with two German officers in it. They had pointed to the red crosses on their arms but Clifford found the vehicle full of arms and he lugged them out. At the same time two snipers had run across to the house on the corner. A tommy with a neat burst killed them as they ran. Mad things were going on. Two Italian officers marched up and demanded in the midst of this confusion that they should be provided with transport to return to their barracks where they had left their waterproof coats.

Meanwhile another patrol of armoured cars had taken the right fork, the Rue de Londres, down to the centre of town. They took the city entirely unawares. Hundreds of Germans were walking in the streets, some with their girl friends. Hundreds more were sitting drinking *apéritifs* in a big pavement café. No one had warned them the British were near. The attack had gone so quickly that here in the town there had been no indication that the Axis line was broken. Now suddenly like a vision from the sky appeared these three British armoured cars. The Germans rose from their seats and stared. The tommies stared back. There was not much they could do. Three armoured cars could not handle all these prisoners. In the hairdressing saloon next door more Germans struggled out of the chairs and with white sheets round their necks and lather on their faces stood gaping.

The three armoured cars turned back for reinforcements.

In this mad way Tunis fell that night. Here and there a German with desperate courage emptied his gun down on the streets and hurled a grenade or two. But for the most part these base troops in Tunis were taken entirely off their guard and there were thousands of them. All night there was hopeless confusion in the dark, Germans and British wandering about together, Italians scrambling in to civilian clothes and taking refuge in the cellars, saboteurs starting new fires and igniting more dumps, men putting out to sea in rowing boats, others grabbing bicycles and carts and making up the roads to Cape Bon, and others again, bewildered and afraid, simply marching along until they could find some one to whom they could surrender. All night the fires burned and they were still going in the morning when the British infantry began to flood into the town in force.

An extraordinary scene of havoc and confusion was revealed by the morning light. The town itself was pretty well unscathed but the waterfront had been ravaged by bombfire out of all recognition. Six-storey buildings had collapsed like pancakes. For days hardly a man had dared to approach the docks. The port of La Goulette outside the town near the site of ancient Carthage was even worse. Ships or parts of ships were blown out of the sea and flung upon the hulks of their sister ships. The stone wharves were split up and pocked with immense craters.

At the two airfields scores of smashed German planes were lying about in the soaking rain, Messerschmitts, Dorniers, Macchis, Folke-Wulfs, Junkers, Stukas and communication machines of every possible sort.

My party had not stayed to explore these things. We had entered the city at fifteen minutes to three on May seventh. The street fighting had held us up until nearly dark and then, through the evening, we made that endless tedious drive back to Thibar to send our messages. We were so tired we scarcely glanced up when a Spitfire crashed close by us at Medjez el Bab. On the way we heard that the Americans had reached Bizerta. It was just six months since the landing in North Africa, just three years since the African war had begun.

Chapter XIX: Bizerta

BY MAY EIGHTH the front was falling to bits in every direction. Even at Alexander's headquarters they did not yet know the overwhelming nature of the break-through. The Allied army had simply picked itself up like a colossal tidal wave and now the wave had burst uncontrollably over that last corner of Axis Africa. No force on earth could have checked its onward course at that moment. The Axis defence was pricked to its heart and now from every direction an ungovernable flood of men and weapons was spilling up the valleys and the mountain roads.

Like every one else we were swept into it that morning. We fondly imagined we could drive back into Tunis and then turn northward up the coast road and enter Bizerta. An hour after leaving Thibar we disillusioned ourselves. There was a sixty-mile traffic jam. This was a traffic jam to end all traffic jams, a solid mass of vehicles blocking every side track. At Medjez el Bab there were only two makeshift bridges and the procession was practically stationary for twenty miles on either side of the bottleneck. Neither persuasion nor cunning could get us through and we turned up the northerly road hoping we could open up a new way across country. If Tebourba had fallen then we knew we might get through. Tebourba had fallen all right but the enemy were still around us. We exchanged a few words with the men who had taken the town and then doubled back on our tracks to Béja. Somehow we felt we had to see the fall of Bizerta. Tunis had been a great triumph and we were greedy for more. By some miracle the back roads were clear. Three hours' headlong driving brought us to Mateur. No firing ahead. We ran straight into Ferryville. The people there were cheering and waving madly but still we could not be sure whether Bizerta had fallen or not. It looked quiet enough across the lake. We doubled round behind the airport and ran through groves of olive trees where thousands of casks of German oil were lying. We were almost into the town before we heard shellfire—shellfire coming towards us. We were rather childishly pleased that we had arrived in time to see the end. It was an odd situation. An American patrol had entered the town the previous day about the same time as Tunis fell but they had come out again in the night. Now, ten hours later, Germans were still fighting in the streets and it was a moot point as to whether the place had fallen or not. The thing was additionally complicated by the fact that more German tanks and gunners were barely a quarter of a mile away across the narrow channel that runs into Bizerta lake. They had a clear view up all the north and south streets running through the town and any one who crossed those lines of fire was in for trouble.

A company of doughboys, moving in single file, was going to have another shot at cleaning up the situation. We parked the car and went along with them.

For the first few hundred yards inside the city wall it was all plain sailing, and there was leisure to look around as we went forward, keeping close to the walls. What a difference there was here. Tunis was alive. This was dead. No town that I have seen in the war has ever been knocked flat, but Bizerta was the nearest thing to it. The very earth had been churned up and broken into dust by high explosive. Tunis was marred at the edges; this was ravaged throughout. I looked at house after house as we walked by and nothing had escaped. Some buildings were turned upside down. The roofs had fallen to the floors and the floors had been blasted up against the walls. Fire had done the rest. The palace, the bank, the administration centre—they were all holed with direct hits and it looked as though some giant claw had scraped away the façades of the buildings. The church steeple still stood. And in the steeple a little group of Germans were sitting around a machine gun. Down below that they had another gun, a full-sized anti-tank gun poking through the grating of a cellar. There were other snipers about.

A Sherman tank lunged down the street of the church, and came back with its nose chipped. Every time a doughboy shoved his head round the corner a bullet flicked by. A Frenchman blithely wished to guide us in a jeep to the upper reaches of the town. We followed until there was another burst of machine-gunning and it was borne in upon us that the snipers were letting the Frenchman go by on his bicycle and holding their fire until we got conveniently close. Our day in Tunis had given me a lively distaste for street fighting and we crawled back to the doughboys. They were working very neatly and smoothly, creeping up on the houses and flinging their hand grenades from the cover of the doorways. Already they had silenced two snipers and the church steeple was cleaned out. Across the river we could see the enemy tanks pulling into a wood and taking the track southward in the wake of the rest of the Axis army. Well, they would not get far. At that we reckoned Bizerta had fallen and was in American hands. The lovely port and its docks had paid the heaviest price that is possible in war. Had the Romans come again with their firebrands and ploughed salt into the ground they could scarcely have done more damage. Bizerta was destroyed. Its inhabitants had fled and not until long after this war will they be able to repair the damage that was done in a few hours of hellishly precise bombing from the sky.

Again we drove back to Thibar in almost a coma of weariness for we had been on the road almost continuously for forty-eight hours. We were forced to a long detour in the darkness because an ammunition lorry had caught fire on the main road and it was again long after midnight before we had our messages done.

Tunis when we got back to it on May ninth had given itself up to song and dance. The town's population had been doubled by refugees and to these was added now a horde of exultant soldiery. The men who had been in the desert or in the moun-

tains for months on end stared with amazement at the riot of
hilarity raging along every street, and then joined in themselves. The French soldiers who came in were nearly smothered
with kisses. Staid old French dowagers leaned over the balconies and screamed, *"Vive de Gaulle"*—they had not yet heard
about General Giraud, and our propaganda units were busy
plastering the town with coloured posters showing Giraud's
features. The *V* sign enclosing the Fighting French Cross of
Lorraine was being chalked up everywhere; it was with some
difficulty that one explained that General de Gaulle was not
after all the man who had liberated them but another general—
Giraud by name. He was just as good, one explained, and they
would grow to like him. Heavens, how the politics of Algiers
stank in this exuberant atmosphere. It was especially embarrassing when some of General Le Clerc's hard-bitten warriors
came in after their three years' fight for de Gaulle in the
desert.

But no one was going very deeply into politics at this moment. The Germans were gone, that was the main thing. How
the French of Tunis loathed the Germans. It was just one black
wall of choking hatred. Not that the Germans had been brutal,
just arrogant and very strict. I went into the local newspaper
office and the French compositor showed me a copy of that
week's *Oasis* he had been obliged to print for the Afrika Korps.
One of the headlines was *"Fair play—Nein."* The compositor
showed me a pile of anti-British and anti-American printing
blocks. With one superb gesture he swept them off the table
and spat.

There was a curfew at night and a car with a loud-speaker
kept driving through the streets to enforce it. But up till eight
the people were free to let themselves go and they did. Tens of
thousands swarmed across the main streets cheering every truck-
load of soldiers that came in.

Tunis still had food and liquor of a sort and the troops made
pretty free with it.

One night I drove out to the headland where the village of Sidi Bou Said is built and after six years of travelling round the Mediterranean I would say that it is the most beautiful village on all the shores of that sea. The snow-white Arab houses are stepped up the cliffs in a haphazard pyramid, and in this vision of bougainvillea and orange groves and terraced gardens the very wealthy people of France and Italy have built their holiday houses. The villas hang above that perfect bay and standing on the balconies one feels suspended between the sea and the sky and the mountains. The show place is the palace built by the international banker d'Erlanger. A niche for this delicate and lovely house was carved out of the cliffs above the Bey's seaside residence. All the old arts of Arab carving in wood and marble and plaster were revived to decorate the interior. A cooling stream plays along a channel through the reception rooms. The books are bound in the rarest leather. A waterfall of flowers and cypresses and orange-trees falls down to the sea.

In the midst of this cultured splendour dwelt La Baronne. She was living in a remote wing of the house when I met her—just a bedroom and a sitting-room. Like herself the sitting-room was fragile and charming and in excellent taste. It was entirely feminine and everything had been chosen with care, even the English books which had just been laid out. The servant, in voluminous white trousers, a turban, a red sash and slippers that turned up to a point, brought us whiskey and soda.

"Thank heavens I have some left," the baroness said. Her English was faultless. "The Germans and the Italians drank all the champagne. I had the pilots living here, you know. They were very correct but there were just a few things . . . The peacocks, for instance. I had ten lovely white peacocks and one day I noticed there were only seven of them on the terrace. It turned out the Italians were killing and roasting them to eat. I had to ask them to stop."

Below us a Moorish fountain, richly tiled, stood among the orange-trees of her private garden, a grotto in the palace. No bombs had fallen here, but away below, the port of La Goulette was an ugly mess. The baroness used to watch the Allied aircraft sail in and plant their bombs on that festering mass of twisted steel.

"But it was all so quick," she said. "Only the day before yesterday the Germans were here and we had no sign at all that anything was wrong. My maid brought my breakfast to me in bed as she always does and she said to me, 'The Germans are going.' I said to her, 'Nonsense. What do you mean? Why should they go?' The next thing she came running in to say that the colonel himself had set off. I looked out the window and sure enough they were throwing their belongings into the trucks and driving off. In an hour or two none of them were left. I had no notion of what was happening. And then a few hours later I looked out again and there they were, the British troops. It was almost too sudden to be believed. I have had such a lot of your generals coming in to see me. They all seem to want to stay here."

I rested luxuriously in another villa a little higher up the hill that night. The bed, as I noted from the books and papers lying about, had been used as late as Wednesday night by the officer in charge of the peacock-eating pilots. An Italian military telephone stood beside the bed.

Back in Tunis one event came crowding on another. The ship that had set off for Italy with the cargo of British prisoners had taken one look at the British destroyers lying in wait outside the harbour and put back into Tunis, its crew preferring imprisonment to death, its precious passengers safe. Everywhere refugees from the Axis were coming out of the cellars and back rooms where they had been living for months—an English clergyman, leaders of the French Socialist party, de Gaullists, tommies who had escaped and found shelter with friendly French people.

General Giraud arrived and when he drove through the streets to the city monument in a fine cavalcade of Spahi horsemen the crowds gave him a good welcome. Already he was becoming well known and it was clear the people would accept him since he stood for revenge on the Germans.

Many hostile Italians were hidden in the city. A proclamation went up stating that all enemy soldiers in hiding were to give themselves up by the following night. Otherwise they would be shot.

Outside the town the prisoners' cages were filling up. Not since Wavell's days had I seen such swarms of men. The compound on the Massicault road overflowed beyond its barbed wire and cactus hedges and the Germans and Italians simply hung around the outskirts waiting to be taken in. A German band complete with its instruments had arrived. The bandsmen stood in a square and played soothing Viennese *lieder*. There must have been five thousand prisoners in that camp and more were coming in at the rate of five hundred an hour. The prisoners were being issued tins of bully beef, packets of biscuits and tins of fruit. There seemed to be plenty. Since neither I myself nor any one in the army had been able to get his hands on more than a spoonful of tinned fruit for the past few weeks I found myself unreasonably annoyed with one German who was pouring away the juice in order to get at the pears in his tin more easily.

At that moment I had not yet begun to know the full story of the prisoners or I would not have been so excited.

While all this peaceful sorting out was going on in Tunis tremendous events were happening outside the town. The Americans had broken clean through the mountains to the west and north of Medjerda Valley and were mopping up prisoners in uncounted thousands. The Seventh Armoured Division wheeled northward from Tunis and pursued its old enemy the Fifteenth Panzer Division up the coast road as far as Porto Farina outside Bizerta. The Germans made one abortive attempt to escape by sea—bodies were being washed ashore for days afterwards—and then surrendered. Those two divisions had been fighting one another across the desert for years.

The fighting French had come through Pont du Fahs in one epic rush and were counting their prisoners by the truckland. On the coast the skeleton Eighth Army was again locked in a most bloody battle around Enfidaville.

But all this did not account for the main bulk of von Arnim's forces. They were in a state of disorder but they were still intact. In a vast disorganized mob the majority of them had made for the Cape Bon Peninsula where arrangements for evacuation ought to have been made. Cape Bon was defensible. A stiff double line of hills ran across its base and von Arnim's last coherent plan was to get as many of his men and weapons as possible behind those hills before the British arrived. There were only two feasible passes through the hills—one at Hamman Lif where the Bey had his palace on the northern coast outside Tunis, the other at the lovely tourist town of Hammamet on the south coast at the base of Cape Bon. Von Arnim himself had retreated to the Zaghouan area and was fighting a hot rear-guard action back towards Hammamet. His northern armies meanwhile were slipping through the Hamman Lif gap in the north.

This was the moment when Alexander turned his decisive thrust on Tunis into a *coup de grâce*. It is fascinating to me now to look back and see a guiding hand in all these vast movements. At the time everything to me was pretty confused; indeed, travelling as I was with the onward sweep of the troops and being without general information from hour to hour it was impossible to know what plan, if any, was being carried out. All I knew was that a major break-through had occurred and willy-nilly one followed the general advance wherever it went.

It was not until a few days later when General Anderson explained to us personally what had happened that I realized what a masterpiece of design the break-through had been and what enormous risks had been taken. In our headlong thrust to Tunis we had left huge numbers of enemy in pockets on either

side of us. It was an extremely narrow thrust and the major
risk was that the enemy might close in behind us and entirely
surround the head of the British army. Fifty things might have
gone wrong. As it turned out the sheer depth and swiftness of
the thrust entirely disorganized von Arnim's command. Von
Arnim himself was put to flight. So were his corps and divisional
headquarters. The result was that the big pockets of fresh fighting troops on either side of the British break-through were without orders. They saw a great column of enemy vehicles and
tanks rushing past them and they simply deduced that the game
was up. They headed at full steam for Cape Bon.

Now, having taken this first major risk and got away with it,
Alexander and Anderson decided to go one further.

They decided to split the German army in two halves by
occupying the Hamman Lif-Hammamet line across the base of
Cape Bon Peninsula before von Arnim could. In that way one
half of the Germans would be bottled up in the Peninsula, the
other half would be isolated outside and neither would even get
a chance of getting to the boats. There was of course not an
instant to lose, and already before Tunis fell the orders went
out to the Sixth Armoured Division: "You will break through
the enemy position at Hamman Lif and then wheeling south between the hills proceed to Hammamet." Even on paper it seemed
to be a fantastic thing to ask of any division. For one thing it
meant their tackling an enemy at least ten times numerically
stronger. But Alexander had the Germans on the run and he
meant to keep them running even if it cost him an entire division
or more. Some of our finest infantry—the Guards—without waiting for daylight—set off into the unknown. The subsequent
march of the Sixth Division must place it and its general in the
very highest place in the military history of the war.

They arrived outside Hamman Lif at nightfall, the evening
after Tunis fell. The village straggles along the main road and
the seashore and it is dominated by the Bey's white palace on
the road and a tall apartment house standing near the sea. There

are half a dozen blocks of smaller buildings and the streets run at right angles. The Germans had set up about twenty eighty-eight-millimetre guns in a field beyond the town. They had also established snipers in every one of the six storeys of the apartment house and there were fighting troops in the village as well. It was an extremely strong defensive position since it had to be attacked frontally.

The general waited until the moon had risen. Then he placed tanks at the mouth of each of the village streets. The Guards infantry clambered up on the outside of the tanks. Then the tanks charged. At each intersection infantry dropped off and went down the side streets mopping up with the grenade, the bayonet and the tommy-gun. Others continued to the apartment house and dealt with it in the same way. The tanks engaged the eighty-eights at short range and knocked them out. In that one epic moonlight charge the town was taken. Some one went into the Bey's palace and apologised to the hysterical officials for the damage that was done and the rest of the division swept on.

They broke clean through to Hammamet inside the next ten hours. They roared past German airfields, workshops, petrol and ammunition dumps and gun positions. They did not stop to take prisoners—things had gone for beyond that. If a comet had rushed down that road it could hardly have made a greater impression. The Germans now were entirely dazed. Wherever they looked British tanks seemed to be hurtling past. Von Arnim's guns would be firing south only to find that the enemy had also appeared behind them. And over on the left. And on the right. The German generals gave up giving orders since they were completely out of touch and the people to whom they could give orders were diminishing every hour. In what direction anyway were they to fight. Back towards Zaghouan? Towards Tunis? Under the German military training you had to have a plan. But there was no plan. Only the boats remained—the evacuation boats which had been promised them. The boats that were to take them back to Italy. In a contagion of doubt and fear the German army turned tail and made up the Cape Bon roads looking for the boats. When on the beaches it became apparent to them at last that there were no boats—nor any aircraft either—the army became a rabble. The Italian navy had not dared to put to sea to save its men. The Luftwaffe had been blown out of the sky. In other words, the Axis had cut its losses and the Afrika Korps was abandoned to its fate.

On May tenth I set off up the peninsula through Hamman Lif to see one of the most grotesque and awesome spectacles that can have occurred in this war—an entire German army laying down its arms.

Chapter XX: Cape Bon

TEN kilometres outside Tunis we began to meet Germans and Italians coming towards us on the road. At Hamman Lif their vehicles had thickened to one every hundred yards. Outside Soliman it was one solid mass and there was hardly a British soldier to be seen anywhere.

All the Axis soldiers were driving. They drove in ten-ton Diesel lorries and by standing upright and close together they had managed to jam about forty or fifty men into each vehicle. Many of the lorries towed a trailer of the same size, and an equal number of men were crowded into the trailer.

For eighty miles this procession was crawling slowly along the roads of Cape Bon Peninsula towards the British lines. Most of the German officers were travelling in blunt-nosed little staff cars adapted from the *Volkswaggon*. Others had ordinary touring cars and saloons and there was a good sprinkling of command vehicles. The Italian officers were in Toppolino Fiats and Lancias. Some of the trucks were very old and much battered by desert wear. They staggered along under their unusual burdens emitting great jets of acrid brown smoke. In the smaller cars the officers had piled up their bedding and any chance thing they had laid their hands on at the last moment—extra gallons of gasoline, packets of cigarettes, a favourite folding chair, a violin, a basket of oranges, a suitcase full of civilian clothing. There were many motor-cycles and sidecars.

When a vehicle broke down its passengers went along the line begging lifts and when they were all absorbed in the over-crowded lorries the procession went on again. The soldiers still wore their insignia showing that they were sailors or soldiers or airmen but they had thrown away their weapons and their steel helmets.

No one was in charge of this horde, not even the Axis officers. No one had accepted its surrender. It was a spontaneous and natural sequence of the Allied victory, a result no one could have foreseen, but still a natural result. The Axis mob had retreated to the tip of the peninsula and found itself unable to get away. They were trapped. They had no orders. The finely balanced Wehrmacht system, the careful stepping down of responsibility from corps to division and from colonel to regiment, from NCO to soldier, had disintegrated into a thousand pieces.

By a natural instinct the men sought the preservation of the last thing left to them—their own lives. In the absence of orders they obeyed their instincts. They clambered into their vehicles and drove back towards their conquerors to surrender. The tide in which they had flooded, like some driven herd of cattle, up to the beaches of Cape Bon now began to ebb back towards Tunis.

A gap—a military vacuum—had been left on the roads by the Sixth Division in its dramatic break-through to Hammamet. The returning Germans and Italians now filled that gap and there were no British troops to take them in charge. Throughout this day my party was outnumbered on the roads by about one thousand to one by Axis troops. None made the slightest attempt to molest us. They shouted instead, "Who do we surrender to? To you?" We were willing to accept any one's surrender but there was nothing that we—four people—could do about it. Like the rest of the British troops scattered here and there along the roads we simply waved the prisoners on and they kept going. I am making no attempt here to write of the astonishment and incredulity with which we saw this mass of beaten men flow by all through May tenth, the eleventh and the twelfth and even for days after that. I want only to explain how it looked and why they surrendered. The prisoners I saw—and I suppose I passed thirty thousand on this first day, mostly Germans—were not exhausted. They were not hungry or shellshocked or wounded. They were not frightened. I saw their dumps under the trees from Soliman to Grombalia and away up the peninsula; and the weapons they had thrown away. They had ammunition and food and water. They had enough weapons and supplies to make a series of isolated stands in the mountains for weeks had they chosen to do so.

But they did not choose because they had lost the power of making military decisions. From the moment of our breakthrough on May sixth orders had stopped flowing through the German machine. It was like an automobile engine running out of petrol. The machine was still there all right but there was no one to put it into motion again. The orders were not given because von Arnim and all his senior generals were forced to strike camp and flee at the most critical stages of the battle. There is nothing new about this. Precisely the same thing happened at Tobruk. Rommel made a swift, narrow and deep penetration of Tobruk perimeter and the South African general in command of the British garrison, General Klopper, was obliged to keep moving his headquarters during the vital stages of the battle. During that time he received no information and was unable to give orders. In the absence of any battle plan, in their complete ignorance of what was happening and because they did not know when to fire or in what direction, the Tobruk garrison was mopped up piecemeal by the Germans and surrendered in one day.

That is precisely what happened to von Arnim. In each case the general and the troops were oppressed by the fact that they had their backs to the sea and that they were trapped without the chance of escape or reinforcement. In each case the bulk of the defending troops had come recently and hurriedly into their new positions and at a time when the enemy was victorious everywhere else. Each position was designed to act as a bulwark in a rout, a peg to halt the retreat. Both at Tobruk and in Cape Bon the defenders were never given time to man their defences, to settle into the trenches, to acclimatize themselves and get the habit of resistance.

With very few exceptions this war seems to have demonstrated that armies are brittle things. Crack them smartly at the outset and they fly to bits. The knockout finishes the fight before the opponent has time to settle into his defence. Thus France. Thus Norway. Thus the Low Countries. Thus Singapore. But not thus in Russia and not thus in Rommel's retreat across the desert, and the difference here was this—the retreating armies had somewhere to retreat to. Behind Singapore and behind Cape Bon was only the sea. At neither place could the defenders play the old game of stretching out the enemy's lines of communication to the point where the enemy was starved and exhausted, a prey to the tactic of throwing in strategic reserves. The Germans had played that game once in Tunisia in the very beginning and got away with it. But now they could retreat no more.

There were a dozen other factors in the Tunisian victory, like our dominance of the air and sea, but this question of the breakdown of the German system seems to be the governing one.

It appeared to me as I travelled among the prisoners, especially the Germans, that they lacked the power of individual thought and action. They had been trained as a team, for years the best fighting team in the world. They had never been trained to fight in small groups or by themselves. They were seldom forced to make adaptations and makeshifts on the spur of the moment because they were usually on the winning side and their almost perfect supply machine had placed the finest weapons in their hands. The German army organization had been a miracle of precision in every phase of the African war. The fighting men always got their ammunition and their food. It used to come by air while we were still using carts. They even got their mail twice a week from home. And so they leaned heavily on the machine and trusted it. They never tried out the odd exciting things that we did—things like the Long Range Desert Group. They were never much good at guerilla fighting or patrolling at night. They liked to do things *en masse*.

I do not want to support that old and easy saying that once the Germans crack they go to pieces. Rommel has shown for all time that the Germans will go on fighting against impossible odds and take impossible risks so long as they are well controlled and officered. Most of the story of the African war shows that the Germans don't crack. They were split up at Alamein and they managed to regroup.

I simply state that the Germans were not trained to band themselves into small autonomous groups whereas often our own troops and the Americans will do so. The British battle schools force men to take independent action in a crisis. The Germans apparently have either not had that training or don't like it. At any rate in Tunisia, when the orders stopped coming, great doubts took hold of the German mind and discipline collapsed. Especially in war it is the unknown that men fear more than anything. As a lonely sentry will imagine a thousand terrors in the night so an army will flounder uncertainly and weakly so long as it is in doubt about the position and strength of the enemy. That is why every battle is preceded with a long period which is called "trying out the enemy." Big operations are laid on with the sole object of getting the enemy to demonstrate his strength and the nature of his weapons. All through this battle we had aircraft and tanks ranging back and forth to tempt the enemy to shoot so that we would know how many guns he had in a certain spot and where they were placed. From May sixth onwards the Germans were forever in doubt and doubt created despair.

I stress the Germans in all this. The Italians at the end showed much more initiative. Indeed, the young Fascists were indignant at several places when their German companions gave up. A few of the Italians at least wanted to fight it out guerilla fashion to the death.

However, the Germans prevailed because of their greater numbers and so for the next two or three days we came on an endless succession of these amazing scenes along the road. At Grombalia the Axis troops were pouring in from the side roads and grouping themselves in a cactus field outside the village. There were, I suppose, thirty British guards for about five thousand prisoners. No one had been able to get word through to a battery of Italian gunners on the heights above that the game was up. They kept firing first in this direction, then in that, and you could almost feel the gunners saying to themselves "Well, what *are* we firing at, anyway?"

In the orchards beside the road the enemy encampments were lying just as they left them—vehicles and tanks dispersed in a circle, motor-cycles lying in the ditches, signals vans standing under camouflage nets and the telephones still working. In their blitz through the Sixth had knocked out an odd truck here and a tank there and these still smouldered beside the track. An ammunition dump had blown up and the sparks had set a haystack alight. At Rebka near to the southern coast we found the vanguard of the Sixth at last. They were entirely surrounded by prisoners, and more coming in every minute. A handful of harassed tank men were forming them into a crocodile that wound slowly away to the north for a mile or two. "God knows where they are supposed to go," a British sergeant said to me. "I just put 'em on the road and tell 'em to keep going."

There was shooting still along the coast to the southwest of Hammamet and we joined a squadron of Shermans that was streaming off in that direction. In the distance a long dark column of enemy vehicles was approaching. The British artillery spotter had just decided on the range and was about to open fire. With his glasses to his eyes he was opening his mouth to give the order when he suddenly snapped, "God damn it. They've seen us and they're hanging out white flags. Cease fire. Try and get some one to round them up."

We turned back and ran into Hammamet, which is more like

a landscape painting in water colours than something in real life. Flowering shrubs and laden fruit-trees hung over the winding lanes. By the tiny beach and the old fort the white villas clustered together in their walled gardens and the sea was shining transparent blue. Just a few hours before we drove in, a violent argument had raged among the German soldiers in the garrison. Some were for surrendering, others for fighting, others for getting away in a fishing smack.

"It was terrible, that dispute," the hotelkeeper said. "In the end they all crowded aboard the boat. They just got round that corner an hour ago." The boat was lucky if it got more than ten miles. By this time the British navy had put a complete blockade across the Sicilian Narrows. Allied aircraft were passing back and forth every half-hour. Both the navy and the air force were feeling a little baulked that the Germans had not at least made one decent attempt to put to sea and that fishing smack would be a welcome sight for a pilot.

Nabeul, the next port, was to have been the major embarkation port but the town was empty when we drove through. Always we kept passing Germans, and Italians. At Korba a group of German and Italian specialists and vital experts had been promised air transportation. They were still waiting on the airfield when the British arrived—along with five or six thousand other prisoners.

Clifford and I were keen to do a little looting, a sport at which we had become adept in the desert. We knew we would have to give the things up to the British military police but still it was great sport to wander about picking up radio sets, cameras, binoculars and typewriters. Everything you saw was yours. If there is such a thing as feeling you are a millionaire for a day then this is it. On this day we wanted cars. "Take your pick," said a British officer who was battling with a disordered mob of prisoners. "Turn out any passengers you like." We did indeed need one car so we selected a Fiat. The Italian officer at once scrambled out with his belongings and we drove off.

The Fiat was not much of a success. It blew up after a bit and then we went hunting for *Volkswaggons*. There were dozens lying about, wonderful little cars with the engine in the back, and they were pleasant to drive. The ignition keys were missing from most of the *Volkswaggons* but in the end we got one going and that was the *Volkswaggon* in which we eventually drove six hundred miles through the mountains from Cape Bon back to Algiers.

Beyond Korba was Kelibia, the most distant of the abortive enemy evacuation ports. A great crowd of Germans were stranded there with their vehicles. Some were forming up to make a convoy on the road, others were rifling a food dump under the olive trees. Enemy colonels and generals seemed to be bustling about in all directions and utterly failing to get any order out of the confusion. Some of the Germans showed us where the cases of choicest food were lying and helped us to extract tins of pork and fruit and packets of whole-wheat biscuits. I lived on German and Italian rations once—they have always been first-class. The soldiers get real Danish butter, not margarine. The Italian tinned fruit and cheese are especially excellent.

The extraordinary thing was that once the enemy troops had decided to surrender they had no thought whatever of taking up arms again. Two days before they were concentrating all their minds and bodies on killing Englishmen and Americans. At this moment they were entirely free to pick up their rifles and shoot us; but they did not seem to be even morose or resentful. They were eager to be pleasant. In dozens they came up to explain the workings of the *Volkswaggon* to us. They were delighted to find Clifford spoke German and they talked with him as though the war had never occurred. Their attitude was, "Well, it's finished for me now. I don't have to fight any more. I can relax a bit."

They had lived such a practical and physical life in the field that they had had no time to develop any grandiose theories about the war and the honour of Germany. They did not worry about the future. Since whole armies were surrendering it did not seem to any one man that he was doing anything extraordinary by giving up. Indeed the whole astonishing spectacle was more and more like another army manoeuvre. They were simply going off to another place—America they hoped. They had heard well of the food and conditions there and they had always wanted to see America.

Indeed the prospect before these prisoners was not a bad one. They had had three years' fighting and they were fortunate to be unwounded and alive. Those who had been in Russia never wanted to go back. They were all sick and tired of army life. They looked forward to having a rest. For the moment the escape from the terrible bombing and shelling was all they asked. They knew their wives and families would be looked after in Germany and Italy as well as might be—they seldom saw them anyway when they were fighting in the Axis armies, so being a prisoner of war would not make much difference.

These men were not soft. They simply felt, "I have done my bit. Let some one else carry on now." They honestly did not have any fixed ideas about whether Germany was going to win or not. If you questioned them they said they thought the war would go on for years. They certainly did not feel that Germany was already beaten. They were glad to be out of it—that was all there was to it. There was in fact a malaise among these men, a malaise of the spirit brought on by too many hard trials that had gone on too long.

We rode back at last to Tunis past the prisoners who now stretched in a procession reaching from the tip of Cape Bon far into Tunisia. Weeks were going to elapse before a final count revealed the total at over a quarter of a million prisoners, the biggest single haul made by the Allies since the war had begun. In all, the Axis had lost close on a million men in Africa. Now they had nothing, absolutely nothing, to show for it.

I personally had expected the African war to finish in havoc, a cataclysm of destruction and death and frightfulness. These friendly, peaceful scenes at the end were almost an anti-climax. In the British army alone the doctors had budgeted for six thousand casualties in the final break-through. Actually they got the astonishing low number of two thousand.

There remained still on May eleventh a large knot of resistance in the mountains between Zaghouan and Enfidaville, where the Eighth Army was still fighting. But in the afternoon General Anderson called us to his headquarters outside Medjez el Bab and gave us the momentous news that von Arnim had been captured near the airdrome of St. Marie du Zit and had asked for terms.

"I told him we want unconditional surrender," General Anderson said. "In my message I said that all destruction of war materials must cease and that we must have a plan of their mine fields immediately. Von Arnim has refused these terms. He has asked to see me. He will be here in a minute. I don't think it will make much difference what he says."

The fact that von Arnim himself had not been able to get away was proof of the speed and completeness of our victory. No Axis aircraft had been able to take off into a sky filled with British and American aircraft, no Axis ship of any size had been able to put to sea. All the Axis generals with only one notable exception had now been taken. One after another the famous units like the Tenth Panzer Division gave up *en masse*. It is doubtful if more than one thousand enemy troops got away to Italy at the last.

Eight minutes to eight o'clock on May twelfth is the official time given for the cessation of all organized enemy resistance in Africa. The last act was for me almost the most dramatic and moving of all. It happened on the coast north of Enfidaville. The two most famous infantry divisions of both armies—the New Zealanders and the Ninetieth German Light—had continued in a bloody battle in the hills long after the war had finished around them. Von Sponeck was the commander of the

Ninetieth Light and his name stood almost as high in the Afrika Korps as Freyberg's stood in the Eighth Army. Their soldiers were the elite of the British and German armies. For two years they had mauled one another back and forth across the desert. We had killed two of the Ninetieth Light's commanders. The Ninetieth Light had almost killed Freyberg. They had charged up to the gates of Egypt in the previous summer and it was the New Zealanders who broke the German division's heart outside Mersa Matruh. There is hardly a major battlefield in the desert where you will not find the graves of New Zealanders and men of the Ninetieth Light.

Now at last it was all over. This war within a war, this private vendetta between the two great divisions, was finished. Von Sponeck saw that he could do no more.

He put on his formal greatcoat, his insignia and his cap and drove down the coast road. His only companions were a driver and an interpreter. Freyberg was waiting for him on the road, *his* road, the road that wound for nearly two thousand miles back to Egypt, the road he had done so much to conquer. The old lion looked a little shabby in his desert shirt, his shorts, his battered cap. He stood a little ahead of his officers on the road as von Sponeck got down stiffly from his car and drew himself up to a full salute. Freyberg saluted slowly in reply. The two generals looked at one another for the first time. Suddenly there was nothing to say. It had all been too long, and too bitter. There were too many dead.

Von Sponeck got back into his car and drove away to gather his men for the surrender. Freyberg turned round and walked down the road.